Reimagining Courts

*To Kathy
who touched my
soul/sorter
Gene*

Reimagining Courts

A DESIGN FOR THE
TWENTY-FIRST CENTURY

Victor E. Flango
and Thomas M. Clarke

TEMPLE UNIVERSITY PRESS
Philadelphia • *Rome* • *Tokyo*

TEMPLE UNIVERSITY PRESS
Philadelphia, Pennsylvania 19122
www.temple.edu/tempress

Library of Congress Cataloging-in-Publication Data

Flango, Victor E., 1942– author.
  Reimagining courts : a design for the twenty-first century / Victor E. Flango,
Thomas M. Clarke.
   pages cm
  Includes bibliographical references and index.
  ISBN 978-1-4399-1167-9 (hardback : alk. paper) — ISBN 978-1-4399-1169-3
(e-book) 1. Courts—United States—States. 2. Court administration—United
States—States. 3. Justice, Administration of—United States—States. I. Clarke,
Thomas M., author. II. Title.
  KF8720.F57 2014
  347.'01—dc23

2014017370

Printed in the United States of America

9 8 7 6 5 4 3 2 1

For Carol R. Flango and Shawn E. Clarke

Contents

PART III. MAKING THE REIMAGINED COURT A REALITY

List of Figures and Tables

Figures

Tables

Acknowledgments

We extend our deep appreciation to Mary C. McQueen, National Center for State Courts (NCSC) president, for supporting this effort and for her commitment to promote this monograph as a spur to dialogue in NCSC educational, research, and consulting activities. We are also sincerely grateful to the many colleagues who commented on earlier drafts of the manuscript, especially Dr. Craig Ducat, Dr. Roger Hanson, the Honorable Steven Leben, and the anonymous reviewers selected by Temple University Press.

Special thanks go to Joan Cochet for tirelessly and cheerfully helping locate resources and citations and for supervising the assembly of the bibliography and index, to Charles Campbell for contributing his editing skills, to Carol R. Flango for contributing her organizational and proofreading skills, to Thomas Haw for his assistance in proofreading and compiling the index, and to Pam Petrakis for formatting the tables and figures.

Overview

L et's begin this overview with a vision of a court process in the twenty-first century.

Vision of the New Court Process

Imagine that you are a potential litigant with a legal problem. You think you want and need a legal decision from a court, but you are not sure. To begin the process, you navigate online to the litigant portal for your jurisdiction. That portal is maintained by a group of legal services organizations, including the courts. Much like TurboTax, the portal asks you a series of simple questions to determine the type of legal dispute. On the basis of your answers, it advises you to either drop the case or to proceed with one of several possible organizations and processes.

If the advice is to proceed with a court case, the portal interacts with you further to solicit additional information about you and your case. On the basis of that information, it advises you regarding your need for a lawyer. If you do not need a lawyer or cannot afford one, the portal suggests the most appropriate and cost-effective form of assistance and provides access to information about that channel of assistance. If you decide to follow that advice and give your permission, the pertinent subset of already-collected information is forwarded to that organization.

Of course, you are free to ignore any of the advice given by the portal. If you choose a different course, the portal still provides any necessary support that it can. Note also that you may not be aware of the portal and instead begin the process by visiting a court, lawyer, or legal services provider either physically or virtually. Any of those organizations may choose to direct you to the portal for evaluation and advice or, alternately, perform a separate assessment and only then make the referral (or not). Thus, there is freedom of decision on both sides.

Let us assume that you decide to proceed with the case through the court system.

The portal next passes you to the case-filing interface, which helps you create and file the initial documents for the case electronically. Again, as with TurboTax, you do not need to figure out which forms are necessary or understand the forms themselves. The portal interface guides you through the process, solicits the necessary information, creates the forms, and files them with the court. If fees are necessary, the portal solicits and collects those as well.

The portal then advises you on the overall process and the next steps. If you have registered with the portal (and indirectly with the court in this case), it receives e-mail notifications and reminders as required to keep the case moving by scheduling hearings and completing necessary actions. What happens next depends partly on you as the litigant, partly on the case characteristics, and partly on the opposing party.

One of the things the portal does is provide you with market information about the case: what the typical costs and times to litigate are and what the typical outcomes are for similar cases. Especially with civil cases, you may have the opportunity to choose between tracks with more or less due process, more or less cost, more or less complexity, and more or less time to disposition. You can then choose which track you prefer.

Let us flip over to the court side of the process now to get a sense of how this new approach is different from what courts currently do. The portal transacts the filing with the court, kicking off internal processes. In addition to the traditional filings, the information collected by the portal is now used by the court to assess what needs to be done with the case and what assistance, if any, needs to be provided to you, the litigant. Let us start with the latter first.

If you have a lawyer, the court may provide no assistance beyond the usual electronic notifications and reminders to you and your attorney. If you want to get a lawyer, the portal separately provides search and screening services for doing so. If you lack a lawyer, the court may still do nothing special if you are assessed to be capable of handling the case yourself. Even in this situation, it may send you messages pointing to information or services that you can use to better prepare your case.

Alternatively, it may determine that you require more direct assistance, which could take the form of a referral to a court self-help center, an appointment with court legal staff, a slot in a court-training session, or a referral to a legal-aid organization. As the portal learns more about you and your case, the court may perform reassessments and change the assistance provided accordingly.

The court uses information from the portal about the case characteristics to select the appropriate initial channel for case management. If you have already indicated through the portal a preference for the case track, the court initially honors that request, although it may separately assess whether your chosen track is appropriate. If it disagrees with your choice, it may indicate so, but the choice is still under your control.

Within the court, the case is automatically assigned to somebody for the next processing step. We describe it this way because who that person is varies dramatically according to the type and status of the case. This is the step where it starts to get interesting.

Several commentators have recently suggested that this revolution in the legal services industry is a good thing, even though it will probably cost the bar jobs and revenue from low-skill tasks that others now perform. Why is that? The answer is that lawyers now spend much more of their time performing high-skill tasks, which is, after all, what they were trained to do. There may be fewer attorneys, but their jobs are more interesting *and* more lucrative. One pundit termed this phenomenon "practicing at the top of their license."

A similar trend occurred over several decades with health care and doctors. Doctors used to see all patients for all types of maladies. Now services are unbundled in two ways. First, limited health care services are provided in a wide variety of local walk-in clinics—some are even available in drugstores—where no appointment or prior relationship is required. Patients can schedule same-day appointments, get test results, or request a prescription, all on their smartphones.[1] This change broke the old model, where patients had to see family doctors or specialists by appointment and hospitals did everything else.

Patients now often see a doctor only after going through a series of encounters with medical staff having progressively more training and capability. They may start with a physician's assistant and then be handed off to a nurse practitioner before seeing a doctor. As a result, doctors also end up practicing more of the time at the top of their licenses. The court system needs to take a similar approach.

Imagine now that a clerk initially screens a new case. Because clerks have no legal training at all, they are empowered only to make an explicit set of decisions on the basis of explicit, predetermined criteria. A case manager, also not likely to be legally trained, may also make decisions about the most appropriate case-management channel and the appropriate next significant event in each case. These decisions are based on a protocol that everyone clearly understands and that the bench has approved.

While these two roles shield other members of the court from performing low-skill tasks and ensure efficient and appropriate initial case processing, they do not really touch the heart of radical triage measures proposed in this book. For that, we must elevate the case to paralegals or staff attorneys.

Staff lawyers have two main tasks to perform. First, they play a starring role in several of the early case-triage models discussed. These are sessions where case issues are evaluated and the cases are disposed of if no contested issues are involved or if the litigants are able to resolve their differences themselves. Alternately, the staff lawyer may find that several issues really are contested or that the issues are serious enough to require the appropriate due process. The case then gets scheduled for the next significant event. Thus, cases that move forward deserve to do so, and the court's scarce resources are conserved for the highest purposes.

Perhaps the most fundamental change in how courts triage incoming cases is the step away from simple rules based on case types. Rather than placing cases within case types on different tracks, our approach to case triage places them in different case-processing tracks regardless of case type. As these cases evolve, they may shift to different tracks as the needs of the case issues dictate. The two keys to these decisions are (1) what kind of case-management strategy does the litigant want and (2) what is the status of the issues in the case?

Litigant preferences drive the choice made between the adversarial and dispositional processes. Given appropriate market information, litigants can decide in civil and family cases between heavy or light due process. That decision carries with it significant differences in process complexity, cost, and time to disposition. In some cases, the court may force use of the adversarial process for social reasons, such as in cases with so-called high stakes: potential loss of liberty, loss of housing, unequal power, and so forth.

In theory, litigants might also affect the choice between adversarial and problem-solving processes. In some criminal cases, the offender might go either way and now has some choice. In some family cases, the parties might disagree with the court about whether a specific case should be handled in an adversarial or nonadversarial way. The wishes of the litigants matter when making these judgment calls.

Some civil and family cases now use the courts solely to provide legal records of the decisions because they are forced to do so. These are matters that could be handled administratively by either the court or some other organization. Many courts are moving to convert citations to payables that are handled only administratively as well. Some case types, such as labor-law cases, in some jurisdictions could be shifted to administrative law courts in the executive branch.

Case issues are the second driving factor in decisions about case triage. The person in charge of the initial review may find that the case literally has nothing at contest. If so, it should be disposed immediately. Presumably, a well-designed litigant portal would prevent most of these cases from reaching the court. Some cases may include one or more issues at contest, but they could be assessed to be easily resolved without requiring a judge by using one of several possible practices. Finally, some issues are real and substantive. The decision then would be to place them before a judge as soon as possible and queue them for trial as required.

Nothing is immutable about case issues. Cases evolve, as do the underlying problems and situations of litigants. New issues may come up. Old issues may ameliorate or become more toxic. Periodic case reviews by competent court staff are needed to confirm that cases remain on the most appropriate processing tracks. Offenders who fail out of problem-solving treatment programs frequently need such reassessments. Another would be juvenile delinquency cases that turn into adult criminal offenses.

Note that all these practices remove low-level tasks from the judge. As the scarcest of all court resources, judges should spend as much time as possible working on the most complex legal tasks. Aside from making the courts more efficient and the judges more productive, this revised process also provides litigants with faster and better service for the most serious cases. Equally important, it makes the job more rewarding for judges and increases the attraction of being a judge for talented potential candidates.

This then is the vision of the modern court: every legal problem does *not* require a court solution. Courts can improve what they now do well and can become even more cost-effective for citizens. In short, the modern court can continue to perform its mission well in an era of permanently constrained resources.

Courts as though Litigants Mattered

Courts have always been a peculiar American institution. For the first 175 years, the judicial system was a separate branch of government in legal name only. Then state court systems realized their potential as a full partner in the governmental monopoly. Now their role in society has grown to encompass not only traditional court business but decisions made by social agencies as well.

The past sixty years have witnessed the transformation of courts from narrow adversarial forums into broad general markets for legal decisions. The transformation has occurred not in a planned, orderly fashion, but very much in an ad hoc way. Although not all judges and court administrators have been happy about this situation, courts floated along until the Great Recession forced a serious reexamination. Now the institutional mission of the courts is very much under attack in many states, and courts must respond in some way to survive.

What caused all these changes? It is frequently noted that courts are conservative organizations, so they rarely change unless they are forced to do so. For the purposes of this book, the modern era of courts in America began in the 1960s. A wave of U.S. Supreme Court decisions on criminal procedural justice radically increased the cost of criminal prosecutions. At the same time, a crime wave unparalleled in modern times motivated politicians, including local prosecutors, to start putting record numbers of citizens in jail or prison.

Court caseloads increased significantly, and case backlogs grew accordingly. Criminal cases crowded out civil dockets because of speedy-trial rules, so all case types started seeing large delays. The reaction of courts to this crisis radically changed them in two ways. First, courts started acting like a real organizational branch of government complete, with their own administrative budgets and staff. The definition of judicial independence was broadened from the previous protection of legal decisions to include administrative independence—the ability of courts to control their own organizational destinies.

The war on drugs and other crimes, also launched in the 1960s in reaction to growing drug use, increased the demand for court services. Soon, more offenders were convicted for drug offenses than had recently been sent to prison for all other crimes. Trial rates for both criminal and civil cases started a long, slow decline as criminal caseloads exceeded the trial capacity of courts, and prosecutors used new weapons to reach settlements with guilty pleas in record numbers. A majority of the felonies were low-level drug cases, and most of the defendants routinely pled out before trial.

Within a few decades, trials became rare events in most courts. Since trials are the single-most resource-intensive event in a court, holding fewer of them contributed to improving court efficiency in disposing of cases.

During the same time period, some courts acquired new, non-case-related functions, such as pretrial and probation services, alternative dispute resolution services, indigent defense, and supervision of guardians, conservators, and guardians *ad litem*. From the perspective of many judges and court administrators, key functions of the criminal justice system would be lost if courts did not step up. From a national perspective, these additions to court functions were patchy and inconsistent because they, too, were acquired during periodic budget crises, creating a surprising disparity in the scope of court missions across jurisdictions.

The Court Response

Around 1990, it also became clear that the war on drugs was not working and that states would not be able to afford the required prisons for much longer. The inevitable backlash spawned a wave of new "problem-solving" courts to treat offenders with drug-addiction problems.

Special driving-while-impaired (DWI) and mental-health courts soon followed. These new types of dockets were institutionally revolutionary in the sense that they were expected to solve social problems using nonadversarial methods.

Problem-solving courts had a precedent. Juvenile courts were conceived as the original problem-solving courts. Even though the pendulum has swung between treating juveniles as children under the protection of the court and making young adults subject to criminal procedures and due-process protections, delinquency courts especially are still viewed as places to reform children—not to punish them. Once delinquency courts set the precedent of a social mission, courts quickly acquired responsibility for solving a second set of social issues involving children. Dockets for dependency and such status issues as truancy were followed by "unified family courts" that appeared and operated with similar nonadversarial sets of procedures. The explicit goal of these courts was not to decide guilt or innocence but to diagnose the problem(s) that brought children to court and to find solutions. Courts quickly learned that both types of new problem-solving courts were very resource-intensive, putting further pressure on court budgets.

Second, a profession of court administration arose, including a comprehensive canon of definitive works on best practices. For the first generation of professional court administrators, the primary goal was a reduction in case backlogs using classic caseflow management techniques, which were also relatively crude. Within case types, two or three tracks were created according to estimates of case complexity. Some attention was also devoted to early disposition of less-complex cases.

The first workload/staffing studies soon appeared to buttress better case management with justifications for additional judges and staff where needed. These studies implicitly assumed that current business processes and practices were ideal and took at face value the reported time allocations of judges and staff. Not surprisingly, courts almost always needed more resources.

As each new wave of court workloads arrived, courts responded by evolving practices that made them more efficient. It was not only trial rates that decreased—average trial times and case-disposition times did as well. To the traditional case tracking that caseflow management recommended, courts added a special emphasis on achieving quick dispositions through a number of techniques, mostly focusing on early interventions and a variety of arbitration and mediation programs. As with calendaring systems, studies found inconsistent results for most of the new programs, and best practices were hard to identify.

These innovations cumulatively enabled courts to handle higher caseloads per judge and staff than was previously possible. However, it was not clear whether the new practices were responsible for the increases or whether judges and staff were simply working harder than in the past. Rumbles about the quality of justice started to reverberate in the background as personnel complained of "burnout."

Ironically, everyone knew that quality was not the primary goal in a monopoly like the courts. Where else could litigants go? The real goal was to clear the dockets by using judges in the most efficient manner. Judges were, and are, the most expensive and scarce type of court resource. If the courts could keep the local bar happy while accommodating judges, so much the better. Courts viewed themselves as having no control over the demand for court services, so litigants were just a fact of life, not customers to be satisfied. Judges were the true evaluators of quality.

Financial Problems

Recessions in 1980, 1990, and 2000 periodically put the entire criminal justice system under short-term fiscal pressure. Fortunately, these recessions always ended quickly, so courts were able to weather the storms using mitigations that left the system essentially unchanged. When the business cycle and government revenues recovered, courts would make up lost ground and restore previous levels of staff.

Then in 2007 the Great Recession arrived, and courts reacted as they always did when recessions occurred: they put in place a wide range of short-term measures designed to wait out what had always been short budget downturns. Such policies as position and wage freezes, delays in calendars, shorter business hours, and furloughs can be used for only a brief period without reducing both the quality of service and the quality of justice. Thus, courts were stunned when the recession grew more severe and persisted for several years.

Their traditional mitigations to budget crises were becoming untenable. As the short-term coping measures remained in effect, the ability of the courts to carry out their constitutional mission was threatened. In response, some courts prioritized case types and stopped processing those deemed to be of lowest importance. Others attempted to reengineer their business processes—with partial success. Still others began to question whether all the functions they were carrying out should be within the scope of their operations.

Nationally, courts quickly united around three strategies. The first (and very traditional) approach was to claim a special budget status for courts as the third branch of government. In this scenario, the judiciary must be funded at a level that enables it to carry out its constitutionally mandated mission and functions. Thus, unlike those of executive branch agencies, its budget cannot be cut as part of general, across-the-board budget reductions. Needless to say, this strategy rarely worked.

Second, the courts considered several simple ways of guaranteeing their "fair share" of existing state and local government revenues. A favorite idea was fixing the court budget as a percentage of the state general fund, with the most frequent number being 3 percent. Because court budgetary needs varied widely from jurisdiction to jurisdiction by court structure and mission scope, a set proportion of the general fund bore no reasonable relation to the actual amounts needed. Therefore, legislatures rightly refused to support such initiatives.

The third and most promising strategy was to review what really belonged within each court's core mission. These "essential functions" were often specified by analyzing the state constitution and existing statutes. What most courts quickly discovered was that those sources of legitimacy supported only the narrow definition of court work—the classic adversarial mission. While some judges liked the idea of returning to the traditional and more comfortable role of courts, many others were appalled. What would happen to all the new cases that required problem solving?

Oddly enough, the least-used method of responding to the budget crisis was traditional caseflow management. Although nothing substantially new had been added to the literature since the 1970s, courts acted as though they had already mined all its nuggets for improving business processes. In fact, most courts were not using proper caseflow management to its fullest extent, and the institutionalization of such practices remained a huge problem. Courts needed two things: a normative way to define their essential functions and a methodology for estimating an adequate budget for those functions. The courts also needed new and improved practices for managing the cases within the scope of those functions beyond classic caseflow management. Fortunately, a number of courts were experimenting with such new practices in bits and pieces, but a more systemic approach was lacking.

The starting point for defining the mission of a modern court must be the recognition that courts have customers: the litigants and the public. Courts must take this view for the first time because they no longer hold a monopoly on the market for legal decisions. As cases were delayed too long, being decided by judges lacking appropriate expertise, or costing too much, litigants began turning to alternate means of settling their legal disputes.

This problem grew especially evident with civil cases. Large complex cases involving corporations increasingly moved to private arbitration. The advent of business courts did not stem the tide in most places. The continuing bar monopoly on legal services and the legal community's resistance to unbundling those services exacerbated a large and growing wave of unmet civil legal needs not found in any other developed country. Faced with unaffordable attorney costs, those litigants who did go to court tried to represent themselves in record numbers. The latter trend quickly spread to family-law cases as well.

The advent of self-represented litigants brought with it a double whammy for the courts. Because litigants and courts were ill prepared for cases to be handled without lawyers, the workload problem grew even worse. Even more alarming, litigants simply lost their cases needlessly in such areas as foreclosure, eviction, and dependency because they often defaulted rather than try to negotiate. Then the wave of judge-intensive problem-solving courts added yet more judicial work, further splitting some benches as to the legitimacy of such courts.

The last cruel twist of fate for the courts came when the Great Recession supposedly ended with an upturn in the business cycle. It took four years instead of one and a half, but revenues finally did bottom out and start growing in most jurisdictions. For states with energy resources or large agriculture subsidies, the recession never did cause much pain. For states with decentralized systems funded by local jurisdictions with adequate tax sources, the fiscal problems were also minimized. For everyone else, budgets were down about 20 percent from their previous high point.

The false dawn of budget recovery resulted from fundamental changes in demographic structure and the ravenous hunger of health care and pensions. As a result, courts are unlikely to escape continuous pressure on their resources for the next couple of decades at least. Court budgets have a "new normal." Faced with this future, courts simply must address the twin issues of mission scope, or essential functions, and improved case management.

Remedies

We argue in this book that courts should respond in three specific ways to the ongoing crisis. First, they must fundamentally reorganize their business processes around the concept of the litigant as a customer. Second, they must identify what their essential functions are on normative grounds and devote their scarce resources to only those areas. Third, they must universally adopt new and radical approaches to case management centered on concepts of case triage. Together, these recommendations offer a new vision of the courts and their modern mission.

Most courts still operate like single-artisan establishments. Much like the way the textile industry was organized three hundred years ago before mechanization and the advent of factories, individual judges operate legal-decision businesses as they wish, with some more centralized support. Business processes and legal quality vary widely within and between individual jurisdictions and even between cases. The public deserves better.

Doctors used to operate this way as well, but they were forced to adopt more consistent and evidence-based practices to the benefit of their customers. Judges and courts need to do the same. Consistent best practices for case processing will significantly improve courts and the legal experience for litigants. The flood of self-represented litigants has already forced courts partway down this path. Some court processes are at least described online, and some court services are also available electronically.

Much more needs to be done with court processes. The current guidance on court case-management systems describes only desired functions at a relatively high level.[2] Courts are still free to implement widely varying processes for carrying out those functions, and the result is expensive and fragile systems software that is hard to change when business requirements demand it. In a separate initiative, the National Center for State Courts (NCSC) plans to identify and document the necessary business capabilities and processes over the next several years.

A fundamental starting point for better business processes is good management information. Toward that end, NCSC established ten national performance measures, called CourTools.[3] In addition, NCSC published an approach for using those performance measures to better manage courts. The so-called High Performance Court Framework starts from the fundamental belief that citizens are the real customers of the courts and should be treated that way.[4] The Framework then lays out a systematic approach to assessing court performance and fixing business problems.

The issue of which court functions are essential is a vexing one. On the one hand, courts do not want essential justice functions to fall through the cracks. On the other hand, they are not well positioned to carry out a number of nontraditional functions. We argue that there are good reasons for reassigning some functions to the executive branch or even outside the legal system entirely. We also provide some guidance on when courts should or should not make these changes.

Aside from the essential functions, it may be worth asking to what extent courts should support the resolution of legal problems outside the formal legal system. The United States is unique in its preference for resolving all legal disputes in the courts. In contrast, many other developed countries have policies that encourage litigants to resolve their legal problems, whenever possible, using more informal processes. While intriguing, that issue lies outside the scope of what we consider in this book.

Most of this book focuses on the third mitigation strategy: case triage. We argue that individual case statuses must be taken much more seriously, since key triage decisions should be based on such information. Courts should not take the route of treating most cases in a certain case type like similar pieces of bread. We further argue that the type of case processing matters more than anything else and should be clearly understood and chosen at all times. Cases in the same case type may require different types of case processing. The same case may even require different types of case processing over its life as its status changes.

Proper case triage requires courts to have a level of detail about individual case statuses immediately available in a way that almost no court does now. Because case-management systems were developed first as docketing systems for clerks and then as case-management approaches based on crude case-type rules, they lack legal detail. Judges and other court staff must read the actual documents and make assessments to access the required information. Needless to say, that requirement makes it too inefficient and expensive to implement a real case-triage approach.

Because these recommended changes in court organization and administration are so radical, we indicate for each type of case processing which specific resources are required and which business processes should be used. We also describe the projected impacts on judges, staff, and facilities. On the basis of that information, a court could reorganize itself to implement case triage with the help of some new functionality in the standard case-management systems.

Our recommendations for case triage are not just academic concepts. Most, if not all, of them have been implemented individually by one or more courts with some success. Many of them are recognized as good practices by many courts, even if they are not widely implemented. Most courts also now realize the need for better management and improved business processes but find it extremely hard to make the desired changes under their current governance structures. Again, NCSC has published useful guidelines on how to solve that problem.[5]

The ideas in this book, together with the other supporting concepts being worked on by NCSC, will bring the courts into the modern world. Many of these ideas would have been immediately recognized in an introductory business management course twenty years ago as obvious actions to take. Although the courts are conservative by nature and design, they can no longer afford the luxury of using that excuse to avoid change. If the courts wish to provide quality justice at a reasonable price to their customers in the future and remain a viable social institution, then they must make these significant reforms soon.

Plan of This Book

Part I of this book contains two chapters outlining the current situation with respect to court reform. Chapter 1 expands on the arguments made in the overview, especially that courts are a victim of their own success. Because courts are among the most respected of government agencies, many disputes now come to court that once were resolved either informally in the family or community or by other governmental agencies using an essentially administrative process. Chapter 2 empirically examines what state courts actually do, thus clarifying the mismatch between our perception of courts and their actual workloads.

Part II contains six chapters outlining our proposals for reform. Chapter 3 suggests the need for triaging cases into explicit case-processing categories, each following a separate resolution process. Courts were originally synonymous with the adversary process—the most costly and slowest form of court decision making. As the types of cases requiring resolution grew, issues inappropriate for resolution by the adversary process came into court, and the adversary process was transformed over time to adapt to changing conditions and meet changing expectations. This transformation, however, was not done systematically or perhaps even consciously but evolved in different forms in different locations. This section suggests that court processes be explicitly and deliberately divided into four methods of dispute resolution and outline criteria by which the triage should take place. A separate chapter describes each process, the types of cases most suitable for resolution by each process, and the ways each process can be optimized to deliver significantly improved services to the public. Because of the recent controversy over use of specialized problem-solving courts, a separate chapter defines and illustrates the problem-solving approach and another describes the consequences of this approach for the justice system as a whole. Each process needs to be recognized and redefined for what it is so that efficiencies can be achieved in each process, as opposed to expecting reform of the basic adversarial process to cover all four processes. Also, each case processing method places different requirements on the judge and therefore has caused the judge's role to evolve.

Part III consists of two chapters. Chapter 9 brings our theory together with suggestions for redesign by showing examples of courts successfully using some of the recommended practices, thus demonstrating how the reforms advocated here can be accomplished in practice. Chapter 10 complements the overview in that it describes a vision of the modern court as well as some of the barriers to implementation.

I

Aligning Image with Reality

Why Courts Need to Be Redesigned

> [D]espite the great variety of ways in which
> human disputes can be resolved over time courts
> have emerged as the most powerful, prominent,
> and influential institution for doing so.
>
> —JETHRO K. LIEBERMAN, *The Role of Courts
> in American Society*[1]

State courts did not come into their own until relatively recently, after 1950.[2] Courts were once defined as institutions for resolving disputes and contested issues by trial, and persist in being associated with trials in the popular mind. Other adjudicatory processes have evolved over time, including those for which expedited processing is the goal or for which diagnosis and treatment are the goals, but they are all described in the adversary language of courts. In practice, this means we treat all the different adjudicatory processes used by courts today as if they were adversary proceedings, where every case is a contest and every case has a realistic chance to go to trial. The role of courts has expanded to include nonadversary matters, which have become grafted onto the adversary process even though they have never really fit there. New and still-evolving principles and practices surrounding "problem-solving" courts are being developed, but they have not yet affected our image of what courts are. Although individual courts have experimented with, and indeed implemented, new practices and procedures, we argue here that the perceptual mismatch between image and reality has impeded a *systematic* reexamination of court processes for resolving disputes. The disconnect between our image of courts and what courts actually do persists. Unless this image is realigned with reality, suggestions for court reform and court improvement are likely to founder.

The Challenge: Burgeoning Caseloads

One major trend, once called the "litigation explosion," was the tremendous expansion of the number and variety of issues now brought to courts for resolution. Law grows from the relentless pressures of technological change, geographic mobility, global economic competition, and environmental pollution—all of which generate social and economic disruption, new risks to health and security, new forms of injustice, and new cultural challenges to traditional norms.[3]

Although discussion of the "litigation explosion"[4] has abated over the last sixty years, the deeper trend toward using courts to resolve not only more disputes but also a greater variety of issues has persisted. Richard B. McNamara has said, "The Courts have changed more in the last 50 years than any other institution in American Society."[5] Regardless of whether that is precisely true, it is unquestioned that the numbers and types of matters litigated have greatly expanded. McNamara notes that the lawyer of 1950 would be "dumbfounded by an explanation of how American courts function today."[6]

In addition to "litigation explosion," other words used to describe the dramatic increase in litigation in the 1960s include "Hyperlexis: Our National Disease"[7] and "legal pollution."[8] A 1983 issue of *Changing Times* illustrates the tone of these articles:

> Outraged by a referee's call, several Washington Redskins football fans file a lawsuit demanding that it be overturned. A young girl breaks her finger catching a fly ball in a school softball game; her parents sue the gym teacher, charging that she wasn't properly coached. The University of Michigan is sued for $853,000 by a student who received a low grade in German. A convict whose sentence is increased for escaping sues the county and its sheriff accusing them of negligence in failing to prevent the getaway. A 9-year-old girl sues the makers of Cracker Jack because her box contains no prize. Welcome to the age of litigation.[9]

Some would argue that Congress passed many new regulations in the 1960s but did not create parallel enforcement mechanisms, so that enforcement was left to courts. Others have cited the civil disobedience of participants in the civil rights movement in the 1960s and the anti–Vietnam War movement, which provided a model for public-interest groups who used litigation to lobby on behalf of environmentalism, feminism, consumer safety, the aged, the children, the poor, the handicapped, and the like.[10] During this period, courts abolished legal immunity from tort liability for government and charitable institutions, changed evidentiary rules in medical-malpractice cases, and imposed "strict liability" for product defects—all making it easier for plaintiffs to win. Congress enacted statutes to enable successful plaintiffs to recover lawyer fees from governmental and corporate defendants but did not require them to pay if they lost.[11]

The "due-process revolution" in criminal procedure and the war on drugs also occurred within the same time frame. In the 1980s, the number of arrests for all crimes rose by 28 percent, but the arrests for drug offenses increased by 126 percent.[12] Approximately half the drug arrests were connected to marijuana. Drug offenders made up 21 percent of all prisoners incarcerated by states. Many believe that the "war on drugs" has been ineffective because its emphasis has been on enforcement rather than treatment.[13]

Litigation continued to increase until the late 1990s, with lawsuits breaking new ground—"children suing parents for wrongful raising, pupils suing teachers for hostile learning environments, lovers suing each other for unfulfilled romantic promises, overweight people suing movie theaters for larger seats."[14]

Patrick M. Garry argues that litigation has entered into areas of American life that were once immune, such as religion, "domestic torts," sports, and education.[15] Medical-malpractice suits, rare in the 1960s, reached 4.3 per 100 insured physicians in 1970 and 18.3 per 100 in 1986.[16] Moreover, judicial hearings have also been extended to other decisions that were formerly private—for example, life-sustaining medical decisions of the terminally ill are sometimes made not by physicians or families but by courts.[17]

Torbjorn Vallinder claims that the trend toward expansion of the courts at the expense of politicians or administrators, or the spread of judicial decision making outside the traditional judicial province, is not only an American trend but also a worldwide trend.[18] Regardless, Robert A. Kagan contends that no other country employs litigation so often to resolve disputes over "delineation of electoral district boundaries, the management of forests, the breakup of business monopolies, the appropriate funding level for inner-city versus suburban public schools, or the effort to discourage cigarette smoking."[19] In summary, many issues previously resolved within the family, the school, the church, and government agencies are now brought to court. Michael Buenger puts the expanding role of state courts this way:

> With abortion, euthanasia, environmental issues, election con-
> troversies, and even the legislative process itself, state judicia-
> ries have become the fora for some of the most vexing political
> and social issues of our time. Unlike the past, state courts are
> finding themselves at the center of, and not the periphery of,
> many divisive political maelstroms.[20]

Acknowledging this expansion of expectations, and the fact that some of the issues identified by Buenger—as well as employment rights, consumer protection, sex discrimination, endangered species, and toxic-waste disposal—have been relatively recent additions to the courts' agenda, Judge William L. Dwyer notes that he would rather not return to an era where "poverty, injury, unfair treatment on the job, ill health [and] loss of savings in a failed bank" had no court redress.[21]

Could it be that courts are trusted by citizens to be a neutral forum—not only a place where they can get their disputes resolved finally and authoritatively but also where they can present their sides of an issue and be heard? Courts, at least as originally designed, are perceived to be such an impartial forum.

Opinion polling does not show such an overwhelming support for courts. Indeed, public distrust of government in general taints courts as well. Most polls dealing with public confidence in public institutions focus on the federal government. In these polls, with regard to the federal courts, and especially the U.S. Supreme Court, people reveal a "fair amount" of confidence in the judiciary.[22] The "courts in my community"[23] enjoy less public trust and confidence. One recent poll found that courts have fewer supporters *and* fewer critics than other public institutions, such as police and schools.[24] Still, if litigation can be considered a form of the public's voting "with their feet," the trend has clearly been toward increased use of courts to resolve a greater variety of issues—regardless of whether they are equipped to do so. In the dramatic words of one observer: "The litigation explosion has conveyed the delusion that the legal process can serve as an all-wise Solomon for American Society—dictating answers to every question, anticipating all future occurrences, remedying every ill, and eliminating every uncertainty."[25]

For much of our history, state judiciaries "simply were not the complex institutions they are today."[26] Along with increases in caseloads came an increase in case-related administrative responsibilities. Courts now supervise many ancillary functions not related directly to decision making in individual cases, such as pretrial services, probation supervision, parole, language interpretation, public defense, conservatorship audits, counseling services, and many others that are sometimes performed by executive branch agencies. While it is rare for one court to perform *all* these ancillary functions, it is telling that some of these functions are performed in all courts. In fact, it could be argued that the courts often control these other functions only because either nobody else wants them or other agencies are doing an inadequate job of managing them. These ancillary functions need to be examined systematically to determine which belong in courts and which would be better accomplished by executive branch agencies.

Countertrends

The countertrends have been the decline in the types of cases once considered the bread and butter of court work as law in some areas becomes more settled (e.g., litigation over railroad injuries) and the number of cases resolved by trial has sharply decreased, giving rise to the phrase "vanishing trials."

Ironically, at the same time that the expansion of litigation was being lamented, courts were also lamenting the loss of the types of cases they were traditionally called upon to resolve—primarily civil cases. Resolving cases through the courts can be an "inefficient, complex, protracted, costly, punitive, and unpredictable method of governance and dispute resolution."[27] Consequently, there has been a countertrend to privatize dispute resolution and resolve legal disputes outside the court system.[28] Courts are under pressure from increasing competition from private agencies claiming to be able to resolve cases more efficiently. Competitors systematically undercut the traditional courts for some case types, such as complex civil cases and some divorce cases, because of lower costs and superior convenience, although Marc Galanter speculates that it is only particular "repeat-player" litigants who are seeking alternatives to courts—namely, corporations and governments.[29]

Numerous mediation and arbitration services exist outside the formal courts and even online. This gradual erosion of the demand for court services is occurring according to market pressures while, at the same time, demand for court services is increasing in new areas.

The arena where disputes are resolved does have consequences for litigants: some research shows that privatization has the potential to undermine the rights of "have-nots."[30]

Financial Crisis: Engine for Change

In the midst of all the pressures and counter-pressures discussed, a funding crisis occurred.[31] This financial crisis increases the urgency to prioritize court services because essential services must be maintained despite diminished resources. On the other hand, the financial crisis provides an opportunity to examine court activities, define those that are most essential, streamline or even eliminate services that are not of the highest priority, and reengineer those court processes that remain. A recent book on leadership puts it this way: "[A]daptation is a process of conservation as well as loss. . . . The question is not only, 'Of all that we care about, what must be given up to service and thrive going forward?' but also 'Of all that we care about, what elements are essential and must be preserved into the future?'"[32]

In the absence of criteria for making cuts in services, courts will either cut services evenly across the board or cut those with the least political clout and weakest constituencies. In the latter situation, often the first types of services to be reduced or eliminated are those that serve the litigants and the public. For example, one study of reductions in court support staff found the reductions translated to reduced public hours at the courthouse, fewer clerks at the front counter, and fewer staff to answer the telephone.[33] Some courts suspend jury trials, which are not only an essential component of court decision making[34] but also one of the key sources of public trust and confidence in the American justice system.[35]

Courts and other state government agencies are being forced to reexamine their work and decide which functions are critical to their existence, which can be modified, and which can be eliminated. This opportunity for self-reflection should not be permitted to pass. Former Chief Judge Judith Kaye of the New York Court of Appeals has noted that "[p]lainly, state courts today need money, but they also need more than money. They need ideas."[36] This observation reinforces a more pessimistic one from the former budget director of New York State:

> Logic might suggest that an environment of scarcity would intensify efforts to provide services through more efficient, customer-oriented models. However, the record of the last few years provides little support for this hypothesis. More typically, tight budgets in state and local governments seem to lead to disruption, which drives out innovation and undercuts efforts to reorient service delivery.[37]

Most Americans do not connect problems in courts to the litigation explosion or to budget cuts but point the finger at the way courts are run. When asked about the factors most responsible for court delays, respondents in a 2012 survey cited the following:

1. "Too many unnecessary lawsuits"
2. "Legal maneuvering by lawyers that drags out cases"
3. "Bureaucratic inefficiency"[38]

The purpose of this monograph is to provide a systematic and thoughtful answer to the following questions:

- Which functions are courts uniquely qualified to perform?
- How can court processes be redesigned to perform those functions effectively and efficiently?

Adjudicatory processes have evolved over time to deal with the quantity and variety of cases brought before courts, but this evolution has necessarily been piecemeal, neither comprehensive nor systematically implemented. The public-opinion survey referenced above did indicate public support for certain investments in court improvements, especially (1) new technology to reduce paperwork and ensure more efficient recordkeeping, (2) mediation programs to resolve disputes without trial, (3) more public defenders, (4) more specialized courts, or (5) more judges, self-help centers, and administrative staff.[39]

Our concern is that each of these investments, though valuable in itself, would be much more effective if implemented as part of a more systemic reform, which requires that the key adjudicatory court processes now in use be defined much more precisely, *realigned* explicitly with the logical structures that support them, and resourced with the right combination of personnel and technology needed to maximize the satisfaction of people who use the courts.

Before getting too far in terms of reforms required, however, let us take an *empirical* and *dispassionate* look at what courts actually do now.

What Courts Actually Do

> The trial court anticipates new conditions and emergent events and adjusts its operations as necessary.[1]

Our *conception* of what courts do and how they do it has not kept pace with a changing world. Courts have changed and must continue to change as circumstances do.

Effective courts are responsive to emergent societal issues, including everything from drug abuse to gender bias to consumer rights and all the other challenges mentioned in Chapter 1. Indeed, Standard 4.5 of the *Trial Court Performance Standards*, cited above, requires courts to recognize and respond to emergent issues in order to provide a stabilizing force in society—consistent with its role in maintaining the rule of law.

In his book *Varieties of Police Behavior*, James Q. Wilson[2] confronts the issue of how to ration scarce police services to the public by deciding how many of which types of requests for which types of services police could respond to. This scenario is a direct analogy to the dilemma facing courts in a time of economic downturn.

In another similarity, he observes a disconnect between the way police departments are organized and where the bulk of their work occurs. Most police departments are organized by the key function of law enforcement, with homicide squads and so forth, yet only a small fraction of cases—less than 10 percent—involves crimes serious enough to make up the FBI crime index; the remaining 90 percent of arrests are for less serious crimes, such as drunkenness, disorderly conduct, vandalism, and other disturbances of the peace. Yet many police departments are organized around the law-enforcement function, even though the bulk of their time is spent on the "watchman" function of maintaining order. With apologies for this oversimplification of Wilson's argument, courts may be subject to this same phenomenon.

Courts are also organized as if their main function were to conduct trials of serious cases, such as felonies, using a full adversary process. Yet what is the actual business of courts? Cases filed in courts reveal not only the number of cases resolved by courts but also the *variety* of cases. These raw case filings accurately reflect the public demand for court services but not the judge and staff work necessary to resolve them.

The examination of the actual court caseloads that follows reveals that at least 50 percent of the caseloads are traffic cases, about 10 percent are small claims, and the remainder includes criminal misdemeanors, family law, and other civil cases. From the customer perspective, these raw case filings are the main business of courts, even though they are not reflective of the court work necessary to resolve them. What if courts were organized according to actual consumer demand for court services?

The major types of cases heard by trial courts in the United States in 2007 and 2008 are listed below (small claims are included in the civil category). More recent data since the 2007 Great Recession show a predictable increase in contract, foreclosure, and some domestic-relations case types in some jurisdictions. Presumably these temporary responses to bad economic times will revert to previous trends as the economy improves.

Traffic	54 percent
Criminal	21 percent
Civil	18 percent
Domestic relations	5 percent
Juvenile	2 percent

Courts Settle Traffic Cases

If the volume of cases were the criterion used to evaluate the work of courts, we would have to conclude that the primary reason courts exist is to handle traffic violations. Of the record number of 106 million cases coming into state trial courts in 2008, 57.5 million were traffic cases. In other words, 54 percent of all filings in state courts are noncriminal traffic violations. Even this number is an underestimate, because not all courts in the United States report complete data on their caseloads. Moreover, in some states, traffic matters do not even go to court but are handled by traffic bureaus.

Obviously, differing definitions of what constitutes a traffic case have tremendous impacts on caseload composition. The Court Statistics Project of the National Center for State Courts (hereafter CSP) is charged with the responsibility of gathering data from state courts in the United States and with doing its best to make the data comparable by using a common classification schema.

The CSP recommends that traffic cases be clearly distinguished from criminal cases and that parking violations be clearly identified, because they inflate the total caseloads in state courts that count them as part of their caseloads and conversely diminish the caseloads in states that have separate executive branch agencies that handle parking tickets.[3] In Hawaii, traffic cases compose 71 percent of the caseload, but 45 percent of these cases are parking violations. In contrast, Illinois also has a high proportion of traffic cases (71 percent of its case filings), but only 5 percent of these are parking violations. Even though traffic cases make up the exact same percentage of overall caseloads in these two states, the composition of these traffic caseloads is very different. At the other extreme, traffic filings make up only 33 percent of the caseload in Florida.

Before becoming enmeshed in the fine points of data analysis, however, let us not lose sight of the key fact that traffic cases make up the largest proportion of state court caseloads, *regardless* of whether parking violations are included as traffic offenses. Moreover, this situation has been true since the CSP began collecting uniform data from state courts for the year 1975.

Traffic cases compose 19 percent of the caseload in courts of general jurisdiction and 61 percent of the caseload in courts of limited jurisdiction.[4] There has been a growing trend in recent years to make more of these cases "payables," in effect decriminalizing them and turning them into quasi-administrative cases. This trend should continue and even accelerate in response to the current and presumably chronic budget pressure that courts now labor under.

Without traffic cases, the caseload composition of courts nation-wide looks like this:

Criminal	45 percent
Civil	39 percent
Domestic relations	12 percent
Juvenile	4 percent

Criminal Cases

Criminal cases can be categorized as 21 percent felony cases and 79 percent misdemeanor cases. Felonies further break down into the following categories:

Drug	29 percent
Property	28 percent
Person	14 percent
Weapon	6 percent
Public order	5 percent
Motor vehicle	4 percent
Domestic violence	3 percent
Other	11 percent

The number of drug crimes rose to the top several decades ago as illicit drug use skyrocketed, with the result being a "war on drugs." Most defendants plead guilty rather than go to trial, and most trials are conducted before a judge instead of a jury. Although criminal cases make up 21 percent of the caseload of courts of general jurisdiction and courts of limited jurisdiction, the composition of the respective caseloads differs. Felonies make up the majority of criminal filings in courts of general jurisdiction, but even here the vast majority of cases are disposed by guilty plea rather than trial. After reaching an all-time high in 2006, the number of criminal cases has decreased slightly since then.[5]

Civil Cases

Civil cases usually attract less attention from the media than criminal cases, except from the ever-present advertisements from personal-injury lawyers. A perhaps dated Civil Litigation Research Project found that in four of the five state courts in its sample, tort cases dominated, particularly cases related to motor vehicle injuries.[6] One reason is that the Civil Litigation Research Project used data from only courts of general jurisdiction, and civil cases make up a larger proportion of the caseloads of general jurisdiction courts (36 percent) than limited jurisdiction courts (15 percent). Tort cases also make up most of the jury trials in civil cases. This attention may leave the impression that personal injury torts are the largest civil case category, but the data below show that half the civil cases involve contract disputes:

Contract	50 percent
Small claims	19 percent
Probate	16 percent
Tort	6 percent
Mental health	2 percent
Real property	1 percent
Appeals	1 percent

The number of contract cases has also grown much faster than the number of civil cases, while small-claims cases have lagged the average growth rate. Civil caseload composition is affected by whether domestic relations are included in the civil totals or counted separately. The major categories of domestic-relations cases are as follows:

Child support	31 percent
Divorce	29 percent
Protection orders	20 percent
Paternity	10 percent
Custody	3 percent
Adoption	3 percent
Visitation	1 percent
Other	3 percent

Averages, however, can be misleading. The proportion of child-support cases in courts of general jurisdiction ranges from 1 percent in Utah to 68 percent in the Courts of Common Pleas in Ohio. Support cases in courts of limited jurisdiction vary from 1 percent in New Hampshire to 80 percent in Alabama.

Juvenile cases are sometimes handled in unified family courts, in separate juvenile courts, or in regular courts of general or limited jurisdiction. The largest proportion of juvenile cases consists of delinquencies:

Delinquency	62 percent
Dependency	20 percent
Status offense	14 percent
Other	4 percent

Of course, these case proportions do not accurately reflect the actual work of the courts, because the major case types vary significantly in the average time required to dispose of a case. For example, although delinquency cases are more plentiful than dependency cases, dependency cases take about twice as long to resolve. Workload is addressed in the individual descriptions of court processes.

Now that we have a rough idea of what courts do, let us turn to the processes courts use to resolve these cases.

Triage and the Four Case-Processing Tracks

3

Triage

Separating Cases by Processing Required

Modern courts currently use many different processes to resolve cases. These existing processes must be disentangled, examined, and perhaps redefined to determine whether they are being used appropriately and most effectively. The issue from our perspective is that the peculiar mechanism for resolving disputes in court was designed to operate in a specific manner for disputes framed in a way to fit the adversary model of resolution. Because many subsequent types of issues did not fit the adversary model, courts developed alternative methods of dispute resolution within the courts umbrella to accommodate them and in the process were themselves changed.

The traditional adversary process was not supplanted when new processes were introduced, but rather coexisted and intermingled with them. Because current adjudicatory processes are intertwined, it is advantageous to separate them conceptually so they can be analyzed separately. Thomas A. Henderson, Cornelius Kerwin, and Hildy Saizow identified three separate adjudication processes used by courts today in varying combinations—procedural (the adversarial process redefined), decisional, and diagnostic.[1]

The Need for Triage

Lawrence Baum observes, "By establishing courts as a forum for dispute resolution, the government provides an important service for its residents."[2] Chief Justice Richard Neely of the West Virginia Supreme Court of Appeals further lays out the case for court services being a "public good."[3]

Courts are available to all potential litigants in almost the same way that the common is available to all farmers. Just as the villagers must be able to afford livestock before using the common, for most cases American litigants must be able to afford a lawyer before they can go to court. Once this precondition is met, however, litigants can use as much court time and resources as they want once their "turn comes up." In most places, of course, their turn does not come up often because of the length of the queue.

Because courts are accessible to all, they can easily be overwhelmed by demands for services under ordinary circumstances. Courts do not have formal control over the number of cases brought to them for resolution, except for jurisdiction restrictions. The size of the backlog of cases—and hence the waiting time—may, however, affect the litigant's decision whether to bring a case to court or to settle out of court. If the backlog and waiting time were to decrease, some litigants who had decided that filing a case was literally not worth their time might decide to file after all. If this premise is true, then courts are likely to have a steady flow of filings, even when the number of cases disposed increases and the backlog of cases decreases. In the absence of guiding principles to determine which issues are most appropriate for judicial resolution, court services are then rationed de facto by delay and cost considerations.

The situation cries out for *triage*—a word used in the medical field for prioritizing patients on the basis of the severity of their condition, a method of rationing treatment when resources are insufficient for all to be treated immediately.[4] Granted, a form of elementary triage or screening occurs now. Cases come to court voluntarily or involuntarily. In criminal cases, the state brings charges, and the accused are required to come to court. In those cases, as well as in some serious traffic cases, prosecutors really do the screening: they can decide to not prosecute a case, which is in effect a dismissal, to prosecute some of the charges but not others, to reduce charges to a lesser included offense, or to prosecute to the full extent of the law. The point here is that mandatory cases do receive some type of preliminary screening before they come to court.

Not so with cases that come to court voluntarily, many of which are civil and family cases. Consumers do make the threshold decision of whether to bring cases to court, but it is our contention that if the court-processing tracks were better understood, consumers would be better able to make the decision about which cases should go to court and, if so, what the tradeoffs are among the processing pathways. For example, would it be worthwhile for a consumer to reduce the dollar amount in controversy to fit the jurisdiction of a lower court if the tradeoff were a quicker resolution of the case? Could a family choose to compromise over the amount of child support if it increased the likelihood that the agreed-upon amount would actually be paid according to a regular schedule? Without taking a fresh look at this problem, it is likely that the vicious cycle of punishing non-support-paying litigants with contempt citations or jail time will continue, without necessarily benefiting their children.[5]

We recommend that triage be done earlier in the process, be done more effectively and transparently, and be focused on issues raised rather than types of cases filed. Individual cases would still receive the individual attention they are due but would be assigned to one of the four adjudicatory processes most suitable for their resolution.

What we are proposing here is a more explicit triage process for cases entering court, with the pathways known and the tradeoffs clear so that consumers of court services can make rational decisions regarding the types of court service most appropriate for their cases. Critics can argue that this concept is nothing new—after all, differentiated case management has been around for a long time. Setting aside the argument that differentiated case management has been implemented in a piecemeal fashion and in very different ways by different courts, we would agree that many of the elements we are about to suggest are not new and that many (or perhaps all) of them have been used by different courts at different times and in different states. What is new, however, is the idea of using these various elements systematically *in combination* to achieve different goals. The foundation principle of case management—*aggressive case management*—will not change. The courts should not be passive, waiting for lawyers to decide what they want to do and when they want to do it or waiting for self-represented litigants to figure out how to navigate the courts. Rather courts need to take control of cases early in the process and manage them actively until disposition.

What we have refined is the specification of triage—that it be done earlier in the process, be done more effectively and transparently, and be focused on issues raised rather than types of cases.[6] The point is that the courts need to establish a repeatable, consistent, and legally responsible business process for ensuring that all cases are handled in the most appropriate and expeditious track.

The specific principles are as follows:

1. Assign cases early to one of four case-processing tracks and provide for the possibility that tracks could change.
2. Assign cases to a track based on issues raised rather than case types.
3. Enable litigant choice of processing strategy to varying degrees on the basis of the assigned track.
4. Make best use of scarce resources by using the least amount of legal expertise required for appropriate disposition.

Four Adjudicatory Processes

Adjudicatory processes need to be clearly defined so that the goals of each are clear and that it is easier for court structures to be adjusted and reengineered to match the redefined processes. Triage is necessary to match the right issues with the right adjudicatory processes. It requires that incoming cases be classified according to the types of processing they require, which in turn depends on the types of issues raised.

We recommend that court business be filtered into one of four distinct adjudicatory processes: (1) the traditional court adversary process, (2) a disposition-oriented process to handle high volume of "ordinary" cases, (3) a nonadversary process for cases requiring the solution to a problem, and (4) an administrative process.[7] The first three are defined somewhat differently than the three processes identified by Henderson and his colleagues, but they are related. To those three, we have added an administrative process that does not necessarily require the attention of a judge and arguably could be accomplished outside a court setting.

Table 3.1 provides a brief overview of the four adjudication processes, and the rest of Part II elaborates on them.

TABLE 3.1. FOUR ADJUDICATION PROCESSES

	ADJUDICATION PROCESSES			
	Adversary	*Disposition*	*Administrative*	*Problem-Solving*
Goal	Justice through due process	Justice through timely decision making	Justice through mechanical application of rules to largely undisputed facts	Personalized or individualized justice
Key Performance Goal	Equality, fairness, and integrity Independence and accountability	Expedition and timeliness	Expedition and timeliness	Access to justice
Role of Judge	Neutral arbiter who is impartial; independent General jurisdiction court	Adjudicator who achieves finality through expeditious case resolution Limited jurisdiction court	Aministrator who applies clear laws to facts; quasi-judge Non-court	Partner in treatment Special jurisdiction court
Role of Support Staff	Minimal; primarily support for trials	Case managers to keep cases moving	Nondiscretionary decision making as well as record keeping	Large staff to locate and evalu-ate treatment programs
Facilities	Full courtroom; regionally based and fully equipped for jury trials	Less-imposing court; county-based in smaller counties, contain-ing many rooms for lawyers to meet to settle cases	Multiple locations within counties, shared with administrative agencies, if necessary, or in easily accessible shopping areas; many transactions carried out online to reduce number of court appearances	County-based with facilities for diagnosis, psychological screening, and drug testing
Cost	High cost; cost is not a consideration if liberty is at stake	Cost is important to both the litigant and the state	Should be cost-efficient; tech-nology should be used to maximum extent appropriate	Long-term cost-benefit analysis—e.g., reduced recidivism

The Adversary Process and Courts Are Intertwined

We contend that the very conception of courts, and therefore the expectations we have of them, was derived from the adversary system. Indeed, one prominent author describing the resolution of a case by courts lists these conditions: "(1) an adversary process, (2) a justifiable issue, (3) ripeness for judicial determination, and (4) an actual disposition."[8] Under this definition, the adversary process is an inherent attribute of courts and vice versa—the key distinguishing features of courts were derived from the traditional adversary process.

The adversary process operates under the simplifying assumption that justice is elusive and that the best way to have it emerge is to have two adversaries vigorously assert their respective positions with a neutral arbiter present to declare the winner. Because the adversary process leaves the work of gathering and presenting evidence to partisans, each side has an incentive to "suppress and distort unfavorable evidence, however truthful it may be."[9] Some would trace this dichotomous process to roots in the medieval process of trial by combat.[10] This perspective is bolstered by a quotation from Justice Robert H. Jackson, who notes that adversary proceedings "[set] the parties fighting."[11]

Please note that *two-sided* in this context does not mean there are only two parties to the dispute or only two issues involved. Two-sided refers to the *structure* of the adversary system, which is bilateral rather than multilateral. Conflicts are presented in a two-sided framework. This assumption does not violate reality in common criminal cases or most civil cases. Cases are initiated by parties—a plaintiff in civil cases, the prosecutor in criminal cases—who assert a claim that the defendant denies. Each side has the opportunity to present arguments in its favor, leaving little room for other participants who may have an interest in the outcome of the case. On rare occasions, courts recognize that a case is multifaceted or that the various people who compose the plaintiff's or defendant's side do not really share a common interest, but nevertheless, the case is still presented as though it were two-sided. Obviously, multiple issues can be addressed, but the case is structured so that the issues are presented sequentially as two-sided issues, usually beginning with the question "Does the court have jurisdiction?" Multilateral disputes with multiple contending interests, or "polycentric" problems, have never been well suited for traditional adversary adjudication.[12] In addition to the adversary process assumption that truth will emerge from an airing of opposing views, the process also assumes that each side wants to win and will command the resources necessary to win. It is further assumed that "having the two sides present their case will expose all pertinent facts and that the rules which govern the trial will allow reasonable men to separate truth from falsehood."[13]

The adversary method of dispute resolution is unique to courts. It developed as a public process from Common Law so that the parties involved present evidence in open trial, the court does not conduct its own investigations or require independent sources of information, and some cases are resolved by a jury of one's peers. Because parties control the gathering of information, delays and high costs are common. A neutral arbiter listens to the arguments presented by representatives of the parties, and a judge or jury makes a decision that is authoritative in that the judgment carries the force of law.[14]

The core of the adversary system is the *form* of participation accorded to the parties. Lon Fuller defines these as the "institutionally protected opportunity to present proofs and arguments for a decision in his favor."[15] Logically, the requirement for the participants to be able to provide proofs and arguments requires a neutral arbiter before whom to present the arguments and a set of standards or laws so that the litigants know the basis on which the decision will be made. The issues in dispute must be agreed upon, or otherwise there cannot be an engagement; the issues for decision must be presented in serial fashion; and reasoned argumentation must have the possibility of affecting the decision.

In summary, and interpreting Fuller's points from the text, which does not present them systematically (with apologies if the translation is not flawless), the key characteristics of the adversary process are as follows:

- A genuine dispute or conflict between two sides
- An impartial third party to make the decision
- An agreement as to the issues in dispute
- The possibility that reasoned argumentation can affect the decision
- A decision based on the arguments presented in court and the evidence presented by the parties
- The serial presentation of issues for decision[16]

How close are these attributes of the adjudicatory process to the traditional definition of what constitutes a court?

Routine Cases: The Dispositional Process

As the adversary process became more refined and cross-pollinated by the inquisitorial system used on the European continent, it was also modified to become more streamlined and more routinized to accommodate the larger caseloads.

The idea that some issues do not merit the full adversarial approach with all its complex and expensive due process should be relatively uncontroversial. The goal for this process is to achieve justice through timely case processing. Here is where William Gladstone's famous utterance "justice delayed is justice denied" is the guiding principle. An injustice is done, for example, when a prisoner is exonerated, but only after a long period in detention. A set sum of money owed but not repaid until a court judgment four or five years later may diminish in value. There are many cases in which achieving finality is important, in the sense that "any decision is better than no decision at all." There is a clear need to have some issues settled quickly and less expensively because the clients can simply not afford to go through the full adversary process to have their issues resolved. Equally true, courts cannot afford the time and resources necessary to provide full adversarial processing to each case.

After all, quick resolution of disputes is the thought behind small-claims dockets and civil dockets in limited-jurisdiction courts. Simpler proceedings do not necessarily imply a disregard for due process; it may be that some cases involve simpler fact situations than those heard in courts of general jurisdiction.[17]

The Problem-Solving Process

Henderson and his colleagues identify a type of case they call "diagnostic adjudication" where disposition does not depend on applying the facts to law but, rather, on clarifying the issues and fashioning appropriate remedies.[18] As we show later, the diagnosis aspect of adjudication has led almost inevitably to a treatment orientation for courts.

The current tension between the use of the structured procedures of the adversary system versus the flexibility of problem-solving procedures in many ways echoes the clash of values in debates over law courts versus equity courts in sixteenth-century England.[19] Note that such family matters as adoptions and guardianships, marriages and divorces, child-support enforcement, probate, mental illness, and even corporate law were originally placed in chancery courts. Juvenile courts are the most common "problem-solving" type of court, although they antedated the current movement by a hundred years. With the development of unified family courts, the specialization has evolved further.

Spurred by perceived inadequacies of the adversary process, courts have developed a more cooperative approach to dispute resolution. Particularly in family law, once a fertile source of trials, the theme is that the adversary system is not suited to disputes involving children.[20] The adversary process is focused on "winning" at trial, which minimizes direct communication between the parties, assigns blame, and generally engenders acrimony between parents. All these consequences harm children whose well-being is affected by their parents' behavior during and after the separation process.[21] These circumstances had led to calls to abandon adversarial proceedings "in favor of more informal approaches with the goal of encouraging parents to develop positive post-divorce co-parenting relationships."[22] Trying to resolve family issues within an adversary framework brings the Constitution to bear on issues that could be negotiated, or in other words, "Courts cannot police every situation."[23] In the words of one observer, "More and more judicial experts recognize the inadequacy of the win/lose system of traditional courts for dispute resolution. A system of mediation/arbitration could let all parties be winners, or at least have their interests be considered promptly and fairly."[24]

In the words of two reformers, "[I]n the last quarter century, the process of resolving legal family disputes has, both literally and metaphorically, moved from confrontation toward collaboration and from the courtroom to the conference room."[25] This transformation of family issues from legal disputes has other consequences: the role of lawyers diminishes, while the roles of mental-health professionals and court staff increase.

On the criminal side, the treatment-oriented approach to case resolution increased greatly in scale with the creation of drug courts, or, more accurately, specialized dockets that focused on repeat offenses and the addictions that brought offenders to court repeatedly.[26]

Problem-solving courts originated not in academia but from the efforts of "practical, creative, and intuitive judges and court personnel, grappling to find an alternative to revolving door justice, especially as dispensed to drug-addicted defendants."[27] They seek to broaden the focus of courts from simply adjudicating cases to changing the future behavior of litigants and ensuring the well-being of the communities they serve.

Figure 3.1 shows how three key questions are asked at case initiation to determine which of the four adjudication processes is most appropriate for the resolution of particular disputes. This chart *does not imply* that once a dispute is sorted into one of the four processes, it must remain assigned to that "track" until resolution. Disputes may change tracks as some issues resolve themselves and others emerge.

Are the Issues Clear and Well Defined?

The first question used to sort cases, regardless of whether the initial decision is made by a prosecutor, attorneys for the litigants, or by the litigants themselves, is "Are issues clear and well defined?"

If the issues are clear and joined, it is easier to know which adjudication process or "track" is most appropriate to use. If they are not, it is necessary to invest the time at the front end to identify the real issues. Many cases, especially family cases, come to court without the participants' having a clear idea of which issues need to be litigated and which issues are not in dispute. One way to identify the issues that should move forward is to have a court team available to meet with the litigants for the purpose of sorting out the issues. Perhaps at this point, a triage staff is necessary to assist in deciding which processing track is most appropriate for the issues raised. Issues may be clear and well defined but still complex and serious enough to warrant a full adversary proceeding. Referral to a triage team may be necessary to help litigants decide which track best fits their issues. Electronic filing portals could use TurboTax-like interrogations to elicit basic information necessary to help litigants decide on the most appropriate processing track.

Some cases are complex because they are an amalgamation of multiple, interrelated, issues—such as a divorce proceeding with issues of domestic violence, child custody, and child support involved—that need to be resolved together. These cases may require early assignment to a mediator or other nonjudge professional to narrow the issues to

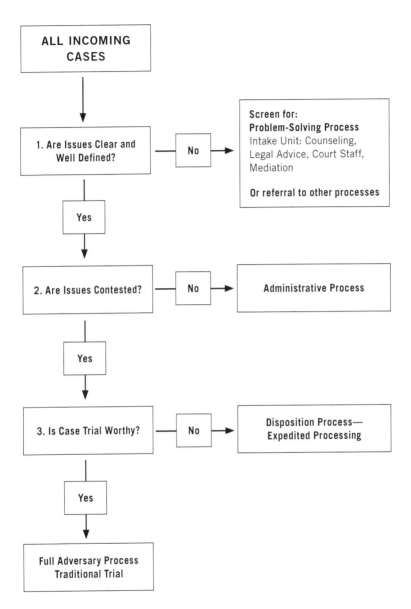

Figure 3.1 The Triage Process

those in dispute, to search for compromise, or to recommend a course of treatment.

Clarity may be even more of an issue for self-represented litigants, many of whom clearly require assistance to make rational decisions about which issues to pursue in which forum. Self-represented litigants make these decisions every day, but the current processes were not designed to be user-friendly for these litigants. For litigants who choose to represent themselves, the processes are rarely described and documented and even more rarely evaluated for effectiveness.

Are the Issues Contested?

Is there a concrete dispute between adverse litigants—that is, parties seeking different outcomes? This principle would apply not only to the classic example of a "friendly" lawsuit, where both parties seek a particular judgment from the court, but also to problem-solving types of cases, such as adoption, where both sides seek to find the best solution. The term *case in controversy* applies to only federal Article III courts, but state courts could adopt the same standard in answering this triage question.

As described more fully in the separate chapter on problem-solving processes, many family cases (other than delinquency cases that would be criminal except for the age of the offender) are not "contested" in the same adversary sense other court cases are. Some are more likely to require "diagnosis" of the problem, a joint search for a solution, and perhaps selection among various treatment options.

Are the Issues Trial Worthy?

Our use of the criterion "potential for trial" raised some concern among early reviewers of this manuscript because it could appear that we were advocating that some people should be denied their right to trial in lower-stakes cases. On the contrary, our esteem for the value of trials is demonstrated by their use as key criteria for triage into the adversary process—precisely to focus attention early on issues likely to require a full trial. The idea that any case could raise issues that not only have implications for the public at large but also affect justice in an individual case is well embedded in the American culture. In

Chapter 4, we argue that the adversary process should be reserved for cases with the potential to go to trial. Trials are important in themselves, but they also are little morality plays that serve a "theatrical or educational" function to instruct the public.[28] As a practical matter, we observe that public trial is too slow and costly to be used to resolve the vast volume of ordinary cases. Trials are certainly not the way most cases are resolved: they are a last resort, used only when all other attempts at resolution have failed. Full-blown trials with all the trimmings do occur today, but for a very small percentage of cases. In fact, trial rates have never been high, but they have dropped significantly over the past quarter of a century.[29] This situation does raise a larger question: how many trials are necessary to ensure the justice system is functioning properly?

We also observe that trials are still used for the "important" large-stakes cases as well as "notorious" cases—mostly criminal cases with sufficient public interest to be covered in the news and perhaps televised. These types of serious, even life or death, issues require attorneys to represent the accused. Self-representation is simply not appropriate for high-stakes cases.

These observations are not a statement of our opinions, just a fact that decisions about which issues are deemed to merit the courts' resources and public expense are now being made every day. Whenever a prosecutor decides to offer a plea agreement or not, whenever a litigant decides on the dollar amount in controversy so as to fall under the jurisdiction of a court with the ability to conduct trials, whenever an accused calculates the odds against the power of the state, a trial-worthy decision is being made.

We fully agree that "trial worthiness" should be defined in each jurisdiction, but we merely ask that the criteria be transparent and clear so that all parties know the rules of the game. We do note, however, that regardless of whether they are articulated, criteria that seem to be used to decide whether a case has the potential to go to trial include the following:

- Cases raising constitutional issues or conflict-of-law issues
- Criminal cases where the death penalty, a life sentence, or another significant loss of liberty is a potential outcome
- Civil cases (contract and tort) with high stakes

Triage by Issue

Triaging cases into four processing queues by early analysis of *issues* involved rather than case type is a fundamental change with many potential impacts on current approaches to case administration. Most courts docket their cases based only on case type. A few larger courts have implemented aspects of differentiated case management to separate cases into several tracks. A switch to triage by issue, however, could mean that four cases of the same case type might literally go into four different case-processing queues. One may be assigned for full adversary processing, another to expedited dispositional processing, a third to problem-solving treatment, and yet a fourth to administrative processing, regardless of whether it is under court jurisdiction. For example, a divorce case can be treated differently if it is contested rather than if an agreement has been reached informally. A further point is that divorces *should be* treated differently depending on whether the couple has children. Without children, the question becomes one of dividing property and other assets—a process quite common in civil courts. With children, the related issues of child support, custody, visitation, and the like become relevant, and the process used to make these decisions is very different. The point to be stressed here is that *the type of case involved is only a rough approximation of the issues involved.*

Reinforcing this point is that if court jurisdiction is assigned by case type, one case cannot be segmented to accommodate different processing. Often, for example, someone charged with driving while intoxicated will want a full adversary process used to determine guilt or innocence. After a guilty finding, it may be that the best sentence is indeed some sort of treatment for addiction to prevent future dangerous driving. Cases triaged by issue would permit different processes to be used at different stages of processing the same cases.

Cases requiring the full adversary process because of the seriousness of the issues raised need to be identified early and assigned to trial. This process would not be much of a change for criminal cases where the state brings the charges and the accused are required to come to court—triage for those cases would continue to be done by prosecutors who decide which charges to bring, which to reduce, and which to prosecute to the full extent of the law.

Clearly, more intense case management by clerk or administrator staff would be required. More sophisticated triaging algorithms would also be needed, complete with objective criteria for assignment that could be reasonably applied by nonlawyers. Dockets might be more diverse in case-type mix than they are now, requiring a different approach to judge assignment and preparation. Technological assistance using a modern case-management system would almost surely be needed for efficient case assignment and scheduling.

Enable Litigant Choice

Litigants now make the threshold decision of whether to bring civil, traffic, and probate cases to court, and they should control the process after cases are filed. To do so, they need to understand the alternative case-processing tracks available along with the due-process protections, costs, and legal expertise associated with each track. If a litigant chooses not to contest a case, he or she could pay a fine or settlement in full or on a payment schedule, perhaps electronically. Would it be worthwhile for a litigant to reduce the dollar amount in controversy to fit the jurisdiction of a lower court if the result were a quicker resolution? Some principles may be worth fighting for in terms of a more protracted, involved, and costly process, whereas in other cases, litigants may prefer faster resolutions even if they yield smaller awards. Why should they not be able to make those choices just like they do in medicine and other spheres of life?

On the last point, note that what constitutes a "correct" queue depends on not only the court's technical legal analysis but also the litigants' preferences for a track based on their assessment of cost, complexity, timeliness, and due process requirements. Litigants can not make these kinds of tradeoffs rationally in the absence of "market" information about these characteristics of case-processing tracks. Many lawyers would also benefit from this type of information.

Make the Best of Legal Resources

Finally, courts should never forget their most defining operating characteristic: judges, who have the most education and greatest legal expertise, are the most expensive court resource. Courts should do everything they can to maximize other staff resources to perform appropriate tasks, including analyzing the issues in a case and managing the case-processing tracks, much in the same way physicians use physician's assistants and senior nurses to assess and treat routine patient complaints. Which issues are serious enough to warrant the attention of a judge?

Triage and Processing Tracks

The suggested methods of triage are intended to sort issues into the appropriate processing tracks. As one way to think about this, cases can be complex because they involve difficult issues of law or difficult issues of fact. Laws can sometimes be unclear, challenged, or perhaps even in conflict with one another. As well, fact situations can be relatively straightforward or complex, clear or unclear. As a model for thinking about this, recognizing that the virtue of models is that they oversimplify to achieve clarity of thought, we propose the forum choice ideal presented in Table 3.2.

The most complex issues—those where the law may be unsettled and the facts are hotly contested—should probably end up being resolved by the full adversary process in a court of general jurisdiction. Cases where the law is settled and clear but the primary issue is factual should probably be decided using a dispositional process. A classic example is a criminal case where the issue is not one of challenging the law but of determining whether the accused indeed committed the crime. Cases where neither the law nor the facts are in dispute can be handled by an administrative process. A classic example is a parking ticket for which the individual admits that the time expired and he or she wants only to pay a fine. The obvious missing box is the problem-solving procedure, which could arguably fit into all these categories but which we have not placed in this chart because we later argue that problem solving is a process that is different from the other methods of adjudication not in degree but in kind.

TABLE 3.2. FORUM CHOICE IDEAL TYPE

LAW CHALLENGED?	FACTS IN DISPUTE?	
	Yes	*No*
Yes	Adversary process	* * *
No	Dispositional process	Administrative process

Appendix to Chapter 3

Functional Equivalents to Triage: Historical Strategies

States recognized early that not all court cases could be conducted using the full adversary proceeding because that process was too cumbersome, costly, and unwarranted for some types of lower-stakes cases. Consequently, several methods of sorting cases were used in the past.

Court Organization

Our interpretation of the evolution of court organization is that states realized that different types of courts were needed to resolve different types of issues. Courts of general jurisdiction were designed to handle the traditional adversarial cases, courts of limited jurisdiction to handle the high-volume cases in an expedited manner, and courts of special jurisdiction to handle cases not suitable for the full adversary process, sometimes because of the age, mental capacities, family status, or other characteristics of the litigants. Even before the era of problem-solving courts, states developed special courts to meet special needs—for example, water courts in Colorado and land courts in Hawaii. Note that even in states that have a single-tiered trial court, that structure is modified by having one court but two classes of judges—full judges for felonies and high-stakes civil cases and associate judges for misdemeanors, lower-stakes civil cases, and domestic-relations cases.

Legal Restrictions

Judicial threshold questions have been used as "gatekeepers" to restrict or enhance access to courts.[1] Threshold questions include jurisdictional challenges, issues of standing, exhaustion of remedies, statutes of limitations, a party's immunity from suit, or whether a claim is ripe or moot, involves a political question, or is frivolous. The doctrines of justiciability place limits on the types of issues courts can resolve. According to Jethro K. Lieberman, "For most of its history, the law was ringed with impediments that kept large classes of people from the courts and hence from any hope of redress."[2] He notes how defects in the language of pleading, for example, could lead to permanent dismissal. Now, justiciability has been liberalized so that "standing" to sue has been interpreted less rigidly, mootness of cases (such as abortion) has been overlooked, and class actions have increased. This liberalization of justiciability has increased to the extent that it has come under some criticism for lacking purpose—"[i]n many cases, justiciability rules do no more than act as an apparently pointless constraint on courts."[3]

Differentiated Case Management

Caseflow management refers to managing, monitoring, and responding effectively to individual court cases and the varied needs of each one, from initial filing to final disposition.[4] It makes sense that cases languish if nobody pays any attention to them. In an age when case-management systems did not routinely produce reports flagging problem cases, such problems could go unattended, so paying attention was the first requirement. Even today, simply having case managers who spend time ensuring that cases move in a timely fashion would improve a court's performance. This is the basic caseflow management tenet of early court intervention and continuous court control of case progress, which results in shorter times to disposition, at least in civil cases.[5]

With the increasing volume and diversity of cases coming to court, it has become apparent that the "first in/first out" approach to case management could be improved. A set of best practices collectively known as differentiated case management (DCM) was developed to sort individual cases by the amount of attention they needed from judges and the pace at which they could be expected to proceed. Literally thousands of court personnel were trained on these concepts, and such training continues to this day.

A key feature of DCM is to assign cases to different processing queues or "tracks" by case type and by case complexity. There is often an expedited track for cases that have a modest need for court oversight, a track for "ordinary" contested cases, and a track for complex cases, each with different scheduled events and timeframes.[6] Obviously, more complex cases require more processing time on average and are more vulnerable to encountering problems that result in significant delay. In David C. Steelman's words, "Courts have long recognized that certain cases may be so complex that they need special judicial attention and call for a departure from procedures typically applied to all cases."[7] Separating more complex cases into a separate "tracks" for increased attention reduces the chances that serious problems will develop.

While these ideas seem obvious and noncontroversial, DCM has been adopted only sporadically in relatively few jurisdictions. Even in those jurisdictions that have adopted DCM, the serious problems that remain have spurred us to seek a more aggressive form of caseflow management.

First and foremost, case pressure on courts and judges is steadily increasing over time, requiring courts to process more cases with fewer staff. This trend has been going on now for more than three decades and shows little sign of abating in the midst of the current budget crisis. Even courts using DCM to keep pace with increasing caseloads may have difficulty maintaining that equilibrium when future increases in caseload demand even higher productivity.

Second, when DCM was developed, courts existed in a less complex world, with fewer diversion programs, mediation programs, and other methods of alternative dispute resolution. The number of self-represented litigants was small. Neither problem-solving courts nor electronic discovery existed. In short, the variety of cases and the number of case-processing alternatives have grown significantly. To make matters worse, cases may contain multiple issues that may require them to shift from one case-processing strategy and process to another, depending on how the issues manifest themselves over the lives of the cases. Classic DCM needs to be updated to accommodate these new complexities and to promote ever-higher levels of case-processing productivity.

The Adversary Process

> The trial is the sun around which all of the planets
> in the law's solar system move.
>
> —JUDGE JAMES BOYD WHITE, quoted in
> Robert P. Burns, *The Death of the American Trial*

Literally hundreds of books have been written about the adversary process by authors more qualified to comment on it than we are. In Chapter 3, we equated the adversary system to the very definition of courts themselves in the United States. Indeed, we argue that the two concepts have become so intertwined that it sometimes blinds us to the other adjudication processes being used successfully. The adversary process, with its emphasis on trials, is critical to our conception of justice in the United States. More cases go to trial in the United States than in most other countries, and more defendants are found not guilty here than in most other countries, adding credibility and legitimacy to the entire justice system.[1]

The Adversary Process Should Be Reserved for Trials

What comes to mind when one thinks of the word *court*? Is it not the image of the trial, more particularly the criminal trial? An adult is arrested for a crime, retains Perry Mason as an attorney, and goes to trial in a wood-paneled and marble-floored courtroom.[2]

Lawrence M. Freedman provides an even sharper image:

> There is a definite image about every aspect of the trial, even
> what the courtroom is supposed to be like; the jury sits in its

box, the judge sits on his or her high bench in a robe with an American flag in the background, the witnesses come in and sit on the witness chair; they raise their right hands and swear; the lawyers and the defendant sit at tables facing the judge. The trial begins with elaborate voir dire—the meticulous process of selecting a jury. The lawyers battle and squabble, trying to stack the jury with people they feel will vote the way they want. The trial itself gets going with opening arguments and statements from the lawyers. The trial itself is long, tense, and full of excitement. The lawyers joust with each other. There is clever and dramatic cross-examination. Lawyers jump up and cry, "I object"; . . . [t]hey end the trial with impassioned arguments. Then the judge instructs the jury, the jury retires to a locked room, and a spine-tingling period of waiting begins. Finally, the door opens, a hush comes over the crowd in the courtroom, and the jury comes in and announces its verdict.[3]

Public expectations of courts may be derived more often from portrayals of trials on television and in the movies than from actual experience.

It should be noted from the onset that the concept of "trial" has changed over time. The adversary trial did not spring to life fully formed but developed piecemeal. John H. Langbein has shown that the adversary system of trial was transformed to a lawyer-dominated process between the 1690s and the 1780s.[4] Before then, trials were an occasion for the defendant to answer charges in person, without the need for defense counsel to serve as an intermediary between the accused and the court. Indeed, defense counsel was forbidden in matters of fact to "pressure the accused to speak in his own defense."[5] Without defense counsel, the trial judge organized the admission and presentation of evidence and examined the witnesses. In this early period (1558–1625), trials were very abrupt, with the average duration of a trial, including time for jury deliberations, calculated at between fifteen and twenty minutes[6]—and these were felony cases that could and did result in death sentences upon conviction. By the mid–eighteenth century, the average trial time had lengthened to about half an hour per trial. So typical was the brief trial that an exceptional proceeding that lasted for some hours became the subject of remark. By the early nineteenth century, ten to twelve trials could be held each morning, with jury deliberation lasting only minutes.[7] English juries sitting in the Old Bailey could try between twelve and twenty felony cases per day.[8]

One reason for this expedition is that English barristers did not file lengthy written submissions to courts but orally educated the court on the facts and the law: "In many cases even the judges' deliberations would be made in open court."[9] This approach had the benefit of making the entire process transparent, interactive, and public, but trials became more elaborate over time. No national norms exist for reasonable trial lengths. Empirical studies report great variation in the length of civil and criminal trials within states and among states but consistently find that jury trials last longer than nonjury trials and that civil trials last longer than criminal trials.[10] The State-of-the-States Survey on Jury Improvement Efforts reports that the median jury deliberation time in state courts for capital felony cases is six hours, for felony and civil cases three hours, and for misdemeanor cases two hours.[11]

In his farewell address as president of the American Bar Association, Eugene Thomas noted, "We know that it should not be necessary for cases that 15 years ago could be tried in two days to require now two months."[12]

Long trials even affect cases that do not go to trial, because many settlements or guilty pleas do not occur until the trial date nears. The length of trials may also help explain the lack of plea bargaining in our early history. As noted above, trials then did not resemble the full adversary process we expect today but were more "quick, slapdash" proceedings, where twelve people were impaneled without voir dire, most defendants were not represented by counsel, little or no cross-examination occurred, few objections were raised, and the jury did not take long to deliberate, thus allowing a jury to hear more than one case per day.[13]

Decreasing Trials

Even with the resources of the National Center for State Courts (NCSC), it is not possible to report complete trial data from state courts. Data on civil dispositions are available for a thirty-four-year period from fifteen courts of general jurisdiction, and the proportion of jury and bench trials from those states is provided in the appendix to this chapter.[14] Figures 4.1 and 4.2 show the decline in jury and bench trials over time.

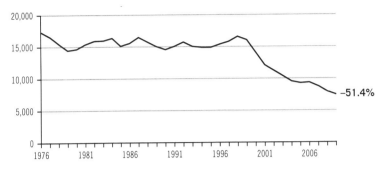

Figure 4.1. Civil Jury Trials in Fifteen Courts, 1976–2009

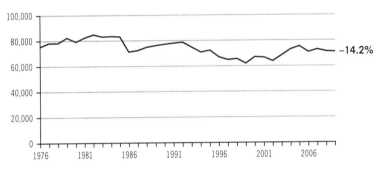

Figure 4.2. Civil Bench Trials in Fifteen Courts, 1976–2009

Between 1976 and 2009, bench trials in civil cases fell by two-thirds from 15.4 to 4.7 percent of dispositions. Civil jury trials fell even further—from 3.5 percent of dispositions to 0.5 percent of civil dispositions.

According to the NCSC's Court Statistics Project, 21.3 million criminal cases were filed in state courts in 2008, and that number is an undercount because of the lack of reporting from some states. Figure 4.3 shows the proportions of criminal cases disposed by jury and bench trials from the sixteen state courts of general jurisdiction that were able to report complete and consistent data for this thirty-four-year period.

One look at the numbers in Figure 4.3 confirms that a full-blown trial is not now, nor has it ever been, a practical way to resolve most

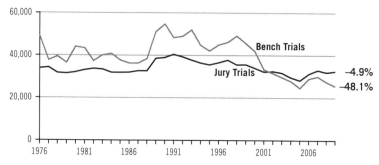

Figure 4.3. Criminal Trials in Sixteen Courts, 1976–2009

criminal cases—even most felonies. In 1976, only 7.6 percent of criminal cases were resolved by trial, and that proportion has declined steadily, dropping to 2 percent by 2008.

The declining percentage of cases resolved by trials does not necessarily mean a reduction of workload for judges. One of the key factors in determining workload is whether a case goes to trial. Even though trials are relatively rare, they require much more time to resolve than cases decided without trials. A workload assessment in Minnesota clearly illustrates the differences. Using a personal-injury case as an example, the study found that pretrial activities required an average of fifty-five minutes to resolve, and postdisposition activities required another fifty-two minutes, *regardless* of whether a case went to trial.[15] The differences in judicial workload for cases that went to trial were dramatic. In addition to the time required for pretrial activities and postdisposition activities, cases resolved without trials required an additional average of approximately an hour to dispose of (62 minutes), whereas cases that went to trial required more than twelve hours (733 minutes).[16] This pattern continued for other case types as well. Again omitting the time required for pretrial and postdisposition activities because they remain constant for all cases, the differences required to dispose of cases between nontrial dispositions and dispositions by trial in selected Minnesota case types are shown in Table 4.1.

From these illustrations of a variety of case types, we can see that the judicial effort required to resolve cases by trial takes between twelve and eighty-seven times longer than the time required to resolve cases without a trial. Case types that have a smaller proportion of tri-

TABLE 4.1. TRIAL AND NONTRIAL: AVERAGE TIME REQUIRED TO RESOLVE CASES IN MINNESOTA

	JUDGE TIME IN MINUTES		
	Nontrial	Trial	Times Longer
Serious Felonies	43	3397	79.0
Other Felonies	13	608	46.7
Gross Misdemeanor DWI	14	375	26.7
Gross Misdemeanor	8	265	33.0
Personal Injury	62	733	11.8
Contract	41	802	19.5
Termination of Parental Rights	13	532	41.0
Marriage Dissolution (Children)	17	674	39.4
Marriage Dissolution (No Children)	4	350	87.5
Domestic Abuse	14	195	13.9

TABLE 4.2. RATIO OF JURY TRIALS TO BENCH TRIALS, 1976–2009

		1976	2009
Civil	Jury	19%	10%
	Bench	81%	90%
Criminal	Jury	41%	55%
	Bench	59%	45%

als obviously require less processing time than cases that have a higher trial rate. The Minnesota Study did not make a distinction between jury trials and bench trials, but we know that jury trials require more judge time to resolve than bench trials do.[17]

The ratio of jury trials to bench trials varies by case type. Civil cases are mostly resolved by bench trials, but criminal trials are much more likely to be conducted in front of a jury (see Table 4.2).

The reasons for these shifts are not clear. The answer to the decline in civil trials may lie in the unhappiness of corporations with the timeliness and predictability of trials. Bench trials may be less susceptible to these criticisms or are at least perceived to be so. The establishment of business courts in twenty-two states may have incrementally helped stem the tide as well. In contrast, the rate of criminal trials has sunk so low that few trials remain that do not require juries.

Trial statistics reported by the states, as noted above, are incomplete. Rather than the comparatively small number of jury trials reported from the sixteen state courts of general jurisdiction, a "State-of-the-States Survey" published in 2007 estimated that 148,558 jury trials are conducted annually.[18] Not surprisingly, California reported the largest number of jury trials (approximately 16,000 annually), and Vermont and Wyoming had the smallest number (reporting approximately 126 jury trials per year). The *rate* of jury trials, which controls for population, also varies widely, from a low of 15 trials per 100,000 population in Alabama to a high of 177 per 100,000 in Alaska (59 trials per 100,000 is the national average). As noted above, most jury trials are criminal (47 percent felony and 19 percent misdemeanor), 31 percent are civil trials, and the remaining 4 percent are family, juvenile, traffic, and other. In addition to incomplete reporting, another reason the national number of jury trials is underestimated is that a much larger proportion of jury trials than expected, perhaps as much as 40 percent, is conducted in courts of limited jurisdiction.[19] The statistics reported in the tables above are based on the number of jury trials conducted in courts of general jurisdiction and suggest the recent trend to eliminate jury trials for less serious offenses has not been as successful as presumed.

Triage: Trial Worthiness

Which types of cases require the full protection of an adversary process? They should be hotly contested between two sides. The two sides may be unequal in terms of power—for example, the government versus an individual, a multinational corporation versus an individual, or a government agency versus a small business, so that the need for an impartial forum to equalize the uneven power is paramount. John H. Wigmore considers the adversary system "the greatest legal engine ever invented for the discovery of truth."[20] Lieberman adds that for a society with a commitment to political freedom, by

> putting the state to an extreme burden of proof and by guaranteeing defendants access to fiercely independent lawyers, we

can in general prevent the state from imprisoning those whom it distrusts or fears. Similarly, a competitive society will look to the forms of trial as the best means of enforcing compliance with contractual commitments and of deterring fraud.[21]

Although we do not presume to recommend criteria to determine which issues are trial worthy, some criteria undoubtedly considered are whether the disputes involve the following:

1. A constitutional issue
2. A novel issue of law or a conflict of laws
3. Notoriety, public attention, and interest
4. High stakes or a large dollar amount in controversy
5. A challenge to government policy
6. A felony with penalties involving a serious deprivation of liberty, including the death penalty
7. Complex issues that have already defied multiple attempts at mediation, arbitration, or other means of settlement
8. Such disparities in power between parties that an impartial forum is critical to justice

Role of the Judge: Umpire

Redesigning this process would involve using judge time for the "highest and best" purpose—conducting trials—and shedding administrative duties to court administrators or other quasi judicial personnel when possible. This change would make judge workload conform to the public expectation, but misperception, that judges spend most of their time conducting trials.

In the early history of the adversary process, defendants spoke for themselves, and judges were much more active in questioning them. Defense counselors were admitted in the 1730s to safeguard against the danger of mistaken conviction.[22] Initially they were limited mostly to cross-examination to supplement the efforts of the accused to conduct his or her own defense. Soon, counsel silenced the defendant and the nature of the trial changed forever, with the focus now on lawyers rather than on the accused. With attorneys gathering and presenting facts for each side, the role of the trial court judge became more passive.

Accordingly, the role of the judge in the adversary process is to preside over the proceedings and maintain order. During a trial, the judge rules on whether any of the evidence the parties want to use is illegal or improper. If the trial is before a jury, the judge gives instructions about the law that applies to the case; if the trial is before the court, the judge determines the facts and decides the case. After the trial, bench or jury, the judge metes out the sentence to the convicted. Note also the role of the judge in this idealized conception—a very passive umpire enforcing the procedural rules of the game. In the language of modern confirmation hearings, the judge is a passive referee who just "calls balls and strikes."[23] As a result, parties have more control over the evidence they present and are able to tell their own story in court. In contrast, judges in the inquisitorial system found on the European continent have much greater control over the discovery process, the witnesses to be called, and the questions to be asked. As a result, judges there have much more control over the facts that will be allowed to appear in public.[24] Some American judges who assume the umpire role have taken a more active role in encouraging litigants to agree to restricted discovery, use expert witnesses, and so forth in the interests of increasing efficiency. It will be interesting to track this development to see whether it is indeed an emerging trend toward a less passive umpire role.

In addition to the judicial role in the adversarial process, it must be mentioned that ordinary citizens, as jurors, do play a key decision-making role in trials: "No other institution of government rivals the jury in placing power so directly in the hands of citizens."[25]

Court Staff

The staff required in the adversary process is minimal when compared to the staffing needed for the other processes to be described. Trials are designed so that the court and/or jury has evidence presented to it by the attorneys. Courts do not independently investigate issues, and so the only staff required are those necessary to make the record and to provide security to the proceedings.

Facilities

The adversary process requires that a judge preside over a court of unlimited jurisdiction with the expectation that cases will be resolved by jury or bench trial. These cases require the full majesty of the traditional courthouse—large rooms with marble and pillars, jury rooms, red velour curtains, and the like. Because of the theater of a trial, the courthouse should be located in large cities, county seats of large counties, or regional centers for smaller counties. Trials are important enough to warrant all the appropriate facilities. Convenience to litigants and other participants is less important in these serious cases, but their inconvenience can be mitigated by high-technology courtrooms with the capability to support high-quality videoconferencing, so that litigants, expert witnesses, underage juveniles, court interpreters, and other key participants can participate virtually—without needing to be physically present. Efficiencies can be achieved if jury selection is done online and panel members report directly to specific courtrooms rather than to assembly areas.[26]

Court Performance

The concept of impartiality is the "heart of the judicial process."[27] The reason people go to court is to get a fair decision made by a neutral arbiter uninfluenced by either external pressures or internal preferences to make decisions. Consequently, for adversary processes, the primary measures of court performance should be derived from Standard 3 of the *Trial Court Performance Standards*—Equality, Fairness, and Integrity—and particularly from Standard 3.3, which requires that court decisions be based on legally relevant factors consistently applied.[28]

Theodore L. Becker considers the concepts of impartiality and independence together to be distinguishing features of courts.[29] However, we believe that if impartiality and fairness are at the heart of the adversary process, independence is a necessary precondition that allows courts to make impartial decisions. To be impartial, judges must be free to decide cases based upon the laws and facts of the case without any pressure to lean one way or the other. Impartiality is impossible unless judges are free from the external pressures of threats, intimidation, or fears of sanctions based on the content of their decisions. In some places, threats to impartiality can be direct and drastic, such as threats on a judge's life, or more subtle pressures can be exerted, such as denial of salary increases, promotions, staff, or equipment needed to do the job. In other words, Trial Court Performance Standard 4, "Independence and Accountability," is important to ensure impartiality, because judicial independence protects the judge from undue influence and, by extension, individuals from arbitrary use of government power. Consequently, the primary measures of court performance for those issues requiring an adversary process for resolution should be those of equity and fairness, supported by independence and accountability.

Proposed Remedies

Because the adversary process is so interrelated with the concept of courts itself, the steep decline in trial rates is troubling. Even if trials are rare, the public expectation is that everyone has a right to go to trial. Indeed, members of the public might be quite surprised if asked to estimate the number of criminal cases resolved by trial versus those resolved by plea agreement. They may have no idea of the proportion of civil cases resolved out of court.

Stephen Landsman has suggested that the decline in trials might strengthen the trend toward a less adversarial and more inquisitorial approach to litigation.[30] The "death" of the trial would mean the end of a forum where a case is presented *"orally and dramatically."*[31] A decline in trials would undercut the adversary process with its elaborate procedural and evidentiary rules, which are necessary to regulate the confrontation inherent in a trial. This decline would also transform the role of the judge to a more "inquiring magistrate who guides cases through a series of what might be described as discovery sessions or pretrial events to an adjudication."[32] In a sense, Landsman may be describing how the adversarial and inquisitorial systems have influenced each other. In this example, some of the pretrial characteristics of the inquisitorial system have resulted in what we describe as the dispositional process. The goal of these proceedings, as described in Chapter 5, is not a public hearing but a fair and equitable resolution of cases with the least cost to the litigants and to the court.

The antidote to this would be to increase the number of trials, which means that trials would have to become more efficient and less costly. Recall from Figures 4.1, 4.2, and 4.3, supported by data reported separately by year in Tables 4.A1 and 4.A2 in the appendix to this chapter, that criminal and civil jury-trial rates among states with data to report are 1.1 percent and 0.5 percent, respectively, while bench trial rates are 0.9 percent and 4.7 percent, respectively. Indeed, we suspect that even the relatively small portion of civil bench trials is an overestimate, because they are likely to include resolutions of some relatively routine cases in courts of limited jurisdiction. Moreover, the definition of what constitutes a trial varies among states and could influence the numbers. Even accepting the most generous definitions of a trial, the trial rates are small and unlikely to increase in the near future.

On the criminal side, William J. Stuntz argues that the lack of transparency in guilty pleas, especially those that occur early in the process, is a problem that would be mitigated if a larger proportion of criminal cases were resolved by trial.[33] Thus, he recommends a greater use of jury trials, with jurors drawn from neighborhoods rather than large metropolitan counties.[34] If the number of criminal trials increased, the public could see how cases are resolved. Stuntz believes that public visibility would improve decision making and increase public trust and confidence in the court system.

Prosecutors and defense attorneys would make fairer plea agreements, knowing the likely outcomes of trials. Plea agreements would then become the way to settle "easy" cases, as opposed to the *primary* method of determining guilt or innocence for most defendants.

How could courts get the resources to conduct more criminal trials? One area being examined now is to decriminalize or reduce the charges for certain offenses, the most notable being possession of marijuana. Because so many crimes are related to substance abuse and mental illness, specialty problem-solving courts have burgeoned, with the goal of reducing repeat business to courts. The advantages and disadvantages of this option are covered in much more detail in Chapters 7 and 8.

Another possibility may be to manage the noncriminal caseloads more efficiently and perhaps even to remove some of these cases from courts. There is a widespread perception that "the civil justice system is too complex, costs too much, and takes too long."[35] Not only low-income but some middle-class members of the public feel priced out of court and the legal representation required for what were once-routine causes of action, such as divorce, foreclosures, and property torts. Although there is not necessarily a direct correlation between the cost of representation and the prevalence of trials, certainly some people are unlikely to risk trial without professional representation, and therefore there is at least an indirect relationship between the two.

The decline in civil jury trials means fewer cases that "have the benefit of citizen input, fewer case precedents, fewer jurors who understand the system, fewer judges and lawyers who can try jury cases."[36] The very legitimacy of courts rests partially on the participation of the public, and the jury is a very valuable point of contact between the public and the courts. Several empirical studies have shown that participation in jury trials is one of the two most important sources of the legitimacy of courts themselves.[37]

The remedy here, as in criminal trials, is to have shorter, more expedited, less costly trials. Toward this end, three prominent court-reform organizations are recommending a "short, summary, and expedited civil action program."[38] In practice, this means doing the following:

1. Limiting the trials to one or two days
2. Adopting a certain and fixed trial date
3. Expediting the pretrial process
4. Driving the pretrial process by favoring rules that promote evidentiary agreements, encouraging stipulations, and narrowing the focus of issues to be addressed at trial
5. Making the expedited track voluntary

In this way, the courts would seek to actively control the scope of discovery, expert witnesses, depositions, and other pretrial events that can get out of control. The benefits of this process to the courts would include reducing the amount of judge and court staff time required to dispose of cases, clearing the dockets faster, and better using judges' time by having them preside only over jury trials.[39] Litigants would benefit because their cases would take less time and cost less. Jurors would benefit by having the opportunity to participate in the justice system, but in shorter, more focused trials.

Another area to examine is the wide variation in time required to dispose of a case of a certain degree of complexity among judges and among the courts. The greatest variation occurs in the amount of time devoted to trials. Examining disposition times in light of performance guidelines may result in a reduction in the amount of judge and staff time required.

Finally, we advocate strongly throughout this book for providing litigants with more and better information about typical costs of representation, court costs, and prior case outcomes (in aggregate percentages) so that they make better decisions regarding whether to go to court, which courts to file in (if there is a choice), and, perhaps most important, empirically based expectations of the likely outcomes. Granted, it may take some time to implement these changes and additional time after that for litigants to understand and use this information to best inform their cost-benefit decisions. It will be interesting to determine the stance the bar takes on the ready availability of this information. On the one hand, attorneys will undoubtedly find this information useful to their practice, but on the other hand, they may resist disseminating information that makes an evaluation of the value added more transparent.

If it is true that American courts are designed to use the adversary process, what happens when courts adapt to changing situations by using other adjudication processes? Can expedited processes be grafted onto the adversary system without threatening its integrity? Can problem-solving processes be added to the adversary system without affecting the perception of impartiality? These are some of the questions we tackle in the chapters that follow.

Appendix to Chapter 4

The Decreasing Number of Jury and Bench Trials

TABLE 4.A1. CIVIL DISPOSITIONS AND TRIALS IN FIFTEEN GENERAL JURISDICTION COURTS, 1976–2009

Year	Total Dispositions	TRIALS			
		Jury	% Dispositions	Bench	% Dispositions
1976	494,405	17,282	3.5	76,157	15.4
1977	519,708	16,579	3.2	78,429	15.1
1978	584,947	15,486	2.6	78,505	13.4
1979	616,803	14,477	2.3	82,095	13.3
1980	649,980	14,689	2.3	79,865	12.3
1981	696,655	15,322	2.2	82,769	11.9
1982	709,707	15,800	2.2	84,755	11.9
1983	757,358	15,922	2.1	83,304	11.0
1984	788,288	16,209	2.1	84,064	10.7
1985	886,985	15,072	1.7	83,548	9.4
1986	893,656	15,453	1.7	71,705	8.0
1987	911,288	16,331	1.8	72,529	8.0
1988	980,259	15,708	1.6	75,440	7.7
1989	1,028,730	15,020	1.5	76,610	7.4
1990	1,049,783	14,511	1.4	77,640	7.4
1991	1,081,129	14,952	1.4	78,750	7.3
1992	1,209,348	15,640	1.3	78,894	6.5
1993	1,130,185	14,980	1.3	75,092	6.6
1994	1,083,820	14,875	1.4	71,165	6.6
1995	1,078,067	14,868	1.4	72,584	6.7
1996	1,084,298	15,314	1.4	67,260	6.2
1997	1,136,744	15,668	1.4	65,520	5.8
1998	1,214,636	16,435	1.4	65,720	5.4
1999	1,162,762	16,009	1.4	62,867	5.4
2000	1,170,923	14,166	1.2	67,700	5.8
2001	1,224,586	12,250	1.0	67,110	5.5
2002	1,221,771	11,289	.9	64,261	5.3
2003	1,259,682	10,382	.8	69,259	5.5
2004	1,305,417	9,598	.7	73,310	5.6
2005	1,291,738	9,200	.7	75,367	5.8
2006	1,243,592	9,319	.7	71,298	5.7
2007	1,282,696	8,742	.7	73,057	5.7
2008	1,387,143	7,824	.6	71,889	5.2
2009	1,496,017	7,443	.5	71,050	4.7
% Change 1976–2009		−51.4		−14.2	
% Change 2000–2009		−47.5		+4.9	

TABLE 4.A2. CRIMINAL DISPOSITIONS AND TRIALS IN SIXTEEN GENERAL JURISDICTION COURTS, 1976–2009

Year	Total Dispositions	TRIALS			
		Jury	% Dispositions	Bench	% Dispositions
1976	1,086,538	33,887	3.1	48,907	4.5
1977	1,136,105	34,389	3.0	37,678	3.3
1978	1,169,955	31,836	2.7	39,146	3.3
1979	1,265,714	31,342	2.5	36,448	2.9
1980	1,298,012	31,962	2.5	43,892	3.4
1981	1,412,070	32,981	2.3	43,300	3.1
1982	1,471,536	33,797	2.3	37,276	2.5
1983	1,506,795	33,263	2.2	39,895	2.6
1984	1,543,106	31,642	2.1	40,793	2.6
1985	1,618,817	31,675	2.0	37,701	2.3
1986	1,701,713	32,161	1.9	36,179	2.1
1987	1,802,972	32,585	1.8	36,228	2.0
1988	1,895,902	32,769	1.7	38,306	2.0
1989	2,032,309	38,218	1.9	50,951	2.5
1990	2,980,280	38,979	1.3	54,350	1.8
1991	3,120,524	40,055	1.3	48,224	1.5
1992	3,116,883	39,216	1.3	48,811	1.6
1993	2,906,431	37,853	1.3	51,761	1.8
1994	2,817,325	36,441	1.3	44,573	1.6
1995	2,876,677	35,538	1.2	42,047	1.5
1996	2,928,933	36,447	1.2	44,878	1.5
1997	2,871,747	37,790	1.3	46,267	1.6
1998	2,838,731	35,673	1.3	49,087	1.7
1999	2,805,800	35,490	1.3	45,610	1.6
2000	2,723,789	33,917	1.2	41,738	1.5
2001	2,698,458	32,486	1.2	33,404	1.2
2002	2,751,672	32,346	1.2	31,367	1.1
2003	2,684,231	31,916	1.2	29,721	1.1
2004	2,676,075	29,684	1.1	27,728	1.0
2005	2,787,667	28,430	1.0	24,675	.9
2006	2,937,652	31,263	1.1	28,981	1.0
2007	2,962,753	32,862	1.1	29,963	1.0
2008	2,915,366	32,152	1.1	27,537	.9
2009	2,884,346	32,239	1.1	25,365	.9
% Change 1976–2009		−4.9		−48.1	
% Change 2000–2009		−4.9		−39.2	

Note: States included in the criminal trend: Alaska, Arizona, California, Delaware, Florida, Hawaii, Indiana, Kansas, Maryland, Michigan, Missouri, North Carolina, Ohio, Pennsylvania, Texas, and Vermont.

The Dispositional Process

B ecause the parties themselves control the gathering of information in the adversary process, delays and high costs are common. Issues most appropriate for resolution by the dispositional process are the more standard "cases" that occur frequently enough so that the law is established and the key determination is whether the facts in question meet the standard of the law. These more-routine cases require facts to be established so that the law can be quickly applied, and sentences and financial penalties are limited so that dispositions can be expeditious.[1] Clearing the docket then becomes very important, and the primary task becomes processing a large number of individual cases, a more streamlined process not unfamiliar to the administrative agencies in the executive branch of government.

Criminal Processing

Most routine cases do not require jury trials, and bench trials are rare. For example, misdemeanor cases are now and have always been handled quickly and summarily without much technicality.[2] Approximately 80 percent of criminal cases are misdemeanors, and most of them (more than 70 percent) are handled by municipal judges, justices of the peace, or magistrates in courts of limited jurisdiction. Even that 70 percent figure is an underestimate, because ten states plus the District of

Columbia and Puerto Rico are unified and thus have only a single-tiered trial court rather than courts of general jurisdiction and courts of limited jurisdiction. (Unified courts do, however, have separate categories of judges—for example, associate judges to handle misdemeanors and traffic cases.) In the sense that these lower criminal courts hear the bulk of criminal cases, including disorderly conduct, drunkenness, prostitution, petty theft, and simple assault cases, they *are* the courts with the most contact with offenders, and the stereotype of "assembly line" justice was created in these courts.[3] One Albany lawyer describes in his blog the situation in the lower courts of New York:

> The biggest problem with our court system is the volume of cases. The volume is so large that the courts have to rely on assembly line justice. It really is an assembly line. The police officer prepares the initial papers and files them with the clerk. The clerk gives the papers to the prosecutor who reviews them and discusses the case with the lawyer or the pro-se defendant. The papers then go back to the clerk, who then hands them to the judge. The judge calls the case.
>
> There's a brief discussion at the bench. Then the papers go back to the clerk, who then processes the result (fine notice, schedule next date, etc.).
>
> Think about this: If a court has 100 cases on for a particular session (a typical number for courts like Colonie, Guilderland, Albany, etc.), and each case takes 15 minutes, that would take 25 hours. That's not going to work. If each case takes only 5 minutes, it still takes 8 hours, so that's still not going to work. Most courts end up at about 1–2 minutes per case. That's assembly line justice.[4]

Chief Justice Kathleen A. Blatz of the Minnesota Supreme Court relates a similar story:

> I think the innovation that we are seeing now is the result of judges processing cases like a vegetable factory. Instead of cans of peas, you've got cases. You just move 'em, move 'em, move 'em. One of my colleagues on the bench said: "You know, I feel like I work for McJustice: we sure aren't good for you, but we are fast."[5]

Prosecutors and Plea Agreements

The section above describes the criminal workload from the court perspective, but in the vast majority of these criminal cases, the judge is not the primary decision maker—the prosecutor is. In most criminal cases, the prosecutor is the key de facto decision maker, because his or her important role in screening cases in effect determines the resolution of most criminal cases. Prosecutors decide *whether* charges will be brought or dismissed, *which* charges will be brought, *how many* counts of each charge will be brought, and *what will be offered* in exchange for a guilty plea.[6] Prosecutors need not follow any protocols when deciding whether to bring charges and need not provide reasons for their decisions. Indeed, this sort of discretion is "widely seen as necessary, and frequently as a good thing: It permits mercy, and it avoids flooding the system with low-level crimes."[7]

Plea bargaining entails the surrender of the defendant's right to trial in exchange for more lenient treatment. More lenient treatment can include such considerations as a reduction in the number of charges/counts, a reduction in the nature of the charge, a recommendation for a lesser sentence within a given range of sentences for specific crimes, a recommendation that multiple sentences run concurrently rather than consecutively, or a recommendation for a particular place of confinement. Unless the defendant is a first-time offender concerned with having the stigma of a conviction on his or her record, most plea negotiations emphasize the likely sentences. The accused can place a ceiling on punishment by pleading guilty to a lesser included offense or by pleading guilty in a court of limited jurisdiction.[8] In return, the prosecutor secures a conviction without the expense, delay, and uncertainty of a trial. It should be noted that the U.S. Supreme Court has held that, within limits, the prosecutor can use these various options in an attempt to secure a guilty plea[9] and that "[p]roperly administered [plea bargaining] can benefit all concerned."[10]

Plea agreements are how most cases are resolved now and have been since they replaced jury trials by the middle of the nineteenth century.[11] Heavy caseloads have long been viewed as the culprit that makes plea bargaining necessary, yet only a small proportion of cases went to trial one hundred years ago when case volume was much lighter.[12] In urban areas today, 65 percent of felony cases end in a guilty plea (with most of the others dismissed by a judge or not pursued by the prosecution), and those pleas represent more than 95 percent of convictions.[13] The equivalent figures for Alameda County at the turn of the century were 41 percent and 63 percent, respectively.[14] From this evidence, William J. Stuntz concludes that less elaborate trial procedures worked to the benefit of defendants, not the government, by making trials and acquittals ordinary events.[15]

It is interesting that most convictions result from guilty pleas, even in jurisdictions that do not permit plea negotiations. In 1975, Avrum Gross, attorney general of Alaska, declared an official statewide ban on plea bargaining.[16] Court processes did not bog down; they accelerated. Rates at which defendants pled guilty did not change significantly, nor did conviction rates, but trial rates did increase. Apparently most defendants in Alaska continued to plead guilty even without plea bargaining, believing that it would be useless to go to trial given the strength of the evidence against them.[17] In 1991, the ban on plea bargaining was reevaluated and the decision was made to retain the ban as official policy, but in a somewhat modified form. Bargaining over charges is fairly common, but bargaining over sentencing has been infrequent. During the fifteen-year period between initial implementation and the reevaluation, the percentage of convicted offenders sentenced to some jail time increased substantially, as did the sentence length.[18] In a recent pair of 5–4 decisions, Supreme Court Justice Anthony Kennedy said, "Ours for the most part is a system of pleas, not a system of trials." Noting that about 97 percent of federal convictions and 94 percent of state convictions result from guilty pleas, Kennedy wrote, "[I]n today's criminal-justice system, the negotiation of a plea bargain, rather than the unfolding of a trial, is almost always the critical point for the defendant."[19]

The courts' role in the bulk of criminal cases then is to ratify plea agreements reached between the prosecutor and the defense counsel. This is not a trivial function, because it does provide a safeguard that the plea agreement was reached using a fair process—that is, without coercion of the defendant—but it is more of an administrative than an adversary process.

Civil Cases

Assembly-line or "cattle-call" dockets can also occur on the civil side, especially for contested traffic, traffic mitigation, small claims, and routine family-law case types. Although large, quick dockets may be efficient for courts, they can potentially damage court legitimacy over the long run if they are not conducted in a way that is perceived to result in procedural justice. Win or lose, it is important for litigants to have their day in court and feel as though they received a fair hearing. How courts should accomplish this is a key facet of dispositional dockets.

Contract-based litigation represents half the civil case filings and increased its share of the caseload between 2005 and 2010, whereas small-claims cases represent 18 percent of the caseload and appear to be decreasing. It would seem that the preponderance of commercial cases would contradict the much lamented migration of complex civil cases to private arbitration, but this is not the case. Since the number of small-claims cases is decreasing, commercial cases represent a steady proportion of a shrinking pie. Also, these are smaller and simpler commercial cases by definition, or they would not be in dispositional courts. On the other hand, the decrease in the number of small-claims cases may be another sign that litigants are being priced out of court.

The full-blown adversary process trial has never been the way courts resolved most cases. Courts have never had the time, resources, or will to resolve by adversary process the following types of lower-stakes cases:

- Cases unlikely to raise constitutional issues or conflict-of-law issues
- Criminal cases involving loss of liberty, but less so than more serious felonies and high misdemeanors
- Civil cases with moderate stakes, including small-claims cases
- Contested traffic cases
- Cases that may have limited interest beyond the interests of the parties themselves

To be clear, we are not advocating a position arguing which issues are more or less important than others. Harking back to the discussion about high-stakes cases in Chapter 4, we are merely observing what actually occurs now and suggesting a more systematic, transparent, and explicit discussion. For example, jurisdiction now is divided between courts of general jurisdiction and courts of limited jurisdiction based upon the sentences that can be levied in criminal cases and the dollar amounts in controversy in civil cases. Indeed, separate courts—most notably small claims and traffic—were specifically created to handle high-volume, lower-stakes disputes. Our point is that these decisions are being made now and that some of them, such as dollar amounts in controversy, should be revisited periodically.

Triage

Dispositional courts focus on speed and cost of dispute resolution. There is certainly evidence that many litigants are being priced out of court. A recent study on the costs of civil litigation examined typical cases in the areas of automobile tort, premises liability, real property, contract, employment, and malpractice and found that median costs to the litigant bringing the charges ranged from $43,000 to $122,000.[20] These costs are clearly outside the range that most litigants can afford and often would exceed any conceivable benefit from litigation. Another study asked litigants in New Mexico what they thought their civil and domestic-relations cases should cost and how long they should take.[21] The gap between what litigants expected and what courts could do was significant for both cost and time to disposition.

Other issues require rapid access to courts to resolve policy issues. For example, a group of litigants wanted trials for their misdemeanor marijuana-possession charges in the New York Bronx court in order to challenge the "stop-and-frisk" policies of local law enforcement.[22] These litigants waited more than five years without getting a single trial date, even though such cases are supposed to be heard within sixty days, according to local speedy-trial rules. If litigants cannot get a trial, they are unable to obtain the kinds of court decisions necessary to force policy change. While the cases themselves may have been relatively unexceptional, the implications were not.

Mediation, arbitration, or some other less costly dispute resolution forum should be attempted before a case is "appealed" to court. Just because a trial is possible does not mean it should be the preferred resolution option. Many cases can be resolved by plea agreement in criminal cases or by settlements or arbitration in civil cases, which preclude the need for trial.

Courts are increasingly using mandatory mediation, early case-settlement conferences, and similar mechanisms to quickly "weed out" cases that have no issues at contest or that can easily be settled. The trend is most obvious in family-law case types, but some civil case types are now being treated this way as well. Moreover, as is explored further in Chapter 6, some lower-stakes cases are now being decriminalized and turned into so-called payables in several states. This strategy is probably appropriate for most citations, especially in traffic cases. Administrative handling of these cases significantly reduces the workload for dispositional courts and provides quicker and simpler resolutions for the litigants.

Of course, courts are setting up these processes to lower case costs and achieve faster times to disposition. Nevertheless, the number and proportion of cases that would normally be handled using a dispositional process, such as small claims, are dwindling. Where are these cases going?

One place is the private sector, which may resolve these cases more quickly and less expensively. We are seeing rapid growth in the availability of online dispute-resolution services. Examples of such services include LegalZoom and Rocket Lawyer. Numerous other examples, such as eQuibbly, ZipCourt, and the Online Arbitration Network (OAN)—some of which offer free services—can be found online for specific case types or causes of action that involve very routine high-volume actions. What these services offer are fast, cheap, and predictable case resolutions for relatively standard cases without complex issues. These private-sector companies may extend their scope of services to other types of cases as the volume grows and they perceive a market.

Courts should not be threatened by this trend but welcome it, because any procedure that removes uncontested or easily resolved cases from court dockets is beneficial. Court dockets can then be reserved for cases that really belong there because they are inappropriate for another forum. Up until now, however, state bar associations (and, by implication, courts) have fought the provision of such private services, with the unfortunate result that cases involving smaller stakes often cannot get hearings in busy courts when they are truly warranted. Deregulating some legal services, or at least "unbundling" them, may reinforce the strategy of first using "disposition-assistance" approaches, such as mediation and arbitration.

Unbundling is an agreement between the client and the lawyer to limit the lawyer's scope of services to reduce the cost. Services that can be unbundled include advice, research, drafting of letters or court pleadings, negotiations, or court appearances. In the latter example, the lawyer represents the client for everything but court appearances. Or, in "vertical unbundling," a lawyer makes an appearance for an emergency hearing on restraining orders, for example, and then withdraws after the hearing is complete.[23]

Outside the United States, such unbundling of legal services has resolved more legal disputes outside formal courts and lowered the cost and the time to disposition of matters that do get to court. In effect, some of the case triage occurs before cases get to court, based on the advice of counsel. Courts could encourage limited-scope representation by giving those attorneys trained to offer limited services priority in scheduling.

To sum up this section, courts triage now for expedited processing on the basis of the amount of money in dispute, the types of issues at stake, and the likelihood of self-representation. Additional ways to sort might include subjective assessments of value, cost of case processing, and speed of case processing. Several states tried over the last several years to force more civil cases from adversarial processing in general-jurisdiction courts to dispositional processing in limited-jurisdiction courts by raising the limit for monetary stakes admissible in the lower courts. However, these rule changes uniformly failed to shift significant numbers of cases from the higher court. While no one really knows why this change did not happen, the total lack of information about relative case costs and the self-interest of attorneys in longer and more complex case processing are explanations worth exploring.

Allowing litigants to choose their forum for civil cases is a more revolutionary approach to triage that we call *self-selection*. As noted above, in some case types and jurisdictions, selection is effectively possible now when courts of general jurisdiction and courts of limited jurisdiction, or two courts of limited jurisdiction, have overlapping concurrent jurisdiction. States could deliberately experiment with changing dollar amounts and types of issues that could be raised in specific courts to maximize efficiency and to provide litigants with a choice. With proper knowledge of processing times and statistics on prior outcomes, litigants could assess the tradeoffs between timeliness of decisions and likelihood of a favorable outcome and then file in the appropriate court. The largest barrier to this approach is the almost total absence of market information that litigants would need to make a rational choice. Self-represented litigants certainly, and perhaps others, would need some help reviewing their options and evaluating the advantages and disadvantages of each course of action.

Role of the Judge: Adjudicator

Professor Henry R. Glick identifies two judicial roles that the disposition-oriented judge could fill—the "adjudicator" who emphasizes deciding cases and the "task performer" who emphasizes processing litigation and maintaining smooth court operations. Here, these two sides are considered aspects of the same role.[24] The "disposition-oriented" or "administrator" role of this judge is to skillfully apply judicial procedures to achieve the swift and consistent disposition of cases. Clearing the docket then becomes very important, and the task becomes to process a large number of individual cases, a more bureaucratic process not unfamiliar to the administrative agencies in the executive branch of government. Keith Boyum has found that judges who emphasized the "administrator" role did indeed take a shorter amount of time, on average, to resolve their cases.[25] Timely resolution is a positive outcome if it does not inhibit litigants from seeking information, including clarification and follow-up questions, or make them believe that their concerns are not taken seriously.

Adjudicators must decide large numbers of lower-stakes cases every day rather than spending days or weeks making a decision in one case at trial, and so the procedures must be streamlined. Consequently, judges may take a more active role in all phases of case processing to move the case along while ensuring that the attorneys, many of whom may be court appointed, are devoting the proper attention to their clients.

By definition, many litigants in dispositional case types are self-represented. Judges in some courts find that they need to expand their involvement in the hearing process and simplify due process to achieve fair and equitable case resolutions.[26] Given the traditional view in adversarial courts that judges should remain totally impartial and above the fray, some controversy has surrounded more active judicial roles. On the other hand, simplified due process is becoming a popular solution to civil-case costs even for more complex cases in adversarial processing tracks.[27] This tricky balancing act can easily degenerate into the assembly-line dockets mentioned above. Victor E. Flango has noted the difficulty of applying the procedural-justice concept to dispositional courts. Can judges be expected to provide litigants with time to tell their stories, to explain and justify their decisions, and still keep ahead of their dockets?[28] The research of Tom Tyler and others on procedural justice points the way for how judges can avoid dissatisfied litigants.[29] Judges must act in ways that ensure that litigants have voice and perceive neutrality, respect, and trust. *Voice* means they have an opportunity to tell their stories and convey their perspectives. *Neutrality* is perceived when the court acts in an open and transparent way, basing decisions on consistently applied legal rules instead of personal opinions. *Respect* is mostly about treating litigants with courtesy and politeness, showing that they are being taken seriously. Finally, *trust* is engendered by judges demonstrating sincerity and caring by acting in the best interests of the parties rather than making decisions based on their own personal attitudes.

Studies repeatedly find that courts delivering procedural justice are viewed positively by litigants even when they lose their cases. This striking finding shows just how important the treatment of litigants is and how careful and thoughtful judges need to be in dispositional courts. The same studies also show that the absence of procedural justice can be particularly common and damaging in dispositional courts with lower stakes and fast-moving dockets. Consequently, judges require special training to ensure that they maintain procedural justice in the eyes of litigants while still moving their cases along in a timely manner.

For the resolution of some types of issues, quasi-judicial officers, such as magistrates and commissioners, could be used as appropriate. In fact, many courts are finding this approach to be cost-effective and more effective from the litigant's viewpoint. The latter arises from the ability of less formal judicial officers to use more informal and less complex due-process procedures to resolve cases.

Surprisingly to some courts, judicial officers in dispositional dockets are often the most resistant to electronic case files, because their current methods for moving hearings using paper are so efficient. It is rational for judges to complain when a technological change actually makes them less efficient during busy dockets due to bad design. On the other hand, judges must also be willing to learn new skills and to become adept at new business processes as court systems evolve. It is not acceptable to simply say that the pace of the dispositional court is incompatible with an electronic court.

Court Staff

The paper flow and scheduling problems created by this volume of cases require substantial administrative support. It falls to court clerks or case managers to keep the cases moving, and indeed these support personnel are largely in control of caseflow.[30] In these high-volume courts, where the time of judges is at a premium, it is most important that court staff treat litigants with respect and consideration. In other words, procedural fairness should be exhibited by court staff as well as by judges.

Moving some of the more routine cases to online transactions can certainly lower the burden on court staff. For example, traffic fines could be paid online, and even traffic mitigation hearings could be virtual. Although online transactions require staff processing, the degree of staff review may be reduced significantly. As courts convert to electronic case files, the burden on courtroom staff to complete case transactions and hearings without slowing down dispositional dockets can also be a significant issue. Well-designed system interfaces and staff training can ease the transition. Because courtroom clerks are typically present to assist with dispositional dockets, the change is more of degree than of kind.

Facilities

The courthouse designed for dispositional adjudication can be less imposing than those designed for trials, and multiple court locations should be accessible to the litigants. Courts should be easy to locate for people who want to pay a fine or obtain court orders.

Large areas of the building should be set aside to handle the many sets of litigants whose cases will be resolved in a single court session. Additional space needs to be allocated for the support staff required to handle the large amount of paperwork involved. Adjoining conference space for lawyers to meet with clients is also desirable.

Virtual facilities are also very important in dispositional courts. We are talking here about the ability of litigants to carry out transactions on the court website. As noted above, these transactions may involve virtual traffic mitigation hearings, notices, services, or payments of fines and fees. The key concept is that litigants should be able to find out what they need to know about the processing of their cases and perform as many required actions as possible without physically traveling to the courthouse. In lower-stakes cases, travel time and time off work to attend court are significant costs. The convenience of virtual courts would also help judges and staff spend their time on tasks that can be performed only at the courthouse.

If a large proportion of the routine case transactions in dispositional cases can become virtual, then less office space may be required for clerk staff. Alternatively, some existing clerk staff can be spared to perform other duties with higher value to the court, such as offering counter help to self-represented litigants or providing more intensive case management. In that situation, the type of space needed in the courthouse may require adjustments.

Finally, more recent reengineering court projects have centralized routine clerk tasks in one statewide facility or contracted out tasks to part- or full-time workers in virtual home offices. In this situation, the space required for clerks in the courthouse itself would be reduced, but new types of facilities elsewhere may be required. Renting or leasing standard office space off site could still reduce overall court facility costs.

Court Performance

Court performance in these cases should be judged by several criteria: expedition and timeliness, cost, and procedural justice. Most often, timeliness will also result in lower costs, especially when the dispositional court makes full use of online or virtual capabilities. But there is a tradeoff between expedition on the one hand and procedural justice on the other.

Because litigants may begin making explicit tradeoffs between these performance goals once they can obtain adequate information about them, their preferences may differ from those of the courts or what the courts expect litigants to want. This will be an interesting empirical question for future research.[31] It is too early to recommend which tradeoffs courts should be making and how their performance should be judged for dispositional processing tracks. In some cases, proper implementation of procedural-justice best practices may actually result in more timely and less costly case processing. This can occur in two ways. First, judges can reach equitable resolutions more quickly by ensuring that litigants believe they are being heard. Second, litigants comply with court processes and orders more frequently when they are explained in simple, easily understood terms. When judges become adept at these practices, fewer case delays and fewer additional case hearings may result.

Implications

The question for dispositional processing is "How much process is due?" How much process is due depends on balancing such factors as (1) the importance of the interest at stake, (2) the risk of erroneous deprivation, (3) the fairness and reliability of existing procedures, and (4) the financial costs and administrative burden to the government of implementing more extensive procedural steps.[32] As courts have added due-process safeguards to the administrative process, they may have failed to consider the administrative burden these new safeguards have imposed. Tight financial times may force a reconsideration of the tradeoff between additional procedural and substantive safeguards on the one hand and the increased cost in dollars, staff time, and processing time on the other. Here again, a renewed effort should be made to identify the *essential basic elements of due process that must be present to have a fair hearing or trial.*

One possible sign that this is starting to happen is the movement in several states to "reform" their civil-case processes in ways that streamline due process. As one practical example, North Carolina business courts proactively adopted local rules to supplement the Rules of Civil Procedure to provide better information and to decrease the cost of litigation.[33] Some of the rule changes are intended to limit discovery and the use of expert witnesses, and other changes are designed to either get a case to trial more quickly or to conduct trials more quickly. What these reforms have in common is an explicit intent to achieve fair resolutions in civil cases at a lower cost and with less case delay.

One of the lessons taught by the devastation of Hurricane Katrina was that in the midst of the disaster, courts had to determine which elements of the adjudicatory process were essential and which could be suspended so that cases could be resolved fairly, but in a timely fashion, when many court personnel were unavailable for duty. This type of reconsideration may need to be accomplished in times of financial crisis. During short financial crises in the past, courts simply delayed minor case types and prioritized high-stakes cases. Since most of the case volume comprises dispositional case types, which often bring most of the revenue collected by courts, such a strategy risks destabilizing the court fiscally while also lowering its legitimacy. Improving adjudicatory processes is clearly a superior strategy.

Many courts are implementing mandatory or voluntary mediation or arbitration processes for high-volume case types amenable to non-adversarial resolution. These fast-track procedures are characterized by strict time limits that apply to the arbitrators as well as to the parties, a limitation of procedural steps (e.g., the number of written submissions), and use of technology, such as e-mail messages and video conferences, for rapid communication. In 2009, Delaware launched a fast-track arbitration process in the hope of attracting international firms that wanted quick, discrete, dispute resolutions.[34] Because of the private nature of the process, it was challenged in federal district court for violating rules on public access to courts and on October 23, 2013, the U.S. Court of Appeals agreed it did violate those rules. Delaware is considering an appeal to the U.S. Supreme Court.

This rapidly growing line of business is likely to continue increasing dramatically as the technology-assisted dispute-resolution movement gains strength. For example, Virtual Courthouse is an Internet-based service that enables parties to submit disputed claims, responses, and supporting material in digital form for resolution by a neutral provider.[35] Another example is a startup called Rezoud, which advertises its ability to reduce costs and the negative corporate reputation of Fortune 500 companies via online dispute resolution.[36]

The number of firms offering different forms of online dispute resolution to various target customer types is rapidly growing.[37] These startups often use the latest Web technology, such as private virtual rooms, online chat, Voice over Internet Protocol (VoIP) for uploading audio and video statements, strong encryption of transactions, and voting features (including countdown timers). The last feature overlaps an automated capability that is rapidly spreading into the dispute resolution world: smart or automated auctions. These algorithms are easily adapted to the mediation of settlements of all kinds.

Redesigning efforts should focus on alternative dispute resolution, especially court-connected methods of resolution, such as arbitration, streamlined local rules to reduce the cost of litigation, and improved systems support for more efficient "back-office" processes. The even broader trend toward centralized and decriminalized processing of most citations and minor misdemeanors as payables is strong evidence of courts trying to perform their constitutional mission more efficiently and, as a result, significantly rethinking their core business processes. While dispositional tracks may be the easiest areas to start with, adversarial tracks are also being reviewed seriously in many states.

6

The Administrative Process

Purpose

Some observers have noted that over time trial courts' workloads have shifted from dispute resolution to routine administration.[1] Should courts address problems that are not appropriate for adjudication? In the words of a former federal judge, "[T]he courts are being asked to solve problems for which they are not institutionally equipped or not as well equipped as other available agencies."[2] Many of these are policy oversight issues that should be addressed by the administrative processes.

At least since 1976, the ABA Task Force, chaired by the Honorable Griffin B. Bell, advocated the increased use of the administrative process *as an alternative to resorting to the courts* (emphasis supplied).[3] The Task Force noted that judicial resources "are never available in overabundance and they should be reserved for the resolution of the controversies and vindication of rights."[4] Its report discusses court involvement in uncontested probate, divorce, and other cases and cautions that "courts should not be quick to assume that conflicts exist when in fact there are none," further explicitly stating that court involvement should be limited "to cases in which a controversy between adversaries has developed."

Caseload

Many perceived injurious experiences *do not* culminate in disputes at all. First, the injury must be recognized (naming), the fault must be attributed (blaming), and then a remedy must be sought (claiming).[5] A claim is transformed into a dispute when it is rejected in whole or in part. Therefore, many grievances do not result in disputes. Individuals may react differently to the same set of circumstances. For example, one buyer of a defective good or service may "lump it" and chalk it up to experience, while another may pursue legal action.[6] When a claim is made, some respondents may decide to make amends and offer redress (in which case, there is no dispute), and others will not. Although resolving disputes is one of the most basic functions of courts, not all disputes should come to court for resolution. Many issues now go to court not to receive court adjudication but simply to have a record made that a transaction was legally concluded.[7] These include records kept in the process of naturalizing citizens, approving name changes, and performing marriages.

Parking tickets are discussed in Chapter 2 as adding to the sheer volume of case filings, but these and similar traffic and ordinance violations do not need to consume judges' time and perhaps should not be handled in courts. Some traffic offenses could be, and are being, decriminalized and handled as infractions without court action at all. Some matters now handled by courts, such as issues related to proof of insurance, registration, and driver's licenses, could be handled by the Department of Motor Vehicles. Others may be handled by administrative tribunals. These issues take on importance because of their sheer volume.

Triage

Uncontested issues do not require an adjudicatory process, which is based on the premise of two sides contending, *even if they remain under court jurisdiction.*

One observer concludes, "Many cases in the courts today are not conflicts at all. For many such cases, new, much less costly technology-intensive pathways can be designed."[8] Cases not in dispute need to be screened out of adjudication as early in the process as possible because of the burden they place on all participants, not just judges. For example:

> To obtain judgment in such undisputed cases, the parties, their attorneys, and any witnesses must travel to court, pass through security lines, wait for the clerk to make roll calls reminiscent of grade school for perhaps a hundred cases (twice in some courts), and wait again for the case to be called and heard. Without the plaintiff, the case is dismissed[;] without the defendant, the plaintiff presents proof of damage at a brief "inquest hearing" before obtaining judgment.[9]

Courts should resolve those types of disputes that they are uniquely qualified to resolve. Both the adjudicatory and administrative processes rely on the application of rules. In adjudication, they constitute the standard judges use to measure the arguments presented by the plaintiff and the defendant, while in the administrative process they constitute durable rules of thumb to decide on service delivery.

The administrative process is best suited to the mechanical application of rules to routine cases, while the adjudicatory process is necessary for cases that are exceptions to the routine. Particularly for cases that initially fall outside the court entirely, one can envision a very different relationship with the executive branch agencies that would administer those cases. In some circumstances, it could become routine for citizens to submit what would formerly have been court cases directly to the appropriate agency. In other circumstances, the court would discover in the course of initial case triage that those issues belonged elsewhere and would then "file" those cases with the right agency. Either because matters came into dispute according to the necessary requirements for court processing or because cases required appeal to court processing, those same agencies would still occasionally need to file cases back in the courts. Thus, the ideal case triage has process steps going both directions.

Role of the Judge: Administrator

The role of the judge in dispute resolution does not come into play if the cases are not in dispute. In the words of one observer, "The failure to distinguish procedurally between cases requiring dispute resolution, and those requiring management needlessly imposes heavy costs on many participants in the court process, and judicial time gets poorly used."[10]

Further, he contends that if courts distinguished between disputed and undisputed cases, most judicial activities could be delegated to less expensive personnel. If many of the current case responsibilities were transferred to other agencies for resolution, there would be no need to discuss the role of the judge. There is no reason why norms of procedural fairness cannot be met in administrative tribunals as well as courts.[11] Indeed, in the more informal setting of limited-jurisdiction courts, especially small-claims courts, litigants can speak for themselves rather than through lawyers and perhaps achieve more satisfaction with their "day in court."

Alternatives

Administrative Units under Court Supervision

If these cases were handled administratively, but under the aegis of the court, the judge would exercise administrative supervision over the hearing officer. One illustration of how this could work may be the civil traffic infraction hearing officers used in Florida. The hearing officer is a judicial employee, has judicial immunity, and is supervised by the Florida Supreme Court through the chief judge of the circuit court.[12] The very existence of the position of hearing officer means that circuit court judges can devote more of their time to other civil and criminal case types. Vermont has a similar arrangement with the Traffic and Municipal Ordinance Bureau, now called the Judicial Bureau, essentially an administrative agency within the judicial branch that operates under the supervision of the Vermont Supreme Court.[13]

In Australia, the existing system requires applicants who want to have their driver's licenses restored after a period of suspension to attend court at least three times: (1) to be told what they need to do, (2) to get a hearing date, and (3) to have the application heard.[14] Only the third step should require a court visit. An online restoration tool could be used by lawyers and traffic agency staff, or the public would obviate the need for the first court visit, and an online application process could make the second visit unnecessary.

Separate Administrative Processing

Some types of cases could be removed from the court system entirely and transferred to administrative agencies that use less formal and less costly procedures. New York City created executive branch adjudicatory agencies called administrative tribunals to decide several types of cases that used to flow through criminal courts—for example, parking violations; noise pollution; sanitation-, fire-, and building-code violations; and health and mental-hygiene violations.[15]

Many of the issues raised in worker's compensation cases could be referred to an administrative process within the judicial or executive branch for resolution, with only contested appeals being referred to court. Failure to reach a resolution in the initial administrative review need not result in an immediate referral to court: many administrative issues could be resolved by appeals to a tribunal *within* the administrative agency before they were referred to court. Indeed, in Western Europe, worker's compensation cases are decided by government-appointed physicians or mixed panels of physicians and social workers.[16]

Robert A. Kagan describes a proactive approach to worker's compensation cases, specifically "functional impairment" claims, in Wisconsin, which significantly reduced costs by employing the following techniques:

1. Prescribing "mandatory minimum ratings," which guarantee the claimant a certain level of compensation for common events, such as back surgery.
2. Using reports from treating physicians to compute presumptive benefits and imposing penalties if the defendant fails to pay or to contest the award promptly (80 percent of the cases are resolved this way).
3. Placing heavy emphasis on disability assessment of the *treating* physician, usually chosen by the worker. If a worker contests the assessment, "final offer adjudication" is used in which compensation judges must choose between either

the treating physician or the company physician's assessment—not an intermediate point. The result is that that physicians who offer extreme ratings (high or low) tend to be screened out.[17]

Administrative panels can be specialized by subject matter. In England, tribunals are used for claims of unfair dismissal, workplace discrimination, and the like. In Japan, fewer than 1 percent of auto accidents involving death or injury result in tort litigation,[18] while in the United States, the comparable figure is 21.5 percent. Japan invests in official investigation of accidents to determine facts and relative responsibilities to parties.[19] (Insurance does not pay if an accident is not reported.) Police reports are rarely challenged in court. Before a case is filed, many contested claims are resolved by nonlitigious dispute resolution—for example, Traffic Accident Dispute Resolution Centers, which provide mediation services, and consultation centers.[20] Compensation is predictable and moderate—Japanese judges have developed a formula for determining damages and assessing liability.[21] Consequently, fewer than 2 percent of accident victims in Japan hire lawyers.[22]

Privatizing Using Insurance

One innovative idea is to have patients waive the right to sue in medical-malpractice cases in return for smaller insurance premiums—in effect, to "purchase" the right to sue.[23] Medical-malpractice liability has been estimated to account for 5 to 9 percent of hospital expenditures, and insurance bills for physicians can cost as much as $100,000 per year[24]—and these are the *direct* costs, not the costs of practicing "defensive medicine" by ordering tests that may not be necessary.[25]

Richard H. Thaler and Cass R. Sunstein argue that the current system is not a deterrent against medical negligence and that, as a practical matter, there is only a small correlation between malpractice claims and injuries caused by medical negligence. They contend, "[M]ost patients who are harmed by medical malpractice do not get any compensation, and many patients who do receive compensation were not harmed at all or were not treated negligently."[26]

This health care plan is analogous to the purchase of collision insurance on your car, with the rate of pay dependent on the deductible chosen. Some patients would opt to eliminate the right to sue for negligence in return for a lower price for health care. Another alternative used in some foreign countries is a "no-fault" system whereby predefined medical injuries receive scheduled payouts regardless of whether the injuries were caused by negligence. This approach too could reduce the burden of determining exactly how much patients should be awarded for their injuries.[27]

In the Netherlands, asbestos-related diseases occurred at ten times the rate found in the United States. Rather than resolving these issues through court, they were handled through the social security system, which covered medical care as well as lost earnings without having to prove that the manufacturer did anything wrong.[28] The U.S. Congress did enact a fund, financed by taxes on all coal-mining companies, to pay for black lung disease,[29] but this solution has not been extended to other types of injuries—such as tobacco-related, asbestos, pharmaceuticals—that use contingency fee–based tort litigation.

This concept of insurance could be expanded to crop insurance, mortgage insurance, health insurance, liability insurance, government-supplied disaster insurance, and others as a way to avoid litigation.

Appendix to Chapter 6

Substituting Court Jurisdiction with Administrative
Jurisdiction: An Example

Here is a brief illustration of a certain class of traffic case—those involving commercial driving violations—that could be removed from court jurisdiction and resolved using an administrative process.[1] In Chapter 2, we note that more than half (54 percent) of all filings in state courts are noncriminal traffic violations, which may be an underestimate because not all courts report completed data on their caseloads. Moreover, some traffic matters do not go to court but are handled by traffic bureaus.

Unfortunately, there is no way of determining how many of these traffic cases involve commercial drivers, because no state reports commercial drivers' case types separately. In 2010, there were 4,237 fatalities in crashes involving a truck or bus, which is proportional to the crash rate of automobiles, unless the number of miles traveled by commercial vehicles is taken into account.[2] Nonetheless, a traffic accident involving a commercial truck is usually more catastrophic than an ordinary accident, because a fully loaded commercial truck can weigh eighty thousand pounds or more, compared to the three thousand pounds the average passenger car weighs.

Courts and Administrative Agencies

Courts and administrative agencies share many characteristics, including following law, statutes, regulations, and rules of procedure to make decisions. Yet one reason courts are perceived to be more independent than administrative agencies is that they hear such a variety of cases that their constituencies constantly change.[3] As courts become more specialized, the distinction between courts and administrative agencies becomes blurred. Administrative agencies were established to do the government's work more directly than the legislature could by enacting laws or then the courts could by interpreting the law in specific controversies.[4] Administrative agencies, such as the Departments of Motor Vehicles (DMVs), are often created by legislatures and placed in the executive branch, but they have functions of all three branches of government. For example, administrative adjudication is "the exercise by an administrative agency of judicial powers delegated to the agency by a legislative body."[5] It was once criticized as contrary to the reservation of judicial powers to courts, but the U.S. Supreme Court ruled in *Crowell v. Benson* (1932) that agencies could adjudicate cases as long as provision was made for ultimate judicial review. It is now a recognized role of courts to review acts of administrative agencies for fairness in uniform application.

As alluded to above, the jurisdiction of administrative adjudication is usually limited to a narrow subject matter, such as labor relations, worker's compensation, automobile operation and inspection, consumer protection, or veteran's benefits, to name a few. Administrative adjudication typically deals with individuals in relationship to the government rather than determining the rights and duties of individuals against other individuals.

Courts and administrative agencies respect precedent and compile written, permanent records.[6] Strictly speaking, an administrative hearing is not a trial, or even necessarily an adversary process. Yet administrative hearings, like trials, resolve disputed questions of fact and can order compliance with laws and regulations. Although often not as formal as courtroom trials, administrative hearings are conducted in an orderly and dignified manner, and most proceedings are open to the public.

Also like courts, administrative adjudication can be empowered to assess various penalties, such as forfeiture of licenses for violation of law or regulation. So should cases involving commercial driving violations be decided by court trial or by administrative hearing?

Commercial Driving Violations

Commercial driving offenses are a narrow specialty area more suited to administrative resolution than to judicial resolution. Other arguments in favor of having most commercial driving violations handled outside the courts are as follows:

Basic Rights Are Not Involved

Unlike rights guaranteed by the Constitution, holding a driver's license is a privilege. Moreover, it is a privilege granted by an executive branch entity, and the privilege continues as long as the licensee displays behavior consistent with holding the privilege. Violations of that privilege may result in the DMV's suspending or revoking that license, be it a regular driver's license or a commercial driver's license. If the state licensing authority grants the license following its own guidelines and testing procedures and has the authority to suspend or revoke the driving privilege, why should administrative processes, such as admitting the offense and paying the fine, be a court concern? If the license holder does not challenge the administrative penalty, there is no reason for court involvement. If the license holder does challenge the assigned penalty, should not the first remedy be an administrative appeal and only after that an appeal to courts?

Case-Processing Efficiency and Timeliness Would Improve

If cases were initially brought to the DMV, a commercial license holder who admits to violating a law would pay financial penalties, fees, or fines directly to the agency that regulates licensing—thus streamlining and expediting the process. One drawback for courts is the fear that relinquishing authority over commercial traffic cases would mean a potential loss of revenue. That revenue loss could be at least partially offset by saving the resources courts use to process, schedule, hear, adjudicate, convict, notice, report, and collect payment on these cases.

From the standpoint of traffic safety, the delay between the time a case is adjudicated in court and the date that report of conviction is received by the state DMV is unnecessary. The delay increases the risk that a commercial driver will be involved in an accident, perhaps with fatalities. This delay would be eliminated if the courts were not involved in routine cases, especially those that are *uncontested*.

Legal Complications Would Be Reduced

Federal law prohibits judges and prosecutors from allowing convictions of commercial drivers to be deferred, dismissed, or left unreported. The Federal Motor Carrier Safety Administration (FMCSA) in federal law 49 CFR 34.226 forbids a state to "mask, defer imposition of judgment, or allow an individual to enter a diversion program that would prevent a conviction" from appearing on a commercial driver's record (no matter where he or she is licensed) for *any* state or local traffic violation in any type of motor vehicle. Masking can occur only in trial courts of original jurisdiction *after* a judgment of guilt has been rendered.

It is interesting to note that some state DMVs impose a penalty required by the language in the law but not imposed by the sentencing court. If an administrative agency can pass judgment independently of the court that adjudicated the matter, why is the matter in court to begin with? If traffic cases involving commercial drivers were initially heard by state DMV, masking would occur only rarely, if at all.

Judicial Independence Would Be Preserved

With respect to sentencing, courts need to be involved in cases where judges can exercise discretion and judgment. In cases involving commercial drivers, federal regulations in 49 CFR 383.51 specify sentences that judges must apply as part of FMCSA compliance imposed on the states. State DMVs, upon receiving notice of conviction, have applied the "mandated" sentence when a judge's sentence does not align with the mandated sentence. This is far more stringent than sentencing guidelines, which were designed to bring some uniformity to judicial sentencing, and is another reason why these cases need to be resolved administratively rather than judicially.

Following the principles articulated here, court jurisdiction would be reserved for only those cases where the commercial driver was challenging the administrative regulations, the uniform application of the regulation, or the application of the penalty.

The Problem-Solving Process

The entire legal profession . . . has become so mesmerized with the stimulation of the courtroom contest that we tend to forget that we ought to be healers of conflicts. For many claims, trials by adversarial contest must in time go the way of the ancient trial by battle and blood. Our system is too costly, too painful, too destructive, and too inefficient for a truly civilized people.[1]

Robert Tobin later echoes the sentiment of Chief Justice Warren Burger quoted above by saying, "The relatively inflexible and formal nature of the adversarial system does not suit most disputes."[2] What are the types of disputes that the adversary process, whether full or expedited, is not designed to handle? What are the problems that go beyond neutral arbitration of legal disputes to "intervention in the individual and social problems that underlie them" through the vehicle of "specialized courts dedicated to discrete problems such as addiction, domestic violence and mental illness"?[3]

In Chapter 3, we note how one of the first responses to new problems brought before the court is to create a new specialized court to handle them. Is this an extension of that trend? In this chapter, we first identify the types of specialized courts that have been created, some rather recently, to handle issues requiring specialized expertise. A separate section is devoted to unified family courts, because they have developed over a longer period of time and so have confronted issues that some of the new problem-solving courts have not yet faced. Among these issues: Which problems are so interrelated that they must be resolved together? How long can treatment be provided, and when does it end? When does the court relinquish jurisdiction and deem a case closed?

Second, we consider how the nature of the workload of problem-solving courts affects the role of the judge, the duties of court staff, the facilities required, and the type of triage needed.

Finally, we consider the development of specialized problem-solving courts in contrast to the previous primary trend in court reform—court unification and trial-court consolidation. Problem-solving courts include case types where the focus is on treatment, such as community courts for "quality-of-life" crimes, gun courts for weapons offenses, gambling courts, homeless courts, and mental-health courts to handle the overrepresentation of people with mental illness in criminal courts. Is the best response to the rise of new problems the creation of more specialized courts, or can case coordination and case management achieve the same purposes?

Specialized Problem-Solving Courts

The principles that underlie the problem-solving approach are as follows:

- Enhanced information—better staff training combined with better information about litigants, victims, and community context of crime
- Community engagement
- Collaboration not only with the justice system but also with social-service providers and treatment agencies
- Individualized justice—linking individuals to community-based services to change behavior
- Accountability—regular and rigorous compliance monitoring
- Evaluation[4]

The principles are implemented by separate problem-solving courts, which are often not actual courts but rather separate dockets of treatment-oriented courts. Specialized courts are established to deal with problems that may benefit from focused and sustained attention. One judge summarizes the appropriate use of problem-solving courts for criminal case types as "where the level of punishment required is diminished by the need to solve the underlying problem and so you'd rather solve the problem than punish the behavior."[5] Resolution of the problem includes a treatment component in an effort to reduce recidivism, which reduces the number of future arrests, prosecutions, and court cases.

The basic characteristics problem-solving courts share include the following:

- Immediate intervention
- Nonadversarial adjudication
- Hands-on judicial involvement
- Treatment programs with clear rules and structured goals
- A team approach that brings together the judge, prosecutor, defense counsel, treatment provider, and correctional staff[6]

This cold listing of characteristics may not give the reader less familiar with problem-solving courts a flavor for what they are and what they do. Before attempting to compare and contrast problem-solving courts with traditional courts, which we cover in Chapter 8, we first want to show the variety of problem-solving courts and the scope of their jurisdiction. Only then can we intelligently address whether the problem-solving principles listed above should be "mainstreamed" to all courts.

Problem-solving courts were originally created to deal with issues involving the family, including juvenile offenses. Because they have experienced a resurgence with the popularity of drug courts, however, we choose to begin this discussion with drug courts and their progeny.

Drug Courts

As we note in Chapter 3, many of the modern problem-solving courts trace their origins to the specialized drug courts that appeared in the late 1980s in response to the dramatic increase in drug offenses.[7] The problem-solving court movement began with the opening of the first drug court in Dade County, Florida, in 1989[8] and spread rapidly on the basis of anecdotal reports of success in reducing recidivism and an infusion of federal dollars.[9] Governor of Arkansas Bill Clinton visited the Miami drug court, and Janet Reno, his appointee as attorney general, played a major role in creating the court.[10] The George W. Bush administration also supported drug courts enthusiastically, as has the Barack Obama administration. By the end of 2009, there were 2,459 drug courts and an additional 1,189 problem-solving courts in the United States.[11] The speed with which the problem-solving court concept spread has been taken as an indicator of the need for an alternative court process *for certain types of cases and proceedings.* Note that this conclusion is not unanimous. One skeptic observes, "[P]erhaps the most startling thing about the drug court phenomenon is that drug courts have so quickly become fixtures of our jurisprudence in the absence of satisfying empirical evidence that they actually work."[12] A more recent, extensive evaluation of drug courts concluded that drug courts are effective in that (1) participants were significantly less likely to relapse to drug use, and if they did relapse, they used fewer drugs; and (2) they reported significantly less family conflict.[13]

Other specialized problem-solving courts have not received the same degree of attention drug courts have, and some have been created too recently to have been evaluated for effectiveness.

Problem-solving courts seek to broaden the focus of courts from simply adjudicating cases to changing the future behavior of litigants and ensuring the well-being of the communities they serve. Some drug courts, often referred to as "drug-treatment courts," emphasize treatment as the way to reduce recidivism. Although there are variations, drug-treatment courts usually include judicial supervision of community-based treatment, timely referral to treatment, regular status hearings to monitor treatment progress, mandatory and periodic drug testing, and a system of graduated sanctions and rewards.[14] The judge provides support and encouragement, but defendants who fail to meet expectations can be removed from the program and given more conventional sanctions.[15]

Community Courts

Community courts were established to handle many of the "quality-of-life" crimes plaguing cities—for example, minor criminal offenses, ordinance violations, and "nuisance" offenses, such as loitering and public intoxication.[16] Although a plea of guilty is a precondition for entry into community courts, these courts do attempt to balance punishment and treatment.[17] The court is then "no longer an impartial arbiter of state power, but instead seeks to serve a victimized community that is in need of repair."[18]

With respect to straight criminal and delinquency cases, without the complicating issues of substance abuse or mental health, the treatment focus is on "restorative justice"—an approach that considers the needs of victims, offenders, and community together. It is based on a theory of justice that considers crime an offense against an individual or a community rather than an offense against the state.[19] Common programs associated with restorative justice include family group conferences, victim-impact panels, "peacemaking circles," and community reparative boards.

Victims take an active role in the process, while offenders are encouraged to take responsibility for their actions by apologizing, making restitution, or performing community service.[20] From this perspective, rehabilitation cannot be achieved until the offender acknowledges the harm caused and makes amends.[21] Therefore, rehabilitative-justice programs are generally voluntary and require offenders to admit responsibility of their illegal act as a condition of participation. Again, because the determination of guilt or innocence is not the key issue to be decided, the question becomes the extent to which these cases are appropriate for resolution in traditional courts. Courts could be involved in the sentencing to treatment, but the ongoing monitoring of progress would be the responsibility of probation departments with court involvement only if treatment were unsuccessful and additional sanctions of a punitive nature became necessary.

Driving While Impaired Courts

The high incidence of crimes committed while under the influence of alcohol, including driving while impaired (DWI), has prompted several jurisdictions to develop sobriety or DWI courts, most based on the drug-court model. Traditional sanctions have not been effective in DWI cases, and least so against repeat offenders.[22] Threats of punishment alone are not likely to change the behavior of individuals, so the philosophy of DWI courts is to treat the problem as well as to punish the offender.

DWI courts were established to protect public safety and to reduce recidivism by attacking the root cause of impaired driving—impairment caused by alcohol and substance abuse. The mission of sobriety and DWI courts is "to make offenders accountable for their actions, bringing about a behavioral change that ends recidivism, stops the abuse of alcohol, and protects the public; to treat the victims of DWI offenders in a fair and just way; and to educate the public as to the benefits of DWI Courts for the communities they serve."[23] Note that this mission seems to expect courts to treat the disease *and* to sanction the offender.

Mental-Health Courts

Mental-health courts, which deal with criminal defendants identified as suffering from mental-health problems, have been called the "closest analogues to drug courts."[24] A high proportion (30 to 40 percent) of criminal defendants seem to have mental illness, and an even higher proportion (75 to 80 percent) of mental-health court enrollees have substance-abuse disorders.[25] A large proportion of incarcerated offenders have mental-health problems (estimated to be 64 percent in local jails and 56 percent in state prisons). The relationship between the problems is so close that the National Drug Court Institute and the national Substance Abuse and Mental Health Services Administration (SAMHSA) support not only drug courts and mental health courts but also "co-occurring courts" for people with substance-abuse disorders and mental illnesses.

People who suffer with mental illness are viewed as blameless for their condition and even more likely to benefit from treatment than from punishment. Legislation in 2000 authorized federal funds to support mental-health courts.[26] A 2009 estimate suggested that more than two hundred mental-health courts currently exist.[27] However, these courts differ from each other to the extent that one commentator notes, "If you have seen one mental health court, you have seen one mental health court."[28]

Veterans' Courts

The Honorable Robert T. Russell, a drug-court judge from Buffalo, New York, established the first Veterans' Treatment Court in January 2008 with the mission of helping military veterans who became criminal defendants.[29] The court's emphasis is on mental-health problems of veterans and is limited to defendants charged with misdemeanors and nonviolent crimes. By 2010, with support from the Department of Veterans Affairs and other federal agencies, veterans' courts, including "combat courts," existed in twenty-one other cities.[30] Again, a special need has been identified, and the response has been the creation of another specialized "court."

Reentry Courts

A related popular program for adults and juveniles is the so-called reentry court, which provides close supervision, links to social services, and intensive case management to offenders returning home after incarceration.[31] Former inmates suffer disproportionately high rates of drug addiction and mental illness. More than two dozen reentry courts are currently in operation in the United States, with more in the planning stages, to help integrate people on probation or parole ("pre-entry courts") into society and thus keep participants out of prison. The Council of State Governments even sponsors a National Reentry Resource Center to assist states, tribes, and corrections working on prisoner reentry.[32] Reentry courts for juveniles are designed to help young people make the transition from out-of-home residential facilities back into the community.[33] Reentry courts also beg the question of why the reintegration of convicted people into society should be a judicial function rather than a probation function under the jurisdiction of state Departments of Corrections.

Unified Family Courts

As noted at the beginning of this chapter, family courts were one of the first arenas to experiment with problem-solving principles, and so in this section we devote more attention to the reasons they were established, the problems they confronted, and the resolutions they reached. Family courts have had to confront the issue of how interrelated cases must be before they are included in family-court jurisdiction and the complementary issue of how often interrelated cases must co-occur to justify the establishment of a separate court process.

In the early history of the United States, many states had separate courts of equity, called chancery courts. Most of these were merged into courts of general jurisdiction in the trend toward court unification so that court clients would be able to seek equitable relief and legal relief in a single setting, although chancery courts still exist as separate entities in Delaware, Mississippi, and Tennessee. The point is that such family matters as adoptions and guardianships, marriage and divorce, child-support enforcement, probate, mental illness, and even matters of corporate law (trusts, estates, and so forth) were originally placed in chancery courts, not "law" courts. It is therefore not surprising that these types of family cases are prime candidates for problem-solving courts.

The therapeutic approach may have been originally used for cases involving juveniles but grew to encompass all interrelated cases involving families.[34] As used here, family-related cases may include juvenile delinquency and domestic relations, including divorce, custody, child support, paternity, domestic violence, adoptions, guardianships, termination of parental rights, and child abuse and neglect. The American Bar Association recommends that the jurisdiction of family courts include the following:

> [j]uvenile law violations; cases of abuse and neglect; cases involving the need for emergency medical treatment; voluntary and involuntary termination of parental rights proceedings, appointment of legal guardians for juveniles; intrafamily criminal offenses (including all forms of domestic violence); proceedings in regard to divorce, separation, annulment, alimony, custody and support of juveniles; proceedings to establish paternity and to enforce [child] support.[35]

The variety of ways in which states handle family jurisdiction caused H. Ted Rubin and Geoff Gallas to create a taxonomy of courts handling six major types of family cases.[36] The variety of court structures used to handle family cases required five categories, ranging from one trial court of general jurisdiction to five separate courts of general, limited, and special jurisdiction. Though dated, the essential truth of that study is that multiple cases involving a single family may still be filed in multiple courts with overlapping jurisdictions. The result could be conflicting court orders and duplicative services ordered, which could exacerbate existing problems as well as create new ones. In the worst scenarios, this situation could result in delays, redundant proceedings, and conflicting orders.[37] Catherine J. Ross cites the "proliferation of venues and resulting illogical compartmentalization of issues" as having "predictably harmful consequences for children and parents."[38] Paul Williams concurs:

> Under the current system, it is not uncommon to have a family involved with one judge because of an adult abuse proceeding, a second judge because of the ensuing divorce, with still another judge because of the child abuse and neglect allegations, and a fourth judge if the abuse allegation led to criminal charges. The fragmented judicial system is costly to litigants, inefficient in the use of judicial resources, and can result in the issuance of diverse or even conflicting orders affecting the family.[39]

Unfortunately, many courts still organize and hear their cases using narrow case types that split families and their problems into multiple cases heard by several judges. Best practices in one narrow case type are developed without regard for other issues that families may have. Others have moved to a unified family court to assist in coordination of interrelated issues involving the family. The term *family court* is used by many courts "without any thought about what the term includes substantively or procedurally."[40] In Rhode Island, Delaware, and South Carolina, the family court is a separate court with its own administration and judges. In Vermont, the family court is a separate court served by judges drawn from the upper- and lower-trial courts. The family court in New York, despite its name, is not considered unified by some because it does not have jurisdiction over divorce.[41] In the District of Columbia, Hawaii, and New Jersey, the family court is a division of the general trial court, and judges may rotate between the family division and other court divisions. Massachusetts assigns family-law cases to a separate department of a trial court.

Family issues were deemed not appropriate for traditional courts using the adversary process for the following reasons:

1. They are so interrelated as to not be amenable to sequential resolution common to the adversary process.
2. They are not really adversarial.
3. They are unlikely to be concluded at judgment or verdict, forcing litigants to return to court for ongoing monitoring.

Interrelated Issues

The issue of interrelated cases will eventually confront all problem-solving courts, if it has not already, and so it is worthwhile to examine the problem. Family-law cases often involve multiple issues, and indeed the problems may not all be obvious initially. A court process is needed to first "diagnose" the real issues involved; search for a mutually satisfactory solution, if the family is to stay intact; and perhaps choose among several treatment options. For example, a couple may have a divorce proceeding with issues of custody, child support, abuse or neglect, or even delinquency alleged. These issues should be addressed together rather than separately. Offenders may have related issues, such as substance abuse or mental illness, that permeate all the other family-related issues. The family can be an invaluable asset to a treatment program. Unfortunately, many individuals with co-occurring disorders may have come to the criminal-justice system after a series of behaviors that alienated some of or all their family members.[42] Dealing with the full complexity of criminal and noncriminal cases is daunting and definitively requires a very sophisticated and clearly understood approach to what works best for each type of participant.

How Close Do Issues Have to Be to Be Considered Related?

How to deal with related issues was first raised and confronted as part of the debate over the ideal jurisdiction of a unified family court. The question was, and still is, are such problems as intra-family crime or elder maltreatment related sufficiently to be handled in a unified family court? Or should they be handled in a separate, non-problem-solving court, even if they co-occur with other family issues and are at least partially the cause of seemingly unrelated family problems?

Criminal Issues

Should criminal matters involving family members be handled along with other family issues, or are they different enough to justify special treatment? Clearly, a risk assessment is necessary to assess danger to family members. If there is potential danger, any discussions among the family members need to take place in a safe environment with ready access to law enforcement. If risk to family members is deemed to be low, on the other hand, perhaps considering criminal issues along with other family issues would promote service delivery to the family—for example, via anger-management classes. In that event, a needs assessment would be helpful to determine the types of services or treatment that would best improve the family dynamics.

Traditionally, the decision about whether to include cases involving domestic violence in the jurisdiction of unified family courts has been most difficult. The conflict is usually over the issue of whether mediation is even possible if one party is intimidated by the other. Some believe that mediation is never appropriate when domestic violence has taken place, while others believe it should be mandatory. Between these extremes lies the idea that mediation can be appropriate, but the decision must be made on a case-by-case basis in consultation with the abuse survivor.[43] Common techniques that mediators use if they suspect abuse or threats of abuse include shuttle or separate mediation sessions, which permit participants to be represented by an attorney or supported by a friend or advocate. Mediation programs often include such safeguards as multiple entry and exit points in the building, separate waiting areas, and escorts to and from vehicles.

Many family courts have resolved this issue by not putting jurisdiction over intra-family criminal cases in their systems. Others, like the family courts in Hawaii, waive criminal matters to the criminal division. Still another compromise, used in Delaware, is to include misdemeanors in family court, but not felonies.

Elder Abuse, Conservatorships, and Guardianships

Are cases involving elder abuse, conservatorships, and guardianships sufficiently related to other family issues to be included in the jurisdiction of family courts? Some would argue that they are.[44] Probate matters can be viewed as the elder version of child dependency—another type of protection case that involves the elderly or those with significant disabilities. Conservatorship cases deal with the money and property matters of people who are incapable of managing their assets. Guardianship cases deal with question of the type and place of care of elderly parents or grandparents. It is not unusual to have mental-health or mental-impairment issues related to people requiring conservatorship or guardianship care.

A presiding judge of the Portland, Oregon, family court finds some advantages of handling these types of cases in this system: "Our judges have lots of scar tissue from their work with families and that enables us to do a really good job with these cases."[45] And clearly, unified family courts may be an appropriate forum for these types of cases. On the other hand, some charges of elder abuse, or conservatorships and guardianships where theft or misappropriation of funds are involved, are actual crimes and should be referred to the adversary process of criminal court. The third alternative is, of course, the creation of a specialized elder protection court. Judge Julie Conger established the first elder court in California's Alameda County Superior Court in 2002. Elder courts were also established in 2008 in Contra Costa County, California, and in Cook County, Illinois, in 2010.[46] These alternatives reinforce the need to triage cases on the basis of issues as well as the need for a thorough evaluation and/or risk assessment.

Do Interrelated Cases Occur with Sufficient Frequency to Justify Coordination?

If cases involving a family were a one-time event, settled in a single court visit, family cases would not need to be coordinated, and record-keeping technology would not be needed to identify other cases involving the family. Regardless of whether intra-family violence, elder maltreatment, or substance abuse is included in the jurisdiction of unified family courts, interrelated issues involving families occur with sufficient frequency to justify a coordinated treatment effort.[47] To positively affect family behavior, many believe this type of integrative approach, which may include participation of other extended family members in such therapeutic sessions as "family group conferencing," is necessary. The case has been made that child- and family-related proceedings are sufficiently different from other court proceedings to justify either separate specialized family courts or family-court divisions of general-jurisdiction courts.

Juvenile cases—primarily delinquency, status offenses, and dependency—easily fit within the purview of family courts, but they are sometimes handled in separate, stand-alone juvenile courts. In dependency cases, courts provide protection to children who have been abused or neglected. Juvenile-delinquency cases are violations of law that would be crimes if committed by adults, but status offenses, such as truancy and running away from home, are noncriminal misbehaviors that are illegal only for minors.[48] Here again, needs assessment and risk assessment would help determine which type of court processing would be most likely to produce the better outcome. The sorting process is difficult, because the concept of juvenile court encompasses issues that are primarily treatment-oriented, issues that are due process–oriented, and everything in between. In their survey of metropolitan juvenile courts, National Center for State Courts (NCSC) researchers confirmed empirically the multiple conflicting goals of juvenile courts and suggested that the major juvenile-court dichotomy of either "traditional" or "due process" was too unrefined to capture the diversity of juvenile courts existing at that time.[49] They identified at least five separate types of juvenile courts based upon their characteristics. Interestingly enough, one type of juvenile court was distinguished by its use of a "triage" process, whereby youth were prescreened for court. Youth determined to be most suitable for treatment and unlikely to be incarcerated were not provided the same due-process protections given to those likely to be incarcerated.[50]

In practice, some families repeatedly petition courts for relief in a number of different but related cases. Of course, the proportion of related cases involving the same family is partially definitional, depending upon the degree of the relationship and the time period examined. The question becomes how often must parties make demands on court services and how related must cases be to justify the effort and cost of case coordination? At what point do the issues become too remote to be coordinated? For example, should the delinquent teenager return to the same court that heard his or her neglect case when the delinquent was a child? These answers can be determined empirically for each court on the basis of how related the issues are and the time span in which they occurred. The other point to be emphasized is that it is *not* the title of the case—for example, "family law"—that determines the processing track but the *issues involved*. One family case in which the key issues are frequency of visitation and living arrangements may go to a unified family court, while another in which the issue is primarily division of property could go to a civil court more accustomed to dealing with the evaluation of property rights. To foreshadow our conclusion, the key distinction about the purpose of the proceeding needs to be made clear early on—is it to treat or to punish? That decision should be based upon a risk assessment and a needs assessment that take into account such factors as physical and emotional safety of participants, their willingness to undergo and cooperate with the treatment plan, and the likelihood of successful treatment. If that process is followed, the treatment or "problem-solving" track could consider a broad range of issues affecting the family, not only those issues that have traditionally been assigned to family court.

Nonadversarial Issues

Many of the multiple, interrelated problems addressed in problem-solving cases are not contested issues in the traditional sense of two parties squaring off against each other in court. Probably most cases involving families fit into this category, including dependency cases, where the goal is finding the best permanent home for a child, not resolving a dispute. An adoption case may be a good illustration of the type of case that requires a search for a suitable family, but it is not necessarily adversarial.[51] In child-support cases, the controversy may not be over the question of whether to pay support but over how much to pay. Questions of degree, as noted earlier in this monograph, are not as well suited to resolution by an adversary proceeding. This category of cases also includes mental-health and substance-abuse cases, both intra-family and extra-family, where finding the appropriate treatment to prevent recidivism, rather than punishment, is the objective. In the cases of addiction and mental health, the issue is likely to be which treatment programs work for which types of problems and people. Three points need to be reemphasized here. First, some sort of triage, based upon needs assessment, risk assessment, or both, should be done to identify the issues involved. Second, those issues that can be resolved by consent of the parties, perhaps with the aid of a mediator or facilitator, should be settled early. Third, only those issues that are seriously contested and that are deadlocked because parties are at an impasse should be scheduled for trial.

Ongoing Issues

Because cases involving children and families are not only interrelated but also ongoing, they lack the same sense of closure that exists in a traditional case, especially those that go to trial. Family-related cases seemingly have no end, because they often involve parties who are enmeshed concurrently in multiple actions, many of which require monitoring after disposition. After a decision is rendered, children and families may need to return to court to review progress, for service and treatment programs, to adjust levels of child-support payments, to review permanency plans, and to hear repeated violations of domestic-violence protection orders. Federal law mandates review hearings of children in foster care for *as long as* they are in care. Many children simply "age out" of the foster care system after reaching the age of majority. This means there is a need for ongoing oversight in these cases and not the finality of decisions achieved in the adversary process.

Although it is clear that many families are dealing with multiple, interrelated issues—some more contested than others—and that these issues are ongoing, there is less consensus over the remedy. One solution, used currently, is the provision of court oversight over these cases until families cease returning to court. Another may be to have the child-welfare agencies in family cases, or probation departments in criminal cases, play a larger role in the monitoring of clients with periodic court reviews. Of course, the argument could be made that courts had to get involved because other agencies were not living up to their obligations and therefore court involvement is essential. The counterargument is that as courts assume more and more responsibilities for outcomes, they may be just as unsuccessful in monitoring because of their overwhelming caseloads.

Workload

Despite the dramatic increase in the number of problem-solving courts, the number of cases resolved as a proportion of total caseloads is still relatively small. Almost by definition, however, cases that go to problem-solving courts are resource-intensive. For example, the average child-welfare/dependency case can take more court resources than the typical serious felony case.[52] That is not surprising when one considers how complicated family problems can be.

Court processes have not remained static but have evolved to match the complexity of the problems. In other words, even if data were available for measuring the workload involved in dependency (child-abuse and neglect) cases thirty years ago, they would not reflect today's case processing. For example, the typical dependency case in 1978 had one hearing—adjudication/disposition. By 1998, the typical dependency case involved a shelter-care hearing (emergency-removal hearing), a pretrial hearing, an adjudication hearing, a disposition hearing, a permanency hearing, and a series of review hearings.[53] The number of participants in dependency cases increased correspondingly. In 1978, the typical participants were caseworkers and custodial parents. Forty years later, they were joined by noncustodial parents, parents' attorneys, children's attorneys or guardians *ad litem*, agency attorneys, court-appointed special advocate (CASA) volunteers, foster parents, and relative caregivers.

The workload problems are exacerbated by the fact that often the parties are not represented by counsel. Studies done in King County, Washington, found that in nearly three-quarters of domestic-relations cases (71 percent), at least one party was unrepresented.[54] The highest percentage of unrepresented litigants was in divorce cases, followed by domestic-violence cases and modifications of child-support orders. Litigants reported difficulty in knowing where and how to file a case, understanding court procedures, completing forms, and even knowing where to obtain forms. Because problem-solving dockets tend to involve a high proportion of unrepresented or self-represented litigants who are unfamiliar with legal procedures by definition, the process takes longer. Judges often need to assist self-represented litigants to ensure fair hearings.

Workload-assessment studies are just now beginning to document the complexity of cases involving children and families in terms of not only judge time but also the administrative and diagnostic support required to resolve these cases.[55] Unfortunately, few, if any, weighted caseload studies measure the effort needed to resolve a case going through the problem-solving process compared to similar cases using the traditional court process. A study of drug courts done in Virginia seems to indicate that the number of minutes judges spend on drug-court cases is higher in problem-solving courts than in traditional courts, but time is still ultimately saved because lower recidivism rates bring fewer repeat cases.[56] Much more research on comparative case-processing times is sorely needed.

A related question is whether nonspecialized courts would perform as well if given the same resources and access to treatment that problem-solving courts have. Critics argue that specialized courts are indeed more successful than other courts because they have so many more resources, which they need if they are to have frequent review hearings, frequent testing for substance use, progress reports from probation officers and addiction counselors, and so forth. Workload is half the equation, however. Do problem-solving courts have benefits

TABLE 7.1. ADULT DRUG-COURT COST-BENEFIT STUDIES

State	Taxpayer Benefits	Total Benefits	Net Costs	Net Benefits	Cost/Benefit Ratio
Virginia	29,049	37,135	17,903	19,234	2.07
New York: 3 yr.	6,198	11,083	5,186	5,897	2.14
New York: 5 yr.	10,330	18,470	5,186	13,284	3.56
California		11,000	3,000	8,000	3.67
Washington	3,376	15,433	4,178	11,255	3.69

Note: The New York and Virginia studies both use the Transactional and Institutional Cost Analysis methodology. The Virginia study reports actual costs and benefits rather than net costs and benefits compared to nonprogrammatic processing. Fred Cheesman and Tara L. Kunkel, "Virginia Adult Drug Treatment Courts: Cost Benefit Analysis" (unpublished paper, Williamsburg, VA: National Center for State Courts, 2012), available at http://ncsc.contentdm .oclc.org/cdm/ref/collection/spcts/id/245. New York results are reported for three- and five-year recidivism results. Mark Waller, Shannon Carey, Erin Farley, and Michael Rempel, *Testing the Cost Savings of Judicial Diversion: Final Report* (New York: NPC Research and Center for Court Innovation, 2013). The California study was performed by Francine Byrne, Nancy Taylor, and Amy Nunez (*California Drug Court Cost Analysis Study* [San Francisco: Administrative Office of the Courts Center for Families Children and the Courts, 2006]). The Washington study was performed by S. Lee, S. Aos, E. Drake, A. Pennucci, M. Miller, and L. Anderson (*Return on Investment: Evidence-Based Options to Improve Statewide Outcomes* [Olympia: Washington State Institute for Public Policy, 2012]) and is available from the WSIPP website.

beyond the number of cases resolved? What is the net impact of costs of case processing versus the benefits to taxpayers of reducing the rate of recidivism?

Table 7.1 summarizes the evidence that does exist on the cost/benefit of drug courts. Caution must be exercised in interpreting the results because of the variations in assumptions underlying the studies. For example, some of the studies report actual costs and benefits, whereas others report net costs and benefits.

The taxpayer benefits are cost reductions for government agencies and show how much is actually saved. These calculations are always tricky, because they take the form of future expenditures that do not need to be made because of the lower recidivism rates brought about by drug courts. Therefore, law-enforcement costs are reduced by not having to reapprehend offenders, and jail and prison costs are saved by not having to incarcerate offenders. Total benefits are dominated by the numbers of people *not* victimized or *not* injured and the amount of property *not* stolen or destroyed. Costs are either net program costs when compared to normal case processing or actual costs. Net benefits are total benefits, including victimization benefits, minus net costs. They show how much society will save. The cost-benefit ratio is simply the total net benefits divided by the net costs (or actual costs in the case of Virginia) and is useful in comparing the relative benefit of establishing a drug court to the relative benefit of creating other innovative programs.

The Washington State study, which is a meta-analysis of available cost-benefit studies, shows a net loss to taxpayers per participant. New York barely breaks even after three years but does much better after five years. New York and Virginia find that the absolute and relative costs for treatment as a component of the overall adult drug court program costs are very similar: $14,270 per participant and 77 percent of total program costs for New York and $14,125 per participant and 79 percent of total program costs for Virginia.

Role of the Judge: Problem Solver

Some basic characteristics of judges are the same in traditional courts or in problem-solving courts: "fairness, consistency, authoritativeness, trustworthiness, respect for the parties, and knowledge of the law."[57] Judges in specialized courts do enjoy some of the advantages of specialization in general, including the ability to craft solutions for individual problems and, in many cases, demonstrating a better understanding of the underlying causes of specific behaviors as well as knowledge of the specific community resources that can offer assistance. Inherent in these advantages are the disadvantages of the potential for loss of perspective caused by immersion in a single problem-solving area and the concomitant risk of burnout.[58]

Here we focus on the dramatically different role requirements of a judge in a problem-solving court versus the role of a judge in an adversarial process. Building on Roger Warren's distinction between traditional and "transformational" courts, which is discussed in more detail in Chapter 8, Jelena Popovic graphically presents the contrasts in role expectations.[59]

Greg Berman and John Feinblatt summarize the differences between the role of the judge in a traditional court and the role of the judge in a problem-solving court. The latter courts encourage judges and attorneys to think of themselves as problem solvers rather than simply case processors. For problem-solving judges and attorneys, a case is a problem to be solved, not just a matter to be adjudicated. Moreover, instead of seeing each case as an isolated incident, judges and attorneys in problem-solving courts analyze the cases in front of

TABLE 7.2. CONTRAST IN ROLES OF TRADITIONAL AND PROBLEM-SOLVING JUDGES

TRADITIONAL JUDICIAL OFFICERS	THERAPEUTIC JURISPRUDENCE JUDICIAL OFFICERS
Dispassionate stance—betray no interest in the litigant as a person, only as a litigant in a legal proceeding	Interested stance—show interest in the litigant's welfare in particular
Impersonal attitude—act as though the litigant is nothing but a "party" in a "case"	Personal attitude—give relevance to the litigant's personal circumstances and make direct inquiries of the litigant
Decision making performed in judicial language and form that satisfies legal requirements, with a particular view toward review by appellate court	Decision making performed in language understood by parties
Limited communication	Open communication—ensure that the story has an opportunity to be heard
Communication with counsel only Eye contact with counsel only	Direct dialogue between judge and parties Eye contact with parties

them for patterns and then fashion responses that seek to change the behavior of offenders, enhance the safety of victims, and improve the quality of life in their communities.[60] See Table 7.2.

Some judges are attracted to problem-solving courts because they have more power to shape outcomes and thus less frustration with the failure of courts to reduce recidivism and improve the lives of defendants. The judge goes "from being a detached neutral arbiter to the central figure in the team,"[61] and many judges enjoy that control over court proceedings and the feeling of satisfaction it brings. In the words of one drug-court judge, "It works. It makes sense. It's cost effective. And it makes you feel good."[62]

The vast differences between the judicial role in traditional courts and this role in problem-solving courts is one of the reasons for the charge that the problem-solving role is more related to the "social worker" or "therapist" role than to the judge role. As team leader, the judge is the link between the criminal justice and treatment systems. The judge assumes, according to Judge Jeffrey S. Tauber, "the role of confessor, task master, cheerleader, and mentor."[63]

In criminal law, this creates tension between concerns for public safety and the dictates of social work, where treatment of the individual client is paramount. Denver Judge Morris B. Hoffman highlights the contrast in criminal cases: "We are judges, not social workers or psychiatrists. We administer the criminal law because the criminal law is its own social end. It is not, or at least ought not to be, a means to other social ends."[64] Judge Raymond R. Norko of the Hartford Community Court counters, "Anything short of jail to a lot of people is not effective."[65] Some problem-solving judges argue that their courts are even tougher than conventional courts, even though they make more use of alternatives to incarceration. Judge Stephen V. Manley notes the complaints against problem-solving courts that judges are social workers and the courts are "soft" and "fuzzy" but continues:

> I think that's a great misconception. Problem-solving courts in my view are the most accountable courts we have because the judge is responsible for each and every individual. There's no passing the buck. They [defendants] are seen more often [and] followed more closely than any other defendants.[66]

Even in child-welfare cases, some perceive that this "social-worker" role conflicts with the traditional role of the judge.[67] In problem-solving courts, the judge not only must consider the impact of his or her decisions on the litigants and perhaps the public at large but also becomes a partner in the "therapeutic-oriented response" in an effort to ameliorate the underlying problems of litigants.[68] Advocates of problem-solving courts respond that most, and probably all, judicial decisions have consequences beyond the immediate court case—it is just a matter of whether those consequences will be taken into account when the decision is being made. In discussing family-law cases, David B. Wexler states:

> Because judges presumably are affecting therapeutic and rehabilitative consequences anyway, a therapeutic jurisprudence approach would suggest that, while they remain fully cognizant of their obligation to dispense justice according to principles of due process of law, judges should indeed try to become less lousy in their inescapable role as social worker.[69]

The collaborative nature of the problem-solving court approach may cause questions to be raised about the impartiality of the judge in criminal cases. Problem-solving courts require judges to be personally engaged with each offender, and this personal involvement is incompatible with the role of a judge as a detached, neutral arbiter. The fact that the judge will deal with the case through frequent, mandatory court appearances allows a judge and offender to develop "an ongoing, working relationship."[70] A *New York Times* article reinforces these differences with respect to criminal cases:

> The judges often have an unusual amount of information about the people who appear before them. These people, who are often called clients, rather than defendants, can talk directly to the judges, rather than communicating through lawyers. And the judges monitor these defendants for months, even years, using a system of rewards and punishments, which can include jail time. Judges also receive training in their court's specialty and may have a psychologist on the staff.[71]

Some may also consider collaboration in "staffings," where the judge and treatment team meet in advance of hearings to discuss the offender's progress in treatment and to reach consensus about rewards and sanctions, to be in conflict with the judicial role.

This role conflict may be less severe in family cases, where the adversary process is relaxed even in traditional courts and the judge is presumed to have the best interests of the family in mind and strives for a socially optimal outcome. The bigger problem here is to clearly define what those outcomes should be. For criminal cases, reduced recidivism and addiction are the primary goals. Noncriminal cases may include multiple goals, which may conflict with each other. Agencies with which the court partners may also disagree among themselves about the preferred outcomes and resist making reasonable tradeoffs among them. Judges must therefore play a leading role in coordinating relationships with supporting agencies and arranging that adequate resources and services are available to promote the desired outcomes.

We must also consider the question of whether judges and judicial officers have the right background to be "therapists" and whether that role should be left to professionals in other fields. Judges typically have no background in sociology, psychology, or medicine and no specific training in addiction treatment or family counseling. What qualifies a judge to play a problem-solving role? The typical rationale is that judicial intervention is needed to compel treatment in order to reduce recidivism. This question of why treatment agencies or even probation departments are not the "therapist" of first choice, with courts receiving cases for punishment when therapy fails, is a question addressed in Chapter 8.

Court Staff

The primary need is for the correct diagnosis of problems on the front end of cases. For criminal cases, this means valid risk and needs assessments for each offender. Triage decisions could then be made on the basis of evidence-based practices. The justice and academic community are now hard at work developing consensus protocols for the triage of offenders in this way, but they have not yet completed this work.

Barbara A. Babb lists the services that may be needed by family courts as including assessment and evaluation, counseling, volunteer, community outreach, and family-support services as well as restitution, probation, diversion, and detention services for courts with juvenile-delinquency jurisdiction.[72] As noted in the caseload section above, courts serving families require more staff support than other courts, including family-court coordinators, liaisons to child-welfare agencies, family-violence coordinators, court-appointed special advocates, and guardians *ad litem*. Without an integrated picture of the family, it is difficult to deal with even the separate problems that may exist.

In some cases, just the effort to disentangle family and significant relationships with respect to biological fathers, putative fathers, family and nonfamily members living in the house, or children living with relatives requires the creation of a relationship chart akin to creating a genealogy chart—and that assumes relationships are present to untangle. Some domestic and civil case types simply do not have parties, usually fathers, even identified.

Either way, these cases require much more administrative support than traditional dockets do. Administrative services required are not only extremely diverse but in very high demand in some cases. For example, judges must have unbiased information about child-placement and treatment alternatives, which requires staff support because the information is not readily available and cannot be provided at trial if there are not attorneys for each side providing information to the court.

Most importantly, services required by children and families are the administrative responsibility of social-service or child-welfare agencies. These services range from the more traditional probation, mental-health, child-protection, and child-custody evaluations to more recent offerings, such as anger-management therapy and substance-abuse counseling. Courts have oversight responsibility to ensure that families receive services.

With regard to criminal cases, risk and needs assessments may be performed at pretrial, at presentence, at incarceration, or during probation. Treatment programs may be assigned at each of these intervention points as well. Some programs outside courts mimic court problem-solving dockets, except for the absence of intensive interactions with a judge. Some probation programs leave the handling of technical violations to probation officers instead of sending the offender back to the court or to jail. Without strong program coordination, justice agencies risk providing both inefficient solutions and conflicting treatment programs.

Facilities

Because hearings in problem-solving cases are less formal and officially not adversarial, the traditional courtroom layout with clearly separated areas for parties, witnesses, and support staff is less critical. In fact, it may be more conducive to such proceedings for the rooms to have a more collegial and informal feeling. The court wants everyone present to cooperate and act as though they are jointly seeking solutions that work well for all participants.

If courts hold less elaborate hearings or any type of mediation sessions, then smaller hearing rooms may be more appropriate. In some cases, it may be useful to have high-quality videoconferencing capabilities in the courtrooms and the hearing rooms to enable parties or staff who cannot attend personally to be *virtually* present. High-quality video is essential to preserve the nature of the proceedings and to not disadvantage any party. Videoconferencing may also be necessary to support remote interpretation—even if both parties understand a language, it does not mean the judge will.

Family cases frequently involve children, who sometimes should not be present in the courtroom. Therefore, adequate child-care facilities in the courthouse may be a key requirement. In the same way, it may occasionally be necessary to conference children into hearings remotely to protect them.

Although they fall under a broad definition of *facilities*, criminal problem-solving procedures rely heavily on treatment and testing information. Many courts now collect, record, and transmit such data manually. When timing and availability are essential, the ability to share such information electronically in near real-time is critical. The same need may arise on the noncriminal side with information from human-services agencies, health-care agencies, and schools.

With regard to court location itself, services in family cases, such as domestic-violence protection orders, need to be delivered quickly from an accessible location. Court facilities need to be designed for customer convenience, located in shopping malls or other readily accessible locations. Indeed, they could be co-located in community centers that house a range of services, as is done in parts of Oregon, so that clients could pay a court fine, locate transportation, find housing, and apply for food stamps or fuel assistance all in the same place.[73] Jackson County, Oregon, is a noteworthy example, with its establishment of family-resource centers that house as many as seventeen agencies in one building. It uses the term *community family court* to represent the commitment to partnerships among the court, community, and service providers.

Triage

Both criminal and family cases need triage for risk assessment to obtain a better idea of the problems identified and to better design services required. For family cases, the possibility of reconciliation versus the dangers of staying together must be assessed. Related cases should be consolidated where possible, which means that administrative-support systems for tracking related cases and prior treatment histories are very important. For criminal cases as well as family cases, appropriate triage may be as much a technical and administrative process as a judicial one.

A study done for the Administrative Office of Courts in California suggested that public defenders could play a critical role in screening and assessment, preferably before arraignment.[74] Objections to this approach were that public defenders would be required to make clinical assessments they were not qualified to perform and that prosecutors would be skeptical of the resulting recommendations, although perhaps this risk could be mitigated if some sort of standardized instrument was used to make the assessment. In the words of one prosecutor, "[The use of] an intake interview, a psychometric [instrument] . . . [would] go on a long way in being able to trust the outcomes and the solutions of the issues."[75]

Ideally, standardized triage questions would be developed by a national-level panel of practitioners and academics based upon evidence of what works. Perhaps the characteristics of problem-solving cases listed above could be considered for inclusion as criteria:

- Is the issue a contest between parties or a search for the best resolution/treatment?
- Is this a single issue to be decided or multiple issues involving multiple parties?
- Is the issue, once adjudicated, likely to involve court oversight of treatment and services?
- Is the goal ultimately to punish or to treat the offender, which involves an assessment of the likely success of any treatment offered?

Screening by issues—really, problems—is useful in all cases but would be especially helpful in cases that now go to problem-solving dockets. Checklists derived from evidence-based protocols could be used to identify problems that need to be addressed as well as to assess amenability to treatment. The occurrence of certain types of issues would dictate the special types of dockets required—for example, substance abuse, mental-health issues, and family violence. Parties to the suit could be screened for the special populations that may be involved—for example, children, veterans, and homeless people. Parties would undergo risk and needs assessments up front, using instruments designed to cover multiple issues. Possible treatments could be grouped by type of services needed.

Needless to say, more thought would have to go into problem-solving protocols, treatment regimens, and assessment instruments before this idea could be implemented. Much more consistency in approach across the various types of problem-solving courts would be required as well. Courts would have to become as sophisticated in their triage and diagnostic processes as doctors in a hospital emergency ward or general practitioners are.

For general cases involving children and families, the principle should be to first identify all problems that involve the family so that the correct docket can be used to achieve the desired outcomes. Perhaps, courts could use nonjudicial professional staff to do preliminary screenings in which the noncontroversial or easily resolved issues are stripped away These professionals could (1) narrow the problems to those that really require solution, (2) frame multiple issues to facilitate substantive outcomes, and (3) settle cases in ways that optimize the desired outcomes. Only after this screening would a case go before a judge. In other words, the only role of the court would be to review any settlements reached for fairness and compliance with the law or to hear contested issues that could not be resolved at screening.

For example, a common issue may be a child who needs a $3,000 set of braces, but the noncustodial spouse cannot afford them. A magistrate or referee would lay out the options to both parties. One option would always be to have each party hire an attorney and contest the case. The referee could indicate typical costs and fees for that approach. Another option would be to temporarily increase child-support payments to an agreed-upon amount until the braces were paid for. Both spouses might be able to live with this compromise, although the custodial parent would have originally preferred payment in full at the time the braces were needed. The point is that an active intervention early in cases can help determine which issues require court resolution and which can be settled by the parties once the options have been explained to them.

The determination of whether an issue is treatable may even require a second screening if there is uncertainty as to the key issues or if one of the parties wants to contest an issue or proposed resolution. This second screen would require a preliminary case conference, but it could be held by quasi-judicial officers.

Cases found not to benefit from treatment or to be appropriate for problem solving could then be transferred to the traditional adversarial process. This option could also be a last resort for people who originally enrolled in a treatment program and failed. Conversely, there is no reason why people adjudicated liable in either a criminal or civil adversary process could not receive treatment as part or all of a sentence.

Can Specialized Problem-Solving Courts Be Reconciled with Court Reform?

Court unification is a concept broad enough to encompass court reform itself, and the two terms have been used nearly synonymously. Indeed, one observer says, "The remedy of unification continues to be the basic prescription for court modernization."[76]

Courts proliferated in reaction to rising caseloads and the public need to have a "local judge,"[77] and the unification movement was a response to the resulting fragmented court systems. For example, a single-tiered trial court of general jurisdiction would preclude overlapping jurisdictions, because only one level of court exists. Some problems under the old court organization, such as cases being dismissed for lack of jurisdiction, would simply disappear.

Unified courts were perceived as the ideal court reform. *Court unification* has been defined as including several different elements, including centralized rule making, administration concentrated at the state level, centralized budget processes, and state funding, but a key component has been a simplified trial-court organization. In the words of two scholars, "If there is a single element that might be considered the heart of court unification it is the consolidation and simplification of court structure."[78] Two other scholars even argued that one statewide trial court of general jurisdiction is all that is required to meet the criteria of unification.[79]

David B. Rottman summarizes the rationale for court unification:

> Simplification makes courts easier for citizens to understand and use, as well as for collateral organizations to service. Flexibility in assigning judges to dockets makes it easier to meet caseload pressures, while also affording judges more diverse dockets. Administrative efficiency is achieved by elimination duplication of facilities and support services.[80]

The court-unification ideology became so popular that some states labeled their courts "unified" even when they were not. Specialized courts became integrated into general-jurisdiction trial courts as separate "divisions." For example, a separate probate court could be relabeled as the probate division of a general-jurisdiction court and still retain a significant amount of autonomy and use the same judge who had heard probate cases before unification.

Court unification, especially trial-court consolidation, had been the dominant theme in court reform since the 1960s, but it has been supplanted by the trend toward the creation of individual problem-solving courts to address each current societal problem from drugs, to homelessness, to veterans' issues, to "drone courts."[81] Court unification was a reaction against the fragmented jurisdictions and corresponding multiplicity of specialized courts. The ideal model of unification was to consolidate courts into one court of general jurisdiction and perhaps one court of limited jurisdiction.

Specialized courts are courts that "possess limited subject matter jurisdiction and are staffed by permanent judges who have substantive expertise in the area."[82] Some problem-solving courts, especially standalone probate and juvenile courts, conform to this definition of a specialized court, but some do not. Rottman notes, "the combination of judicial expertise and permanency of assignment is rare in the new specialized courts, at least at this point of their evolution."[83] He further notes that court divisions and specialized dockets are often referred to as "courts," although they do not meet the definition of autonomous courts and are often subsets of "parent" courts. Regardless of how they are labeled, problem-solving courts seem to be reinstituting the overlapping jurisdictions and multiple "courts" that trial-court consolidation was designed to remedy. Can these positions be reconciled?

Problem-solving courts arose in reaction to specific problems—for example, juvenile delinquency, domestic violence, and substance abuse. Soon the interrelationship among problems became evident, and the mission of single-issue problem-solving courts began to change. Let us examine the overlap between family issues and substance abuse in some detail and then elevate the discussion to a more general consideration of specialized courts versus general-jurisdiction courts.

Substance abuse would not ordinarily be considered a type of family case, but it is often inherent in affecting, if not causing, family dysfunction. A strong correlation exists between parental substance abuse and child maltreatment.[84] An estimated 60 to 80 percent of substantiated child-abuse and neglect cases involve substance abuse by a custodial parent or guardian.[85] New York found that three-quarters of all new abuse and neglect petitions involved substance-abusing parents.[86] Because of the prevalence of this connection, separate family-treatment courts or family-dependency treatment courts were created as a combination of family courts and drug courts to address the poor outcomes of existing family-unification programs for substance-abusing parents. These courts attempt to provide a safe and secure environment for children while intensively treating the parent's substance-abuse issues.[87] The first court was established in Reno, Nevada, in 1995, and now more than three hundred programs exist.[88]

Stand-alone juvenile courts became integrated into family courts, and family problems caused by substance abuse led to "family-treatment courts" to address both problems. (Similar specialization occurred as drug courts were created to deal with adults only, juveniles only, college students, truants, and veterans.) Courts designed to focus on mental illness or veterans found those problems had an overlapping clientele who needed their issues to be addressed holistically, and when veterans suffering from battle-inflicted trauma were treated with prescription drugs, substance abuse was added to the mix. These combinations of specialized courts may result in multispecialty courts at intermediate levels of specialization, such as drug courts for "co-occurring" disorders.[89] One cannot help but wonder whether these various combinations of specialized courts will lead a latter-day Roscoe Pound to suggest that all single-issue problem-solving courts be consolidated into one unified problem-solving court. Actually, a unified problem-solving court is consistent with the triage process we are suggesting, because it would enable issues brought to court to be evaluated early and to have diagnostic, testing, and treatment resources services available for use regardless of the particular "problem" that brought litigants to court initially.

Are Triage and Coordination the Answer?

Our interpretation of the development of problem-solving courts, based in part on issues raised in Chapter 8, leads us to conclude that triage into a problem-solving track is necessary to coordinate treatment services, but coordination *does not* require the establishment of separate courts, although separate dockets of a more general problem-solving track may be justified on the basis of the number of litigants seeking court services. Recent evaluations have supported the effectiveness of drug courts, but some of the other courts, such as mental-health courts and veterans' courts, have been too recently established to be evaluated scientifically.

Problem-solving approaches *can be* appropriate for serious criminal cases, *but only for the sentencing phase.* As John Feinblatt, Greg Berman, and Derek Denckla cogently state, "Problem solving courts emphasize traditional due process protections during the adjudication phase of a case and the achievement of a tangible, constructive outcome post-adjudication."[90] Especially in criminal cases with a substance-abuse component, the full adversary process with all its due-process protections should be employed until guilt has been established. *After* guilt is established, problem-solving principles designed to prevent repeat offenses could be used to select the best sentencing options, be they therapeutic or punitive.

An even larger issue is triage of problems where the conclusion is that courts are not the best forum for their resolution. Judge Steve Leben, although sympathetic to problem-solving courts, recognizes they have limitations and cites the Elián González case as an example.[91] He notes judges are usually not psychologists nor social workers, have no special training in discerning who is telling the truth, and simply take too long to resolve a case, especially from the perspective of a child waiting for a final decision. To recapitulate some key points made in this chapter, some problem-solving courts, notably unified family courts, have resulted in a more integrated approach to family law issues. Others on the criminal side, which include drug, mental-health, DWI, domestic-violence, and veteran's courts, began their evolution as separate programs, funding streams, and dockets. That is extremely unfortunate, because many offenders come to court with multiple, interrelated issues. Having to choose from among several separate problem-solving courts with overlapping jurisdictions is confusing and inefficient.

Triage needs to be conducted and the appropriate processing track chosen based upon whether the goal is treatment or punishment. Treatment should be an option *only* postdisposition. Existing assessment instruments will undoubtedly need to be improved and enhanced to better predict which cases would be best served by which processing track. If courts would employ evidence-based protocols for triaging offenders, they could then design dockets rationally around the most appropriate treatment approaches. Actually, use of triage will undoubtedly increase the need for and use of assessment instruments and will thus encourage their improvement.

Finally, even with exemplary assessment instruments, it will sometimes be necessary to switch processing tracks as it becomes clear that either treatment or sanctions are necessary.

Consistent data on litigant preferences are required to fully implement the triage process. For the first time, courts may be able to predict reliably which resources they need to carry out their mission and to estimate the measurable reductions in litigant satisfaction that would result from inadequate resources. State legislatures and county commissions could make more rational decisions on court funding if the consequences of various funding levels were known.

Implications of the Problem-Solving
Approach for Court Reform

The problem-solving process is not just another variation on the adversary theme, as are the dispositional and administrative processes,
but a different model of justice. If this premise is correct, what are the
implications of the problem-solving process? In this chapter, we argue
that the problem-solving process and the adversary process are based
on fundamentally opposing philosophical foundations—a medical
model of individual treatment and a legal model of treating like cases
alike. Consequently, it is unwise to try to graft problem-solving principles onto adversary-based court proceedings, at least until after the
judgment is made. If that is so, what is the justification for having
courts rather than probation departments be responsible for treatment?

Two Separate Processes: The Legal Model and
the Medical Model

Here we confront directly the underlying philosophical basis for the
tension between advocates for traditional courts and advocates for
problem-solving courts—between the legal tradition of treating like
cases alike and the medical tradition of fitting the treatment to the
individual.[1]

Medical Model in Corrections

Interestingly enough, this current debate is in some ways a replay of
the controversy over sentencing conducted a half century ago in the

field of corrections, where the medical model was used to promote "reformation." The medical model, with its focus on rehabilitation, was abandoned by corrections, undoubtedly for many different reasons, including the lack of commitment of staff, financial, and treatment resources to rehabilitation programs.

In 1977, Professor Donal E. J. MacNamara reviewed the lack of empirical validation for the medical model in corrections, subtitling his article "Requiescat in Pace." His description of the medical model in corrections resonates today:

> In its simplest (perhaps oversimplified) terms, the medical model as applied to corrections assumed the offender to be "sick" (physically, mentally, and/or socially); his offense to be a manifestation or symptom of his illness, a cry for help. Obviously, then, early and accurate diagnosis, followed by prompt and effective therapeutic intervention, assured an affirmative prognosis—rehabilitation.[2]

In corrections, diagnosis was the function of the presentence investigation, therapeutic intervention was decreed in the sentence and made specific in the treatment plan, and the parole board decided when the offender was "cured" and could be released back into the community. The medical model also assumed a triage process to disqualify offenders who would pose a danger to the community, a wide variety of treatment alternatives, and a large staff of probation and parole officers as well as social-services officers to monitor and supervise treatment.

Ironically, many "new penologists" at that time advocated a return to the justice model based on individual responsibility, with uniform penalties imposed for like crimes and the abandonment of indeterminate sentencing, wide judicial discretion, and coerced participation in rehabilitation.[3] It is interesting to speculate what lessons courts could learn from the corrections experience.

Medical Model versus Legal Model in Courts

How does problem solving affect court behavior? As noted in Chapter 7, the problem-solving movement is defined by two characteristics:

- A focus on treatment of the problems of the individual defendant
- The relaxation of the adversarial process in favor of increased cooperation among court participants[4]

Treatment Focus

The focus on treatment reflects a much earlier debate on sentencing: should the punishment fit the crime or fit the criminal? In a sense, this is really a much broader distinction between a legal approach and a medical approach to crime.

The basic premise of the traditional legal model is that humans are all equal before the law. In practice, that means treating "like cases alike"—that is, fairness requires that everyone who commits a similar offense receive a similar consequence.[5] In other words, the law does not address problems presented in legal cases by individualizing justice. Conditions for finding an accused at fault should be the same for all individuals in similar circumstances. To do otherwise would undermine citizen respect not only for courts but for law and government as well.

The premise of resolving similar disputes similarly also helps explain the importance that law places on precedent. Reasoning by analogy permits the judge to decide how a case presently before the court is like or unlike previous cases and therefore which legal rule to use to resolve the issue. The rule itself is not just a solution for a particular individual but must fit an entire category of cases—those with similar fact patterns. The opinion keeps courts accountable by requiring a justification for the decision that is transparent to all. By requiring judges to state reasons for their decisions, arbitrary and capricious decisions are discouraged. Adherence to precedent encourages consistency in outcome and therefore predictability of expectations.

The basic premise of the medical model is *treating the individual*. For example, a doctor may not prescribe the same medicine to two people even if they exhibit the same symptoms—for example, some individuals may be allergic to a medicine that is perfectly suited to another individual. Treatment requires diagnosis of the problem and development of an individualized treatment plan—which by its very nature is antithetical to treating like cases alike.

The procedural implications of these two models are very different. The different approaches to abuse and neglect cases may provide an apt illustration. The strict legal approach to handling parents who are suspected of abusing or neglecting their children would be to have the police investigate, make an arrest if warranted, and then have the prosecutors charge the alleged perpetrator or perpetrators. The role of the court in this scenario is to determine guilt or lack thereof based upon a high standard of proof (e.g., "beyond a reasonable doubt") and to sentence the guilty as it would in any other type of criminal case. This is a very public process that could result in incarceration, job loss, and formal dissolution of the family.

The medical approach would view the problem more broadly as one of family dysfunction, treat the entire family to determine whether improved interactions among all family members would reduce violence, and perhaps result in some alternative coping mechanisms. Most treatment programs begin with an admission that a problem exists, and in this scenario it is often difficult for the alleged perpetrator to take this first step. Consequently, the alleged perpetrator must be assured that admitting "guilt" will not lead to punishment but to treatment for the problem and that the treatment will be kept confidential, as any medical issue should be. Incentives to encourage treatment would be couched in terms of being able to avoid incarceration, retaining a job so that the family would be supported, and keeping the family unit together.

Thomas Henderson and Cornelius Kerwin describe the objective of "diagnostic adjudication" as "to identify the problems that are the source of the dispute" to devise a solution that will assist "both the persons before the court and the broader societal interest at stake."[6] "Treatment focus" better describes the purpose of these proceedings, because the search for a remedy certainly goes beyond diagnosis to extend to treatment.

The legal approach is more limited in the sense that it seeks the *status quo ante*—that is, the restoration of things to where they were before the crime was committed or the injury was inflicted. The legal remedies then are limited to punishing someone or awarding compensation.

The medical approach goes much further into correcting the problem. The goal of the medical approach in family cases, for example, is to restore or perhaps create family harmony, not necessarily to punish the offender. In the words of the Governor's Task Force in Maryland:

The goal of a court dealing with family disputes should be more than simply resolving the particular issues before them. Rather, such resolution should leave the family with the skills and access to support services necessary to enable them to resolve subsequent disputes constructively with minimum need for legal intervention.[7]

These goals require a different method of implementation than do sanctions applied using an adversarial process. The role of the court here is not to adjudicate guilt or innocence, but to closely monitor offenders and to ensure that the agreed-upon treatment regimen is adhered with the implied, if not explicit, threat that if treatment is not completed, more public sanctions will be imposed.

The difference in approach between the legal and medical models are being further exacerbated and at the same time blurred by advances in neuroscience. The prospect of using incarceration as a deterrent is viable only for people with normal functioning brains. The problem is that prisons have become "our de facto mental-health-care institutions—and inflicting punishment on the mentally ill usually has little influence on their future behavior."[8] The development of specialty "mental-health courts," discussed in Chapter 7, combines treatment with confinement in a structured environment. As the criminal-justice system becomes more informed by science, more emphasis will be placed on customized sentences, incentives for good behavior, and opportunities for rehabilitation. Unfortunately, a good illustration of the mental-health issue has been found within the court community itself. According to John Leo:

> When Sol Wachtler, the chief judge of New York State's highest court, was arrested for extortion and threatening to kidnap the fourteen-year-old daughter of his ex-lover, many New Yorkers were under the impression that some crimes may have been committed. Not so, according to John Money, a prominent sexologist and medical psychologist . . . [who] wrote that Wachtler "was manifesting advanced symptoms of . . . Clerambault-Kandinsky Syndrome (CKS) . . . a devastating illness. The law-and-order treatment of people with CKS is the equivalent of making it a crime to have epileptic spells.[9]

The medical approach tends to look to causes that may be genetic, environmental, social, or economic—in other words, almost always beyond the control of the individual. Indeed, prominent psychiatrist Dr. Karl Menninger advocates treating all offenders as mentally ill.[10]

The legal approach is to determine responsibility for an offense, and by that we mean who is at fault. The law is not looking for the ultimate cause of wrongful behavior—for example, was a child abuser also abused as a child? A trial is designed not as an inquiry to determine the root causes of crime but as a more narrow inquiry into whether the defendant is to blame. The key questions are (1) "Did he do it?" and (2) "Did he mean to do it?" because it is difficult to prove guilt without showing motive. The law assumes that individuals have the capacity for rational choice and had the opportunity to choose whether to break the law at the time the crime was committed.

Certainly, people without the capacity to make rational choices need to be treated differently. Patients with fronto-temporal dementia frequently end up in court to have their lawyers, doctors, and family explain that the perpetrators were not at fault, because their brains have degenerated and medical science has no remedy.[11] David Eagleman attributes the shift from blame to biology to the effectiveness of pharmacology, which has shown that some symptoms can be controlled by medication.[12] He quotes a senior law lord with saying that the law makes several working assumptions, including that adults have free will, act rationally in their best interests, and can foresee the consequences of their actions: "Whatever the merits or demerits of working assumptions such as these in the ordinary range of cases, it is evident that they do not provide a uniformly accurate guide to human behavior."[13]

Eagleman suggests dispensing with the concept of blameworthiness altogether and focusing on what needs to be done *moving forward*—for example, how is the person likely to behave in the future? Are criminal actions likely to be repeated? Can incentives be structured to deter future offenses?

This suggestion comports very well with what Douglas B. Marlowe suggests in a very intriguing interview. He states that the treatment versus punishment dichotomy has not been helpful and contends that the critical question is how to match offenders to the best programs that meet their needs, protect public safety, and do so at least cost.[14] He recommends a four-fold classification scheme to guide intervention based on the two dimensions of "need," the offenders' clinical diagnosis and need for treatment, and "risk," or amenability to treatment. Actually, the levels of risk and need for treatment must be assessed throughout the offenders' involvement in the criminal-justice system because the requirements may change (between the pretrial stage of the proceedings and the postsentencing stage, for example).

Why the Two Processes Must Be Kept Separate

Roger Warren, president emeritus of the National Center for State Courts (NCSC), has compiled a summary of the key differences between traditional and problem-solving court processes.[15] This side-by-side comparison illustrates how distinct the two processes are (see Table 8.1).

We contend that the adversary and problem-solving processes need

TABLE 8.1. A COMPARISON OF TRANSFORMED AND TRADITIONAL COURT PROCESSES

TRADITIONAL PROCESS	TRANSFORMED PROCESS
• Dispute resolution	• Problem-solving dispute avoidance
• Legal outcome	• Therapeutic outcome
• Adversarial process	• Collaborative process
• Claim- or case-oriented	• People-oriented
• Rights-based	• Interest- or needs-based
• Emphasis placed on adjudication	• Emphasis placed on post- adjudication and alternative dispute resolution
• Interpretation and application of law	• Interpretation and application of social science
• Judge as arbiter	• Judge as coach
• Backward looking	• Forward looking
• Precedent-based	• Planning-based
• Few participants and stakeholders	• Wide range of participants and stakeholders
• Individualistic	• Interdependent
• Legalistic	• Common-sensical
• Formal	• Informal
• Efficient	• Effective

Source: R. K. Warren, "Reengineering the Court Process," presentation to Great Lakes Court Summit, Madison, Wisconsin, September 24–25, 1998, reprinted in David Rottman and Pamela Casey, "Therapeutic Jurisprudence and the Emergence of Problem-Solving Courts," *NIJ Journal* (July 1999): 12–19.

to be kept separate and distinct because they require different methods of decision making, different support staff, different monitoring practices after sentencing, and so forth. Conflicting characteristics are the reason why the two processes cannot be merged, and *problem-solving principles cannot be grafted onto traditional courts without doing damage to each process*. What is the point of treatment-oriented adversarial proceedings or sanction-oriented problem-solving courts? Can we force technically innocent people into treatment programs before guilt has been adjudicated? Can judges be detached *and* engaged or expected to be detached in some cases and engaged in others? Can court processes be both austere and formal as well as welcoming and informal at the same time?

Courts Cannot Be Both Adversarial and Reconciling

The problem-solving approach is clearly *not* adversarial and therefore requires a different processing track. The goal of problem-solving proceedings is to achieve justice using a nonadversarial process—the emphasis is not on finding guilt or liability but on fashioning an appropriate remedy. The prosecution, defense, judges, and other court participants share an interest in treating the condition that has caused the defendant to commit criminal offenses. Defendants are either diverted from standard court processing before guilt or innocence is determined or encouraged to plead guilty in order to be admitted into a problem-solving court (postadjudication treatment program). This characteristic of the problem-solving approach has led one scholar to state, "[I]t is not a court if you have to plead guilty to get there."[16] Actually, because the defendant must admit culpability to be ready for treatment, we argue that postadjudication treatment is the more appropriate model and preferable to deferred prosecution.

With regard to sentencing, the adversary process by its very nature must try to harmonize sentences among offenders so that all are treated fairly. In the problem-solving process, sentencing is explicitly tailored to the needs of the individual, *regardless* of how others similarly situated were sentenced. In treatment-oriented processes, addiction patterns, mental health, and other individual-based characteristics must all be factored into the proposed treatment plans if those treatments are to be effective.

Courts Cannot Both Treat and Sanction

Bruce Winick and David Wexler contend that traditional courts benefit from judges familiar with problem-solving techniques. Problem-solving courts have served to raise the consciousness of many judges concerning their therapeutic role, and many former problem-solving court judges, upon being transferred back to courts of general jurisdiction, have taken with them the tools and sensitivities they have acquired in those newer courts.[17]

We would argue that it is not possible for courts to be both helper and punisher—which is why treatment should be offered *only* after an admission of guilt. These are clearly two separate and distinct roles, which is why we argue that courts should triage cases into separate, distinct, and well-defined adversary or problem-solving processes—so that litigants as well as court participants know which set of rules is being applied and which role the judge is playing.

Again, our concern here is that grafting problem-solving practices onto traditional courts contaminates the integrity of both processing tracks. Obviously the two separate tracks can interact, but the integrity of each track should be maintained so that consistent focus is on *either* sanctions *or* treatment. If during the course of treatment it were determined that treatment was not the right course of action, the defendant could be switched to the sanction track and vice versa. What we should *not* do is tinker with the integrity of the case-processing tracks, lest we be left with only one hybrid process with mixed objectives.

Mainstreaming Problem-Solving Principles

Because problem-solving processes are labor-intensive, Alex Aikman argues that problem-solving courts will remain "one tool among many being used by only a fraction of all trial judges on a fraction of the caseload."[18] Indeed, some advocates argue that the problem-solving approach works precisely because its caseloads are so small that all attention can be focused on a few particular cases and their related problems.[19]

Advocates of problem-solving courts agree that these courts reach only a small proportion of litigants who might benefit and have suggested two methods of increasing their reach: *either increase the num-*

ber of specialized courts or apply the core principles of problem-solving courts to traditional courts.

A California focus group favors the first option, because problem-solving courts (called collaborative justice there) seem to work:

> [We] focus the attention of all parties . . . on a particular problem, train them and try to get the resources together. You lose that efficacy once you start trying to make it into a general proposition. And therefore, . . . the more practical [approach] is to continue to do these small boutique courts. . . . We can focus our attention on some of the solvable problems.[20]

Moreover, they fear that if specialized courts were discontinued, they would return to the prior situation of inconsistent practice and the loss of treatment resources in a larger court. Because adding a significant number of cases would change the very nature, and hence effectiveness, of problem-solving courts, experts now are trying to determine which offenders can best be served by such courts.

The second option is to expand selective problem-solving principles into traditional courts. The Conference of Chief Justices (CCJ) and the Conference of State Court Administrators (COSCA) supported the latter approach in a resolution passed on August 3, 2000, and confirmed it by a second resolution passed on July 29, 2004. Point 4 of the original resolution calls upon state courts to

> [e]ncourage, where appropriate, the broad integration over the next decade of the principles and methods employed in the problem-solving courts into the administration of justice to improve court processes and outcomes while preserving the rule of law, enhancing judicial effectiveness, and meeting the needs and expectations of litigants, victims, and the community.[21]

Again, the California focus group of experts expresses reservations about expanding problem-solving practices too quickly and not balancing those practices with concerns for public safety. They fear a "backlash" if the expansion were not managed correctly.[22] The experiment with juvenile courts, the first "problem-solving" court, may serve as a cautionary tale as to how other problem-solving courts may be transformed over time. Juvenile courts were established to focus on treating individual adolescents but reacquired some of the characteristics of a traditional court, resulting in a hybrid that was neither fully treatment-oriented nor sanctions-oriented.

In 1995, John DiIulio created a new theory around the notion of a new generation of street criminals—"super predators" who were impulsive, remorseless youth with no respect for human life.[23] Public fear of juvenile crime has caused most states to limit the juvenile-court jurisdiction over serious, violent cases, especially those perpetrated by repeat offenders. Necessarily these cases have been shifted toward the punitive track, and many states now list punishment of offenders as one of the purposes of juvenile court.[24] Laws have also been modified to make it easier to prosecute juveniles in adult-criminal court, which increases the possibility of a prison sentence rather than placement in a juvenile facility offering rehabilitative programs.[25] The point is that a court created to be distinctive from a traditional court with an adversary orientation ended up in the "muddled middle," neither a traditional court nor a treatment court.

In practice, juvenile courts did not change practice as much as their proponents had hoped, one reason being that judges who presided over juvenile courts did not all share the treatment orientation that underlay the creation of these courts.[26] Critics note, "Aside from a few celebrities, juvenile court magistrates did not share the therapeutic orientation"[27] and juvenile courts "provided new bottles for old wine."[28] Treatment orientation in juvenile courts declined over time until the U.S. Supreme Court's 1967 decision *In re Gault* restored most due-process rights to juvenile defendants.[29] As the Court noted a year earlier in *Kent v. United States*, "[T]here may be grounds for concern that the child receives the worst of both worlds: that he gets neither the protections accorded to adults nor the solicitous care and regenerative treatment postulated for children."[30] This lesson may also be applicable to the modern version of problem-solving courts as their principles are "mainstreamed" to traditional courts.

Is Treatment a Court Responsibility?

The larger question underlying this whole discussion is whether treatment should be a function of courts at all. After all, we begin this chapter with a short description of the function of rehabilitation in corrections. Should courts' responsibility end at the determination of guilt, or do they have a responsibility to rehabilitate or at least monitor the rehabilitation of offenders? Or, should the rehabilitation function along with the punishment and reduced risk to public safety be a responsibility of the probation departments perhaps with court oversight? Courts edged into this arena because someone had to do it, but the historic mission of probation departments has been to engage in the type of monitoring and service provision that the treatment approach recommends.

With respect to family cases, must ongoing monitoring be done by courts? Could child-welfare agencies monitor progress, with the proviso that they bring to the court's attention those clients who are not participating in the prescribed, perhaps court-ordered, treatment plans, are not making sufficient progress in the treatment programs, or have repeatedly been unsuccessful in achieving treatment goals?

With respect to criminal matters, what benefits does court monitoring have over probation programs that apply most of the same principles as problem-solving courts without the intensive participation of a judge? How is judicial monitoring of problem-solving clients different from intensive supervision probation,[31] with monitoring done by the probation departments under the state departments of corrections? Indeed, it may be possible to have services provided by treatment teams staffed by representatives from different agencies, including education, health, mental health, and housing.

Probation agencies and associations claim that those programs are at least as effective while costing less. Courts and their supporting organizations are equally adamant that the participation of judges is a critical success factor. These kinds of issues need to be sorted out empirically in a way that wins the support of the entire community.

As a step in this direction, the Pew Charitable Trusts' Public Safety Performance Project, the American Probation and Parole Association, and NCSC jointly sponsored a conference on effective administrative responses in probation and parole supervision in December 2012.[32] At the conference, the strategies of "swift, certain, and proportionate sanctions" to respond to violations and the use of incentives to promote and reinforce compliance were discussed. The authority of issue sanctions and reward compliance can be given to courts *or* to the agency. One of the key lessons learned is that regardless of who does the supervision, it requires an investment of resources.[33] If done administratively, implementation of this program would increase the workload of probation and parole officers, though it may reduce court staff time. Moreover, if administrative proceedings were used, the state may not be required to provide counsel. If a sanction were proposed, best practices would require that the probationer have the right to appear at the hearing, present evidence, and be provided with a written copy of the decision. However, if the probationer contested an administratively imposed sanction, the recommendation would be that he or she be provided with the opportunity for an independent administrative review. Finally, if a state does not wish to establish a separate administrative hearing procedure, the probationer should be able to choose whether to waive the right to a hearing and accept the administrative sanction or to go to court.

The best response to why courts need to be involved is found in a description of the key elements of a reentry court:

- Ex-offenders require a powerful intervention to change their behavior.
- The judge as an influential authority figure can influence behavior.
- The reentry court, through rigorous monitoring, can hold collaborating agencies and offenders to a higher level of accountability than other interventions can.[34]

These are excellent hypotheses, but they should be verified by empirical testing. It may be too late to change the course of development for problem-solving courts and responsibility for treatment, but the discussion should at least clarify the respective role of courts and the role of probation services in providing treatment. Indeed, some die-hard advocates of the traditional adversary system would question whether it is even a goal of courts, rather than corrections, to reduce recidivism.

In sum, *when does the treatment focus end?* At which point in the process should clients exit the treatment "track" and be transferred to the adversary track? Because we believe that the adversarial and treatment tracks need to be separate and distinct, the points at which clients are not engaged in treatment, are deemed not suitable for treatment, or are not successful in completing treatment programs and, more generally, when the focus becomes punishment rather than treatment are times when those individuals should be switched to the adversarial, due-process track. Conversely, when judges believe that participants in the adversarial system could benefit from treatment and that treatments would reduce the probability of recidivism, those defendants should be switched to the treatment track.

Making the Reimagined Court a Reality

Case-Triage Strategies in Action

The triage strategies discussed in previous chapters require significant investment in protocols and procedures to develop decision trees appropriate for clerks, paralegals, and staff lawyers, but they have yielded impressive results in the few places they have been attempted. Perhaps a few illustrations of these triage strategies from courts around the country will illustrate the potential of what can be done using enhanced case triage and, at the very least, encourage more experimentation.

Reducing Jurisdiction

Rather than adding more types of cases to the courts, some courts have gone the opposite way and curtailed jurisdictions.

One experiment in New York eliminated family-court jurisdiction over status offenses. In 2004, at least 159,000 status-offense cases were processed in the United States, or approximately 12 percent of the juvenile dockets of general- and limited-jurisdiction courts.[1] Status offenses are behaviors that are offenses only because the persons involved are minors and include truants, curfew violators, and runaways.

Taking a similar tack, the Vera Institute of Justice has been developing new programs to assist families with adolescents in crisis. Rather than taking these youth to court for proceedings that could result in detention, probation, and out-of-home placement, parents, schools, and police are focusing on community-based assistance, which has shown promising results in family stability, outcomes for children, and reduced financial burdens on the state.[2]

Increasing Litigant Choice

Given our interest in increasing triage as well as litigant choice, one attractive solution is to use an interdisciplinary team of lawyers who work frequently with social workers and parent advocates to represent parents *before a petition is filed*.[3] This process allows the parents to access the expertise of a multidisciplinary team in law, social services, and life in a confidential setting. In Jane M. Spinak's words, "The parent advocate who can draw on her own experience in proposing solutions may be as important to the case as the social worker who accesses services or the lawyer who gets the case dismissed."[4] In other words, the parent's advocacy team is supporting the family rather than having a problem-solving court create and monitor a solution.

The preliminary results in New York City have been impressive, with 95 percent of the children served avoiding foster care and those for whom a petition had already been filed reducing their length of stay in foster care.[5] In other words, this model has the potential to significantly diminish the need for court intervention.

Adopting a similar strategy, the Maricopa, Arizona, family court decided to put the initial case-triage decision in the hands of litigants after providing appropriate guidance via its website and detailed court rules. The court discovered that about half the family cases required only an entry of decree or judgment by default or consent to dispose, so it decided to use technology in a very innovative way by offering Decree on Demand and Default on Demand capabilities through its website. Litigants could then receive the desired court decrees without ever physically going to the court. Judges produced the decrees more efficiently, and court staff avoided unnecessary appearances and file manipulation. The website provided detailed guidance on which case characteristics would qualify a litigant for an online decree.

In a related innovation, the court initiated an aggressive Early Resolution Triage Program for contested cases using an attorney case manager. Uncontested matters were disposed of immediately. Cases with no remaining contested issues were also quickly disposed of.

Cases with remaining contested issues were then fast-tracked for hearing dates to resolve those issues. In 2007, the Maricopa family court was disposing of only a bit more than 50 percent of its cases within seven months. After fewer than three years of implementing these new approaches to case triage, more than 80 percent of all family cases are being resolved within seven months.[6]

The Elkins Family Law Task Force conducted a comprehensive review of family-law proceedings to increase access for family-law litigants, including the self-represented. Its report to the California Judicial Council suggests helping litigants navigate the family court, streamlining forms and procedures, and "Expanding Services to Litigants to Assist in Resolving Their Cases."[7] The task force recommends a "continuum of services," including providing legal information, assisting with forms, explaining legal processes, providing mediation assistance, and providing representation in trial and appellate courts. If this variety of services is needed to ensure access, there is also a need for a process to identify which litigants need which services.

Streamlining Processes

New York City Housing Court has empowered judges to handle their cases with simplified processes in informal settings.[8] The lessons for courts facing significant issues with self-represented litigants are instructive. The court permits representation by professionals or family members who are not lawyers. Judges use a set of best practices to ensure that all parties are effectively represented in terms of consistency and fairness during the hearing without acting in unlawful or unconstitutional ways. In addition to relaxed rules of due process and evidence, judges are beginning to consider holding virtual hearings.

The Multnomah, Oregon, civil court has embarked on an ambitious civil-reform project intended to speed up the average processing rate of civil cases without sacrificing legal quality. An initial case-management conference is held within ten days, and a firm trial date is set within four months. The court aggressively manages the parties' discovery plans. A pretrial conference produces stipulations limiting exhibits, expert testimony, and motions. A voluntary expedited track is provided for civil jury trials. A number of other features ensure a speedy, significantly more predictable, and less costly trial process.[9]

Utah is piloting a broader project to control civil discovery, based on the principle of legal proportionality. The court shifts the burden to the parties to demonstrate their entitlement to discovery. A number of features ensure that discovery is relevant and timely. Limits are set on depositions, interrogatories, requests for production, and requests for admission. A presumptive time limit for discovery is also set.

In Minnesota, Early Neutral Evaluation provides another example of the type of triage that is available early in the process. This program is a voluntary, confidential, and affordable alternative dispute resolution (ADR) process focused on generating durable settlements in child-custody cases.[10] It is not mediation but an alternative to custody evaluations that consists of (1) voluntary referral, (2) a first meeting within fourteen days of the initial case-management hearing, and (3) a confidential process in that evaluators cannot be deposed and cannot testify in any subsequent court hearing. "Social" neutral evaluations address custody and parenting-time issues and are conducted by a male/female team working in pairs to avoid any appearance of gender bias. Often, one team member is an attorney and the other a mental-health professional. "Financial" evaluations address support and marital-estate issues and are usually conducted by one evaluator. The evaluators set the stage by explaining the process, permit each client to present his or her "story," consult privately to exchange impressions or to determine whether more information is necessary, deliver an opinion, and then reconvene to discuss each side's reaction to the decision. Most participants are willing to negotiate, a settlement is crafted, and the court is informed of the results. A high percentage of cases settle. If the negotiation is unsuccessful, parties often stipulate to case-management options suggested by the evaluators, which expedites issuance of subsequent orders.

Early Case Management requires intensive judicial involvement early in the litigation and consists of five steps: (1) an initial case-management conference within three weeks of case filing; (2) submission of two-page "preliminary data sheets" by each party to provide basic information; (3) the judge's perception of the choices available for resolution on each issue; (4) stipulated, tailored case-management plans; and (5) continued case management that may be accomplished by a telephone conference, letter submission detailing progress, pretrial conference, or in-court hearing. Cases are often settled early when no significant contested issues exist. Use of relief hearings and formal discovery has largely disappeared. The average time to disposition for family cases is now fewer than six months.

As a side benefit, when court processes are streamlined, they become easier for self-represented litigants to access. Richard Zorza suggests the need to make court processes more welcoming; to provide additional information to litigants, along with plain-language paper and automated forms and self-help centers; and to restructure hearings to streamline the process and increase access.[11]

Optimizing Scarce Resources

Two very different examples illustrate how scarce resources can better be used. The first example suggests a more efficient approach than the traditional problem-solving court strategies. The second example suggests some possible case-processing efficiencies in the back office.

We contend that problem-solving approaches are appropriate for serious criminal cases, *but only for the sentencing phase*. As John Feinblatt, Greg Berman, and Derek Denckla cogently state, "[Problem-solving courts emphasize] traditional due process protections during adjudication and the achievement of tangible, constructive outcomes post adjudication."[12] Especially in criminal cases involving substance abuse, such as driving-while-impaired (DWI) cases, the full adversary process with all its due-process protections should be employed until guilt has been established. After guilt has been established, problem-solving principles designed to prevent repeat offenses could be used to select the best sentencing options, be they therapeutic or punitive. This should at least mitigate the role conflict between judges with a traditional orientation toward law and advocates of the more "transformed" process of problem-solving courts.

This raises the question of the appropriate role of problem-solving courts in general. If evidence-based probation is, indeed, a functional equivalent to a problem-solving court, is it not a more cost-effective alternative?[13] Evidence-based probation is founded on similar principles: use of proven strategies for changing the behavior of certain types of offenders, positive reinforcement, and swift and certain sanctions for violations.[14] At least some corrections officials believe that sentencing costs per client can be lower and the outcomes just as good, if not better, with evidence-based probation than with problem-solving courts. The possible reason might be that success with high-risk offenders requires an individualized response of "graduated sanctions" based on each offender's drug abuse and criminal history. Is it wise to employ high-cost judges in this high-intensity effort rather than lower-cost probation officers? The number of times judges are involved with low-risk offenders does not seem to affect outcomes.[15] Given that scenario, would evidence-based probation without intensive judge involvement work just as well as problem-solving courts, at least for drug cases?

Switching now to the court back office, consider how the clerk's office has literally been reinvented in Utah.[16] As the traditional data-entry and case-file-manipulation tasks became more automated, clerk staff saw less demand for the simple skills they had commonly performed. As a result, all job descriptions have been completely rewritten to emphasize case-management and litigant-support skills rather than low-level data-entry and paper-case-file-management abilities. The clerks have also been reorganized into cross-trained teams better positioned to provide help and move cases forward. The result has been impressive. Staff turnover has decreased significantly. The number of managers needed has been cut almost in half. The average clerk is now more capable, better educated, and better paid, so more work is accomplished with fewer staff. More importantly, more resources have been made available to assist with the key tasks of case management. Litigants and judges are better supported at every point in the case-management process.

Implications for Judicial and Court Staff Selection, Education, and Training

The examples of case-processing strategies discussed above are encouraging. Many of them are being pursued by major courts in some locations, but no single court has implemented them all. Thus, it is difficult to assess the total impact on productivity and customer satisfaction that might result if they were employed collectively. What is clear is that the courts have a pathway to improving their case-processing performance.

If the major ideas presented in this book are taken seriously, they will have implications not only for court management but for judicial selection and education as well.

Judicial Selection

In Chapter 8, we note that different case-processing tracks require different skills and perhaps different judicial personality types, yet we persist in picturing the ideal judge as a neutral arbiter—stoic, speaking only to attorneys, and above the fray. Yet we also note in Chapter 7 that the problem-solving judge should demonstrate an entirely different set of characteristics—engaged, involved, communicating with litigants, interested in the success of treatment. These differences are easily observed because they are so clearly contradictory, but keep in mind that the disposition-oriented judge requires yet another set of traits—an ability to be in the fray, dealing with multiple cases in many different ways to promote expeditious resolution.

In addition to these basic role differences, problem-solving courts, where they are successful, are likely to rely on the judge's prestige and standing in the community to coordinate the resources housed in different organizations and to take the lead in advocating for new resources. This is another aspect of the problem-solving role that is not part of the neutral arbiter role. Although some aspects of the problem-solving role can perhaps be taught, others cannot. Some participants in the California focus group referred to earlier believe that "even with training or experience in problem-solving courts, colleagues without the right personality traits would be ineffective."[17] This opinion would suggest that judges should be explicitly selected to serve on problem-solving courts.

While proposing remedies to judicial selection goes beyond the scope of this book, we do recommend that current methods of judicial selection be adjusted to take into account the different requirements of different judicial positions. At the very least, judges wishing to serve on a specialized court should seek that position specifically rather than accept a general assignment in an area of law in which they are not much interested and wait until a rotation puts them on a docket they really desire. This change may require diversifying the pool of candidates for judicial office to include not only those who excel at being dispassionate, analytic neutral arbiters but also those with more right-brained interpersonal skills concerned with creating harmony. Consideration of appropriate judicial roles should change the requirements by which nominations for appointments are made (gubernatorial, legislative, or merit plan) and the way candidates for election are chosen and election campaigns are conducted.

Changes to the selection process require that methods of judicial assignment and rotation also be taken into account. The theory of rotation in judicial assignment was designed to protect the neutral arbiter from becoming too close to any one type of case and preclude the possibility of becoming captured by special interests, as some administrative agencies are. Advocates for problem-solving courts consider assignments to these courts as a method of educating traditional judges about the process and a way to carry those skills to subsequent general calendar assignments.[18]

Yet if judges were selected for positions on problem-solving courts because of their interest in, aptitude for, and experience in a specialized area of the law, what would be the point of frequent rotation off the specialized docket, except to avoid burnout?

Judicial Education and Training

The issues surrounding problem-solving courts also raise the question of judicial qualifications for presiding over specialized courts. Currently, most law schools focus only on training for the adversary process, so where do problem-solving judges obtain the qualifications necessary to run a problem-solving court? Furthermore, how useful is a legal education as preparation for a role as a problem-solving judge? Research on the attributes of attorneys suggests they rely disproportionately on analytic, rational thought and are not "interpersonally sensitive"—that is, not attuned to the "emotions, needs, and concerns of other people."[19] This may argue for the use of nonlawyers as judges or quasi-judicial officers to staff problem-solving processes.[20]

The California focus group recommends judicial colleges and judicial orientations as the best way of disseminating information on problem-solving courts, with some favoring mandatory training.[21] This requires that candidates for judicial office, and those already in office who sought the position on the basis of expectations about the judge's role in an adversary setting, be trained for a totally different problem-solving role. One focus group member says, "You are talking about evolving or changing the role of the judicial officer and the colleagues. . . . [T]he judicial officers who [came in] 20 to 25 years ago as a general rule don't perceive the position that way."[22]

The alternative is a much-longer-term solution of introducing problem-solving techniques into the standard law-school curricula that will produce the judges of the future. Although problem solving has been incorporated into some law-school courses in an ad hoc fashion, advocates would like to see it become an explicit part of the curriculum.[23]

Court Staff

As courts require fewer judges and more lawyers and paralegals, not only will the number of court staff be affected; the roles they fill will change as well. Court clerks will need to have higher skill sets, education levels, and salaries than they do now. Staffing by case type, especially for back-office clerks, may no longer make sense. Case-management systems would need to support easy assessment of the status of case issues and include contingencies to support dynamic shifts to other case-processing tracks. Much more information would need to be elicited from and provided to litigants at the beginning of their cases to enable initial placement in the correct case-processing queues.

Although the implications are not entirely clear, this situation might require cross-trained clerk staff who work in teams and employ a more generalist approach to case processing. Utah is testing that kind of clerk-office organization, moving away from specialization by case type. Evaluation will be required to determine whether this approach is successful.

In an article based on a survey of court managers looking toward the year 2025, the authors conclude that "courts will hire staff with a broad range of skills, including computer technology experts, interpreters, accountants, mediators, conciliators, grant writers, webmasters, forensic psychologists, public information specialists, and security analysts."[24] The nature of work performed by paralegals will change as the technology of data mining is used to scan thousands of cases to assist in pre-trial research.

The American Bar Association reports that some law firms have started training their staff lawyers in nonadversarial methods, partly because there are so few trials.[25] But other opportunities exist as well. For example, many courts are implementing mandatory or voluntary mediation or arbitration processes for high-volume case types amenable to nonadversarial resolution. While some of these may be handled by court staff, others would use outside lawyers. This could create a new specialty for law firms, but one for which few law schools are preparing.

Putting It All Together

As noted in the Introduction, most of our recommended practices have been implemented successfully in one or more courts. Many of them have proven to be spectacularly successful at reducing times to disposition and case costs while maintaining judicial quality. Both the courts and the litigants win as long as resources are conserved and litigants perceive justice to be done. The real innovation in this book is the framework that integrates these new practices into a consistent approach and suggests that courts should reorganize around that framework. Otherwise, incremental adoption of selective practices produces jarring discontinuities of process to litigants and confusion about court approaches to case management for everyone.

Implementing the Vision
of a Modern Court

We have presented a daunting array of proposals for realigning and reconciling the functions of courts with the methods of case processing. The suggestions for redesigning internal court case processes are equally challenging. Perhaps the best way to start is with some fundamental concepts.

The Worldview of the Modern Court

A small set of concepts encapsulate our new way of looking at the court, constituting a sort of worldview, if you will. It is hard to understand the motivation for many of our proposed innovations without first accepting the worldview that lies behind them.

Courts no longer have a monopoly on legal decision making. For too long, courts have acted as if they held a monopoly on legal services—at least those involving formal legal decisions. Although they did not control demand, they totally controlled supply. As such, their primary problem was not to provide high-quality services to happy customers, but to match the supply of their services to whatever demand came through the door. This is what government agencies do.

The problem with that mindset is that it is simply not true. Criminal cases are the classic example of a service where the courts maintain an unquestioned monopoly. In fact, criminal cases overwhelmingly settle before going to trial and often before going to court in any meaningful way. In a sense, the court is just a threat used to force a settlement. One might conceivably achieve the same result by enforcing a simple algorithm for dealing with offenders. Rather than selecting the small set of meaningful criminal court cases randomly or politically, the algorithm would select them according to criteria such as seriousness of the crime. Of course, there would still have to be the threat of trial for all cases, or they would not settle at a high rate.

Courts do deal with high-stakes criminal cases and that is appropriate. Even there, individual courts and state court systems vary widely in the extent to which they try comparable crimes and in the sentences that result. Although offenders may have no choice about which courts hear their cases, courts themselves seem to have a lot of latitude in how they handle specific types of cases.

The situation is even more open for civil and family cases. A growing number of complex civil cases are now handled outside the courts by private arbitration. These are high-stakes cases where the parties have found the courts to be undesirable forums. The reasons include cost, time to disposition, and predictability of result. The last concern directly implies a belief that the courts are literally not capable of deciding such cases consistently. On the other hand, the market for court cases involving family law seems to be exploding in some areas and imploding in others. Divorces with children, child welfare, dependency, and abuse cases are now handled by courts rather than, or in addition to, more traditional approaches. Although the reasons are probably complex, this growth in court involvement seems to reflect a market failure on the part of other institutions, like churches, that used to handle these problems exclusively.

The courts are no longer an attractive market for simple divorce cases. Litigants feel as if they should be able to receive a divorce without court involvement. Indeed, some courts now recognize that they are performing an entirely administrative role by granting qualified divorce decrees without any meaningful court action or review.

Many potential litigants now think that they should be able to carry out not only divorces but also other routine legal actions and receive legal decisions without going through the slow, complex, and costly legal processes of courts. One can certainly imagine a world where companies like LegalZoom and Rocket Lawyer help litigants perform legal actions without a physical lawyer present and receive binding legal decisions from online arbitration services. Only the self-interested monopoly of the state bar associations prevents that kind of legal service from being realized now.

Finally, huge markets for legal services are handled by administrative law courts and various forms of non-court arbitration and mediation. Many private industries now embed specific requirements for legal arbitration, rather than court litigation, in their standard consumer contracts for products and services. In a country where there are large populations of recent immigrants, many ethnic communities retain and operate traditional informal methods for resolving legal disputes. Their problems become visible to the formal courts only when their own cultural mechanisms are unequal to the task.

One might view the shift of some legal decisions from the courts as one form of a more general trend to privatize certain functions formerly performed exclusively by government agencies. If so, the courts have not done so consciously. It has happened because potential litigants were unhappy with the services provided by courts. Courts could try to manage these changes more thoughtfully by following the recommendations in this book.

The Legal Market Will Become More Transparent

The typical potential litigant knows absolutely nothing about what his or her case will cost, how long it will take, and what the chances of winning are. This kind of fundamental information about the market is nowhere available and may sometimes be deliberately so. Even so, most potential litigants in civil cases quickly find out that they cannot afford even the most minimal legal representation. The costs are simply too high. That explains the exploding proportion of cases with self-represented litigants who are not poor and could in theory afford an attorney.

Surprisingly, the lack of accurate market information extends even to the bar itself. While large legal firms dealing with *Fortune 500* companies do have a lot of insight into the legal market for the services they provide, most other law firms and legal practitioners do not. They may result from the long-standing and almost universal practice of charging by the hour and treating each case as if it were totally unique. In a recent study of civil legal costs, the National Center for State Courts found that even most experienced lawyers were unable to report what the typical costs for common case types might be.[1] They were simply unused to thinking about their costs that way and had not made any attempt to gather the necessary data to identify costs.

Under the current pressure of competitors both within and without the courts and the bar, the market is beginning to expose data on legal services. Law firms are starting to offer fixed prices for certain services and compete on the basis of those prices. Competitors to the courts already offer such fixed prices for those litigants with enough knowledge to use them. As we argue below, it is in the interest of courts to tell potential litigants what they know about similar cases so that litigants can make informed decisions to use or not use the courts.

Legal Services Will Become More Unbundled

The legal industry itself is telling us that the traditional bar monopoly model of legal services is coming apart at the seams. This process probably started some years ago, but it quickly reached crisis status under the pressure of the Great Recession. The unbundling takes three forms on the bar side. Lawyers are starting to offer limited legal services, sometimes at a fixed price. Bar associations are starting to regulate the provision of limited legal services by non-lawyers. Finally, law firms are creating novel forms of organization that blend bar and non-bar resources. Of course, there are attempts by non-lawyers to simply violate the bar monopoly and offer what are usually considered legal services without sanction. These services tend to be popular, especially when provided online at an attractive price, but they are usually short-lived when the local bar association finds out.

Courts may offer their own version of unbundled legal services. Not every litigant needs the same level of assistance. Providing the right kind of service to the right litigant is very much a court problem right now. Doing so in the most economical way while ensuring that litigants are not put at a legal disadvantage is an even more acute issue.

Finally, courts are beginning to unbundle their internal legal services to themselves. Not too long ago judges considered almost everything they did a legal service. As a consequence, a typical judge juggled paperwork almost as often as he or she made decisions—a clear waste of the most valuable court resource. Having trained staff lawyers, case managers, or clerks perform tasks that do not require a judge's attention is a compelling strategy and one that the health care industry has developed over the last several decades with considerable success.

Courts Will Retain a Monopoly in Only Certain Segments of the Legal Market

There was a time when Ford and General Motors were what is called a vertical monopoly. That is, they made everything that went into a car, starting with the steel. Now, most of the car-manufacturing process is outsourced to a host of vendors who specialize in different parts and do so more efficiently than the car companies ever could. Some car companies no longer attempt to compete in all markets for different types of vehicles. In fact, only a handful still can and they do so by simplifying and reusing common parts across what looks to us like different vehicles.

In a similar way, courts acted as full-service monopolies, offering to process each and every type of legal case from speeding tickets to corporate lawsuits to death penalty cases. Now that menu has expanded to truancy and permanency for children and drug addiction recovery. It is becoming clear that courts will not be able to compete effectively with other organizations for some of these case types and possibly should not even try for others.

Simple low-end cases can probably be done better using either administrative processes or non-court services. Much of what many limited jurisdiction courts now do will fall into this category. It is not clear that most courts will ever recapture the complex civil cases that business courts are intended to service. Many court systems cannot economically provide business courts with sufficient expertise. Finally, the non-adversarial processes of problem-solving courts can and often are performed outside a court by simply eliminating the involvement of the judge or using them in a less intensive way.

Suggestions for Reform

Courts Should Help Potential Litigants Understand When Court Services Are Appropriate

If a court is not a monopoly and if that court accepts that it is not the right forum for every legal dispute, then the court should help litigants understand when using the court is appropriate and when it is not. This is partly a matter of data transparency about the market (as discussed above) and partly education about when other legal solutions or forums are a better choice. Sometimes, the advice might be to just drop the legal process entirely (when there is no real dispute or little likelihood of winning it).

As a corollary of this responsibility, courts should help self-represented litigants better understand when they need help, what kind of assistance is most appropriate, and how to get it. The court should advise them when they should not proceed without legal representation because the stakes are too high or the processes too complex.

The Courts Should Partner with Other Legal Services Providers to Offer Potential Litigants a Seamless Set of Legal Services

If courts are not always the answer and if courts should not always provide services and assistance, then logically they should make referrals to other organizations when appropriate. The courts are not in the business of trying to maintain a monopoly or growing their business. They should handle only cases that they can most appropriately resolve. Courts are unusually qualified to handle cases requiring the classic adversary process and are therefore likely to retain a monopoly of those cases.

There are strong business-process and information-sharing implications for this view of the world. One can imagine a sort of litigant portal that courts would jointly sponsor with other groups that provide legal services. That portal would help litigants make decisions about how to proceed and with whom. Supporting information might be provided by multiple organizations and litigant information might be shared with multiple organizations. Litigants entering the process through interactions with other organizations might be handed off to courts, along with their supporting legal and demographic information.

The Courts Should Tailor Their Legal Services Appropriately and Explicitly for Litigants

The mindset of many courts is so foreign to the idea of litigants as customers that courts should perhaps start by imagining that they are for-profit organizations that must attract customers to survive. Although that idea is repellant to many judges and court staff, the thought experiment is instructive. It helps courts understand the gap between how they interact now with litigants and how those litigants want with the courts to handle them.

It is a truism that core court processes are organized first and foremost for the benefit of the court itself and usually of the judges. Next in importance is the local bar. Trailing far behind are the litigants themselves. This perspective must be stood on its head for the courts to compete and provide valuable legal services. Otherwise, an increasing proportion of its business will simply go elsewhere.

Courts Should Innovate Continuously to Offer Valuable Legal Services

This is an idea that is even more foreign to courts. If you are a permanent monopoly, then innovation is not necessary or even desirable. It is only when funding crises threaten the viability of courts and the quality of justice that courts begin to think about improving their business processes. Because they are not structured or trained to innovate, attempts to do so are extremely difficult, traumatic, and exhausting.

If a court goes through a reengineering process with any degree of success, there is little support to repeat the process. When the funding crisis or increased competition forces the court to do so, morale drops even lower and fear levels rise. Courts need systematic training in how to continuously innovate, or they will disintegrate under the constant pressure to raise productivity and service levels.

Court managers are not trained to do this, and presiding judges are even less equipped professionally to do so. In fact, the business literature teaches us that an organization must be completely restructured in deep and thoughtful ways to institutionalize innovation and become a learning organization. Government bureaucracies, and some would include courts in this characterization, are usually the opposite of learning organizations. That must change.

Barriers to Implementation

It is easier to say what should happen with courts, but much harder to get courts to experiment in the real world. Not all of the resistance is traditional conservatism. Some of the ideas in this book will be hard for courts to implement for valid reasons. Of course, that is not an excuse for delaying the transition to a more modern court system. It just means that plans must take those barriers into account.

Given the fiscal situation that government faces and will continue to face for decades to come, perhaps the biggest initial hurdle is the need to save money with any innovation proposed. While one of our goals here is to create a more productive court system, not all implementation projects will reduce budget costs. Courts will need to bundle their innovations so that the overall effect of any particular project is a cost savings. Otherwise, funders are unlikely to support projects that try only to improve the quality of justice for litigants. This might seem counterintuitive, since litigants are voting citizens after all, but the simple fact is that voters do not rank court problems high enough to influence political agendas directly.

Converting what are now court cases into purely administrative matters, some of which are handled outside the courts, is not difficult technically but can be so politically. Perhaps the easiest step is converting traffic tickets and other low-level citations or misdemeanors to strictly payable noncriminal offenses. A number of states have already done this successfully, so we know it can be done.

It will be harder to shift some case types completely out of the courts. Administrative law courts exist in every state, but the executive branches may resist taking on new workloads in these times of tight finances. This should not be an excuse for courts not to try if it is the right thing to do. It just means that a good case must be made, and courts must be politically adept at promoting the changes.

Treating uncontested divorces without children as administrative matters is surprisingly controversial in some jurisdictions. This attitude seems to be the last gasp of governmental paternalism about marriages. At one extreme, spouses can get a divorce decree in Maricopa County, Arizona without even appearing in court and using an online transaction if they meet the qualifying criteria. At the other extreme, some states like Alaska still mandate "cooling off periods" and require judge review of every case to ensure that both parties are getting a fair shake, even when those parties have already voluntarily agreed to a settlement.

Another very difficult problem is achieving a more integrated and consolidated process for criminal problem-solving dockets. The primary obstacle here is a political one. Separate types of problem-solving courts for offenders are sponsored, funded, and supported by separate federal government agencies and legislation. Although actual offenders cross these artificial boundaries, and justice agencies (including courts) desire a more integrated and coordinated approach to their treatment, such stove-piped organizations are extremely resistant to change for obvious reasons of self-interest.

There is a second level of resistance at the state and local level to better coordination of procedures for dealing with offenders. Multiple agencies, including the courts, receive separate funding to perform risk-and-needs assessments and to carry out treatment regimes. In essence, courts now compete with pretrial agencies, probation and parole organizations, jails, and prisons to provide such services to reduce recidivism. Each responsibility and program comes with a budget, which represents power and influence in any government bureaucracy. Overcoming these very real barriers is not a trivial act.

Even if these agencies were willing to cooperate in good faith, it is still necessary to know what the evidence-based practices should be. We still face significant gaps in knowledge about how best to deal with particular offenders. The research community is starting to develop an overall protocol for triaging offenders as they move through the criminal justice process, but we are still a long way from required comprehensive and non-overlapping solutions.

One timely example of this tension contrasts traditional drug courts to probation programs that apply most of the same principles without the intensive participation of a judge. Probation agencies and associations claim that those programs are at least as effective while costing less. Courts and their supporting organizations are equally adamant that the participation of judges is a critical success factor. These kinds of issues need to be sorted out empirically in a way that achieves consensus of the entire community and that funders will systematically support.

Another huge problem is providing the market information litigants need to make rational decisions about how best to resolve their legal problems. It is a vast understatement to say that both lawyers and courts have been reluctant to reveal such data. The bar had a strong conflict of interest in doing so, since its business model was to charge by the hour, instead of offering services with fixed prices. That is now starting to change under the current fiscal crisis, so attorneys may precede the courts in this area.

Courts could rather easily provide market information on several critical areas, but they have chosen not to by policy. One example would be litigation records for particular attorneys. How many cases of a particular type have they litigated? What proportion of those cases did they win? What were the settlements? Another example would be data on typical court costs and times to disposition for specific case types. Some litigants might even want to know how often a judge was overturned on appeal. In principle, all of this information could and should be knowable, but courts have resisted making it available.

The creation of litigant portals seems more realistic in the short-run. Supported by a variety of access-to-justice organizations, courts are just now beginning to consider what such portals might look like, how they would work, what data would be needed, and how courts would coordinate and integrate with other legal services agencies to operate them. Some research is now being conducted on the necessary litigant-triage protocols, including those for self-represented litigants. Parallel research is also going on to clarify what the optimal forms of assistance by courts should be for different kinds of litigants and cases. Pilot portals may appear in the next couple of years.

Another significant barrier, but technically possible to surmount, concerns new types of data needed to make appropriate case management decisions. Current case management systems, even new ones, lack necessary data on the issues within cases and the status of those issues at any point in the life of the cases. Without such data readily at hand, courts will literally not have the information required to carry out the case management strategies recommended in this book. It is an urgent task to work out what the supporting data models should look like and convince vendors of case management systems to incorporate those functionalities into their off-the-shelf products.

Two other barriers are much more fundamental to courts. Virtually every court still organizes and operates their case management in the back office according to major case types. In larger jurisdictions, clerks specialize in certain case types and learn those processes deeply. Business processes become optimized for the handling of similar cases over time. In some jurisdictions, cases that would be considered adversarial or dispositional in this book might be handled by more than one type of court. These are very practical obstacles to the transition away from case-type-based approaches to case management.

One can certainly imagine a court structure that would better suit a case-process and issue-based approach. First, there would be only one trial court type to facilitate the transition of cases between processes as needed. Second, clerks and others would use information about litigant capabilities and preferences, case issues, and case status to properly manage their cases. Third, case management systems would make it easy to do so for all court participants.

Assume that those structures and capabilities are in place. There is still a requirement to create new job roles with graduated legal capabilities and responsibilities analogous to what has evolved in the health care industry. That kind of internal legal unbundling will not happen quickly. It took health care decades to develop the definitions of those new positions and set up processes for institutionalizing and governing them.

A significant part of that process is the development of protocols for what each role can and should do. Courts have not done anything seriously in this direction, since they traditionally assumed that judges handled all legal analysis of cases and clerks stayed away from the practice of law. Only intermediate appellate courts have used the role of staff attorney to do something similar to what is being suggested here.

While these barriers to implementation are real, they can be overcome. Progress need not occur in a big bang. Incremental improvements and parallel efforts are possible. Some of these experiments are happening as we speak and the future looks promising. Perhaps what is most needed is a general agreement in the court community on what needs to be done. As Yogi Berra famously said, "You've got to be very careful if you don't know where you're going, because you might not get there."

Getting There from Here

The recommendations made in this book collectively represent a very comprehensive and integrated court design effort. This type of fundamental change is never easy. Nevertheless, the redesign of courts should be done because it will help improve courts and deliver better services to its customers.

Three key themes underlie our suggested redesign of state and local courts:

1. A strong customer focus
2. Increased access to justice
3. More efficient delivery of services to litigants and other court stakeholders

An emphasis on court customers first emerged with the publication of the High Performance Court Framework.[2] The Framework stresses the importance of building court services around the needs of court customers by using measurable standards to ensure that those services actually improve. One implication of a customer focus is an explicit effort to treat parties with respect and dignity by implementing the best practices of procedural justice.[3]

One variation on the theme of customer focus that runs through this entire book is increased transparency. Right now, most litigants (and many lawyers) have little understanding of the different court processes they might use to obtain a legal decision. Courts need to provide customers with a choice of alternative court processes and information about those processes that enables them to choose the process that is best for them.

In a country where up to half of all demand for civil legal services goes unmet and almost half of court caseloads involve self-represented litigants, courts cannot avoid the need to increase access to justice. Some steps, like better use of existing facilities, are both obvious and straightforward. The provision of online services is another strategy that all courts should embrace. Improvements in the availability, accessibility, and timeliness of information about courts and cases are already empowering litigants and citizens like never before.

Public perception of court legitimacy is bolstered by direct experience with courts. Jury duty is perhaps the foremost occasion for such personal contact. Although many courts have made strides toward better public service at the counter and in the courtroom, many, perhaps younger, citizens find court services lag behind their experiences with private companies, which set the standard of expected service. Any improvements to court processing that lowers case costs and improves efficiency should therefore have a positive effect on courts.

The latest recession underscored the absolute criticality of courts improving the efficiency and productivity of their business processes. Here again, technology can be a great enabler of streamlined service delivery. The courts must emulate other modern government organizations by using performance standards and managing based on objective data (evidence-based practices) to continuously improve their operations.

Many of the recommendations in the book have been implemented successfully in one or more major courts demonstrating empirically that they work. The only untested proposals are the more integrated approach to problem-solving court triage and the shift from case types to case issues as the organizing strategy for case management. Some unbundling of legal services has not yet occurred in this country, but has been done successfully overseas. The creation of new legal roles has also not yet progressed too far, but the analogous process in the health care industry is encouraging for courts.

Expecting a significant amount of new money from funders to redesign the courts is simply not realistic. On the other hand, courts that have started down this road through reengineering projects have often been granted budget-cut reprieves or delays from supportive funders. Doing nothing costs the courts credibility, but trying to do the right thing, even if unsuccessful, usually gains strong support.

Almost any court can begin by piloting some of the narrower recommendations. With some thought and care, it is possible to bootstrap from modest beginnings to major changes. The sequence must be carefully thought out, so that a court may use savings from the initial steps to fund the next steps.

A healthy market for legal services is beneficial for everyone. It helps potential litigants solve their legal problems in the most socially efficient way. It makes it easier for courts to organize around their core functions and improve them in a measurable way. It even recognizes parallel fundamental changes going on in the world of lawyers and law firms. We cannot put the genie back in the bottle, and we should not want to do so. The new design of the courts will create a healthier institution that does a better job of carrying out its legitimate and critical court mission of resolving disputes impartially, economically, and swiftly.

Notes

Overview

1. "Disruptors, Health Care," *Forbes*, April 15, 2013, 96.
2. National Center for State Courts, *Court Case Management System Functional Standards: A Development Road Map* (Williamsburg, VA: National Center for State Courts, 2005).
3. See www.courtools.org/.
4. Brian Ostrom and Roger Hanson, *Achieving High Performance: A Framework for Courts* (Williamsburg, VA: National Center for State Courts, 2010), available at www.ncsc.org/hpc.
5. NCSC and the Harvard Kennedy School sponsored a series of papers from the Executive Session for State Court Leaders in the 21st Century. Particularly relevant papers for court governance are "Governance: The Final Frontier," by Mary McQueen (2013); and "A Case for Court Governance Principles," by Christine Durham and Dan Becker (2013).

Chapter 1

1. See also National Conference of the Council on the Role of Courts, "Final Report," St. Louis, Missouri, May 7–9, 1982.
2. Robert W. Tobin, *Creating the Judicial Branch: The Unfinished Reform* (Williamsburg, VA: National Center for State Courts, 1999), viii.
3. Robert A. Kagan, *Adversarial Legalism: The American Way of Law* (Cambridge, MA: Harvard University Press, 2001), 6.
4. Maurice Rosenberg, "Court Congestion: Status, Causes and Proposed Remedies," in *The Courts, the Public and the Law Explosion*, ed. H. W. Jones

(Englewood Cliffs, NJ: Prentice-Hall, 1965). Former Chief Justice Warren Burger refers to the "litigation explosion during this generation" in his article "Isn't There a Better Way?" *American Bar Association Journal* 68 (1982): 274–277.

5. Richard B. McNamara, Memo, "Innovation Commission," June 8, 2010.

6. Ibid.

7. Christopher Manning, "Hyperlexis: Our National Disease," *Northwestern University Law Review* 71 (1977): 767.

8. Thomas Ehrlich, "Legal Pollution," *New York Times Magazine* 6 (1976): 17.

9. "Everybody Is Suing Everybody," *Changing Times,* April 1983, 76. See also Victor E. Flango, Robert T. Roper, and Mary E. Elsner, *The Business of State Trial Courts* (Williamsburg, VA: National Center for State Courts, 1983).

10. Kagan, *Adversarial Legalism*, 38.

11. Michael S. Greve, "Environmentalism and Bounty Hunting," *Public Interest* 97 (1989): 15.

12. Austin J. McVey, *The 1989 NCCD Prison Population Forecast: The Impact of the War on Drugs* (San Francisco: National Council on Crime and Delinquency, 1989).

13. The situation has changed. In 2000, the U.S. budget for drug control was $18.4 billion, half of which went to law enforcement and one-sixth went to treatment. Only three years later, 53 percent of the budget still went to law enforcement, but 29 percent went for treatment and 18 percent went for prevention. See Jonathan Alter, "The War on Addiction," *Newsweek,* February 12, 2001, 37–43; and "How Goes the 'War on Drugs': An Assessment of U.S. Drug Problems and Policy" (RAND Corporation Drug Policy Research Center, 2005).

14. Patrick M. Garry, *A Nation of Adversaries: How the Litigation Explosion Is Reshaping America* (New York: Insight Books, 1997), 2.

15. Ibid. With respect to the recent decision by California judge Rolf M. Treu to throw out the state's teacher-tenure laws, in a *Washington Post* commentary, Jay Mathews notes that "teachers are finding ways to improve their ranks that are better than relying on the courts, which are a crude instrument when trying to fix schools" (June 23, 2014).

16. Donald Dewees, Michael Trebilcock, and Peter Coyte, "The Medical Malpractice Crisis: A Comparative Empirical Perspective," *Law and Contemporary Problems* 54 (1991): 217–251; Lois Quam, Robert Dingwall, and Paul Fenn, "Medical Malpractice in Perspective," *British Medical Journal* 294 (1987): 1529, 1597.

17. Jethro K. Lieberman, *The Litigious Society* (New York: Basic Books, 1981), 170.

18. Torbjorn Vallinder, "When the Courts Go Marching In," in *The Global Expansion of Judicial Power,* ed. C. Neal Tate and Torbjorn Vallinder (New York: New York University Press, 1995), 13.

19. Kagan, *Adversarial Legalism*, 7.

20. Michael L. Buenger, "Of Money and Judicial Independence: Can Inherent Powers Protect State Courts in Tough Fiscal Times?" *Kentucky Law Journal* 92 (2003–2004): 1019–1020.

21. Judge William L. Dwyer, *In the Hands of the People: The Trial Jury's Origins, Triumphs, Troubles, and Future in American Democracy* (New York: Thomas Dunne Books, 2002), 125.

22. Bureau of Justice Statistics, University at Albany, *Sourcebook of Criminal Justice Statistics Online*, available at table 2.0031.2011. A more recent survey conducted in April 2012 and reported in a joint publication of Justice at Stake and the National Center for State Courts, *Funding Justice: Strategies and Messages for Restoring Court Funding* (Williamsburg, VA: National Center for State Courts, 2012), revealed that only 18 percent had a "great deal of confidence" in the U.S. Supreme Court, but that number was higher than respondents' 17 percent confidence in the state governor, 13 percent in the state court system, 6 percent in the state legislature, and 3 percent in the U.S. Congress.

23. David B. Rottman and Alan Tomkins, "Public Trust and Confidence in the Courts: What Public Opinion Surveys Mean to Judges," *Court Review* 36 (Fall 1999), found that respondents had less confidence in courts than in medical professionals, local police, the U.S. Supreme Court, the governor's office, and public schools. Only the state legislature and media ranked lower. This result is not too different from a 1999 survey in which the American public gave courts in their communities only an average grade.

24. David B. Rottman and Randall M. Hansen, "How Recent Court Users View the State Courts: Perceptions of Whites, African-Americans, and Latinos" (Williamsburg, VA: National Center for State Courts, n.d.).

25. Garry, *Nation of Adversaries*, 139.

26. Chief Justice Paul J. De Muniz, "The Invisible Branch: Funding Resilient Courts through Public Relations, Institutional Identity, and a Place on the 'Public Radar,'" *Kentucky Law Journal* 100 (2011–2012): 811.

27. Kagan, *Adversarial Legalism*, 4.

28. See, for example, Marc Galanter and John Lande, "Private Courts and Public Authority," *Studies in Law, Politics and Society* 12 (1992): 393–415; Shauhin Talesh, "The Privatization of Public Legal Rights: How Manufacturers Construct the Meaning of Consumer Law," *Law and Society Review* 43 (2009): 527–562.

29. Marc Galanter, "A World without Trials," *Journal of Dispute Resolution* 7 (2006): 32.

30. Shauhin A. Talesh, "How Dispute Resolution System Design Matters: An Organizational Analysis of Dispute Resolution Structures and Consumer Lemon Laws," *Law and Society Review* 46 (2012): 463–496.

31. A special issue of the *Kentucky Law Journal* was devoted to a Symposium on State Court Funding and lists the background and consequences of the current funding crisis. See *Kentucky Law Journal* 100, no. 4 (2011–2012): 729–870.

32. Ronald Hiefetz, Alexander Grashow, and Marty Linsky, *The Practice of Adaptive Leadership* (Cambridge, MA: Harvard Business Press, 2009), 23.

33. In his analysis of the impact of court support staff on the smooth functioning of courts and service to the public, Steadman classifies duties performed into four categories: (1) those required by the constitution, legislation, rules,

or ordinances; (2) those that aid the public welfare and the judicial branch of government; (3) management duties that involve regulating, supervising, or directing activities within the office; and (4) political duties that involve interactions with elected officials. Clerks were asked which duties would be delayed or neglected if a number of support staff were inadequate and, conversely, which tasks would be performed if additional staff were hired. Additional staff would be used to improve court performance, especially in the areas of expedition and timeliness by improving the integrity of court records and access to justice by improving responses to questions from the public. Steven R. Steadman, "Structured Factorial Sort Survey: Wisconsin Clerks of Courts' Perception on Compliance and the Need for Staff across Their Typology of Duties," in "Analysis of Court Support Staffing Levels in Wisconsin," by Steven R. Steadman and Kathleen M. Murphy (unpublished paper submitted in partial fulfillment of Court Executive Development Program requirements of the Institute for Court Management, National Center for State Courts, May 17, 1991), 4, 8, 38.

34. A November 11, 2009, *New York Times* editorial, "State Courts at the Tipping Point" (available at http://www.nytimes.com/2009/11/25/opinion/25weds1. html?th&emc=th), illustrates this point by showing that state courthouses are closed for business on the third Wednesday of every month in California, civil and criminal jury trials are suspended in eight of ten county courts for one month each in New Hampshire, and magnet security machines are no longer regularly staffed at local courthouses in Maine.

35. American Bar Association, *Perceptions of the U.S. Justice System* (Washington, DC: American Bar Association, 1999), 62.

36. Judith S. Kaye, "Constructive State Court Intervention: Turning Crisis into Opportunity," in *The Book of the States 2010* (Lexington, KY: Council of State Governments, 2010), 295.

37. Dall Forsythe, quoted in Steven D. Gold, ed., "State Fiscal Problems and Policies," in *Fiscal Crisis of the States* (Washington, DC: Georgetown University Press, 1995), 6, 34.

38. NCSC and Justice at Stake, *Funding Justice,* 4.

39. Ibid., 8.

Chapter 2

1. National Center for State Courts, *Trial Court Performance Standards with Commentary* (Washington, DC: Bureau of Justice Assistance, 1997), 20.

2. James Q. Wilson, *Varieties of Police Behavior: The Management of Law and Order in Eight Communities* (New York: Atheneum Press, 1970).

3. Search for Court Statistics Project on the National Center for State Courts website: www.courtstatistics.org/Other-Pages/StateCourtCaseloadStatistics .aspx.

4. R. LaFountain et al., *Examining the Work of State Courts: An Analysis of 2009 State Court Caseloads* (Williamsburg, VA: National Center for State

Courts, 2011), 4. Available at www.courtstatistics.org/Other-Pages/StateCourt CaseloadStatistics.aspx.

5. Ibid., 20.

6. Joel B. Grossman et al., "Dimensions of Institutional Participation: Who Uses Courts and How?" *Journal of Politics* 44 (February 1982): 9.

Chapter 3

1. Thomas A. Henderson, Cornelius Kerwin, and Hildy Saizow, *Structuring Justice: The Implications of Court Unification Reform* (Washington, DC: U.S. Department of Justice, 1984).

2. Lawrence Baum, *American Courts: Process and Policy* (Boston: Houghton Mifflin, 1998), 8.

3. Richard Neely, *Why Courts Don't Work* (New York: McGraw-Hill, 1982), 172.

4. The process of prioritizing treatment still continues in the medical profession. A March 8, 2010, *Newsweek* article by Mary Carmichael titled "The Doctor Won't See You Now" decries the lack of primary care physicians but also suggests that "young, healthy patients" with simple medical needs should see a nurse or physician assistance for routine care, with physicians being reserved for only more complex problems: "There is absolutely no reason to force all primary-care providers to have an M.D." (47).

5. Hon. Jim Rausch and Hon. Tom Rawlings, "Integrating Problem-Solving Court Practices into the Child Support Docket," *Juvenile and Family Justice Today* (Winter 2008): 16–19.

6. Richard Zorza has proposed triage as one of the key elements of the "emerging consensus" on providing access to justice for self-represented litigants. Zorza, "Access to Justice: The Emerging Consensus and Some Questions and Implications," *Judicature* 94 (January–February 2011): 156–167.

7. Victor E. Flango and Thomas Clarke, "Which Disputes Belong in Court?" *Judges' Journal* 50, no. 2 (2011): 22–30.

8. Henry J. Abraham, *The Judicial Process*, 3rd ed. (New York: Oxford University Press, 1975), 134.

9. John H. Langbein, *The Origins of the Adversary Criminal Trial* (Oxford, UK: Oxford University Press, 2003), 103. According to Langbein, this "combat effect" of the adversary process was made worse by the "wealth effect" caused by "[p]rivatizing for hire the work of the adversaries who gathered and presented the evidence" because most criminal defendants were indigent (332).

10. Anne Strick, *Injustice for All* (New York: G. P. Putnam's Sons, 1977), 21.

11. Quoted in Abraham, *The Judicial Process,* 100.

12. Lon Fuller distinguishes between the dichotomous types of issues that the adversary system was designed to solve and "polycentric" problems unsuited to solution by adjudication. See Fuller, "Forms and Limits of Adjudication," *Harvard Law Review* 92 (1978): 353.

13. Herbert Jacob, *Urban Justice* (Englewood Cliffs, NJ: Prentice-Hall, 1973), 99.

14. William P. McLauchlan, *American Legal Processes* (New York: Wiley, 1977), 19.

15. Lon L. Fuller, "Adjudication and the Rule of Law," *Proceeding of the American Society of International Law at Its Fifty-fourth Annual Meeting* 54 (1960): 2.

16. We are indebted to Professor Craig Ducat for clarifying this argument, especially for pointing out the sixth criterion of the necessity to have arguments presented in serial fashion. Justiciability doctrines, including cases in controversy, mootness, and ripeness, were partially designed to ensure that a real dispute exists.

17. Thomas A. Henderson et al., *The Significance of Judicial Structure: The Effect of Unification on Trial Court Operations* (Washington, DC: National Institute of Justice, 1984), 57.

18. Ibid., 62.

19. Abraham, *The Judicial Process,* 15. Given the narrowly defined scope of "Law Courts," an alternative method was developed as early as 1340 in England whereby a disappointed litigant could petition the king for "justice" or relief when common law provided no remedy. The king typically referred these petitions to his chancellor, who, until the Reformation, was always a cleric and often the king's confessor. Unlike courts of law, which were based on formal causes of action, the lord chancellor could decide cases according to equity or fairness rather than according to the strict letter of the law. Ultimately, the volume of these petitions led to the establishment of the Court of Chancery.

Because equity developed from canon law, it was a more private process that was (1) written as opposed to oral; (2) more prospective in that judges could order preventive measures and even remedial ones, such as injunctions or restraining orders; and (3) more reliant on judges, rather than juries, to make decisions.

20. See, for example, Gregory Firestone and Janet Weinstein, "In the Best Interests of Children: A Proposal to Transform the Adversarial System," *Family Court Review* 42 (2004): 203.

21. See Robert E. Emery, *Renegotiating Family Relationships: Divorce Child Custody, and Mediation* (New York: Guilford Press, 1994), 205.

22. Jane C. Murphy, "Revitalizing the Adversary System in Family Law," *University of Cincinnati Law Review* 78 (2009–2010): 895.

23. Dahlia Lithwick, "Whose God Wins?" *Newsweek,* March 8, 2010, 22, notes that family courts interfere with constitutional freedoms "all the time"— for example, freedom of speech when the judge bars a person from speaking ill of his or her former spouse in front of the children, freedom to travel to move a child away from a former spouse, and freedom of religion when different faiths are involved.

24. Gene Stephens, "Participatory Justice," in *The 1990s and Beyond,* ed. Edward Cornish (Bethesda: World Future Society, 1990), 100.

25. Andrew Schepard and Peter Salem, "Foreword of the Special Issue on the Family Law Education Project," *Family Court Review* 44 (2006): 516.

26. The conventional term "problem-solving courts" has passed into the language even though most are not separate courts but separate dockets or calendars of larger courts or divisions. In most instances, they involve a single judge periodically handling a single type of case.

27. Quote is from David B. Wexler, "Therapeutic Jurisprudence: It's Not Just for Problem-Solving Courts and Calendars Anymore," in *Future Trends in State Courts 2004*, ed. Carol R. Flango et al. (Williamsburg, VA: National Center for State Courts, 2004), 87–89.

28. Lawrence M. Friedman, "The Day before Trials Vanished," *Journal of Empirical Legal Studies* 1 (2004): 689.

29. The entire issue of the *Journal of Empirical Legal Studies* (November 2004) was devoted to the "vanishing trial."

Appendix to Chapter 3

1. See Erin B. Kaheny, "Appellate Judges as Gatekeepers? An Investigation of Threshold Decisions in Federal Courts of Appeals," *Journal of Appellate Practice and Process* 12 (Fall 2011): 257.

2. Jethro K. Lieberman, *The Litigious Society* (New York: Basic Books, 1981), 17.

3. Jonathan R. Siegel, "A Theory of Justiciability," *Texas Law Review* 86 (2007–2008): 75, 78.

4. Maureen Solomon, *Caseflow Management in the Trial Court* (Chicago: American Bar Association, 1973).

5. David C. Steelman, John Goerdt, and James McMillan, *Caseflow Management: The Heart of Court Management in the New Millennium* (Williamsburg, VA: National Center for State Courts, 2004), 3. Steelman, Goerdt, and McMillan list differentiated case management as the third element of caseflow management, right after early court intervention and continuous court control of cases. See also John Goerdt, Chris Lomvardias, and Geoff Gallas, *Reexamining the Pace of Litigation in 39 Urban Trial Courts* (Williamsburg, VA: National Center for State Courts, 1991), 55. A recent doctoral dissertation found caseflow management to be key to the timeliness of civil and criminal cases in Colorado, but management did not affect the timeliness of domestic-relations cases. See Peter M. Koelling, "Caseflow Management and Its Effect on Timeliness in the Colorado District Courts" (Ph.D. diss., Dekalb: Northern Illinois University, 2013), 184.

6. U.S. Department of Justice, Office of Justice Programs, *Bureau of Justice Assistance Fact Sheet: Differentiated Case Management* (Washington, DC: U.S. Department of Justice, 1995).

7. Steelman, Goerdt, and McMillan, *Caseflow Management*, 4.

Chapter 4

1. David L. McKnight and Paul J. Hilton, "International Comparisons of Litigation Costs: Europe, the United States, and Canada" (paper produced by

NERA Economic Consulting for the U.S. Chamber Institute for Legal Reform, May 2013).

2. Charles E. Silberman, *Criminal Violence, Criminal Justice* (New York: Vintage Books, 1978), 375.

3. Lawrence M. Friedman, "The Day before Trials Vanished," *Journal of Empirical Legal Studies* 1 (2004): 690.

4. John H. Langbein, *The Origins of the Adversary Criminal Trial* (Oxford, UK: Oxford University Press, 2003).

5. Ibid., 2.

6. Ibid., 16, and quoting Edward Powell, "Jury Trial at Gaol Delivery in the Late Middle Ages: The Midland Circuit, 1400–1429," in *Twelve Good Men and True: The Criminal Trial Jury in England, 1200–1800*, ed. J. S. Cockburn and Thomas A. Green (Princeton, NJ: Princeton University Press, 1988), 78–116.

7. Ibid.

8. John Langbein, "Understanding the Short History of Plea Bargaining," *Law and Society Review* 13 (1979): 262.

9. David R. Cleveland and Steven Wisotsky, "The Decline of Oral Argument in the Federal Courts of Appeals: A Modest Proposal for Reform," *Journal of Appellate Practice and Process* 13 (Spring 2012): 125. See also Suzanne Ehrenberg, "Embracing the Writing Centered Legal Process," *Iowa Law Review* 89 (2004): 1167.

10. Dale Anne Sipes, *On Trial: The Length of Civil and Criminal Trials* (Williamsburg, VA: National Center for State Courts, 1988).

11. Hon. Gregory E. Mize (ret.), Paula Hannaford-Agor, and Nicole L. Waters, *The State-of-the-States Survey of Jury Improvement Efforts: A Compendium Report* (Williamsburg, VA: National Center for State Courts, 2007), 38, available at www.ncsc-jurystudies.org/State-of-the-States-Survey.aspx. For each category of cases, jury deliberation time for cases heard by federal courts was longer—for example, 10 hours for capital felony cases, 4 hours for felony and civil cases, and 2.5 hours for misdemeanor cases.

12. Eugene Thomas, as reported in the *San Francisco Recorder*, August 11, 1987, and quoted in Sipes, *On Trial*, 1.

13. Friedman, "The Day before Trials Vanished," 692.

14. The original data for the appendix and figures in this chapter were from Brian J. Ostrom, Shaunna M. Strickland, and Paula I. Hannaford-Agor, "Examining Trial Trends in State Courts: 1976–2002," *Journal of Empirical Legal Studies* 1 (2004): 773–777, but they have been updated by the authors to cover 2003–2009.

15. Brian J. Ostrom et al., *Minnesota Judicial Workload Assessment, 2002* (Williamsburg, VA: National Center for State Courts, 2003).

16. Ibid., 27.

17. Brian J. Ostrom, Victor E. Flango, and Heidi Green, *Determining the Need for Judgeships in Wisconsin* (Williamsburg, VA: National Center for State Courts, 1996), found that a jury trial added 5 hours to the *average* amount of time necessary to dispose of a misdemeanor case and more than 16 hours to the average amount of time necessary to dispose of a personal injury case. In con-

trast, a bench trial added only 2 hours to the average time necessary to resolve a misdemeanor case and 2.25 hours to the average amount of time necessary to resolve a personal injury case.

18. Mize, Hannaford-Agor, and Waters, *State-of-the-States Survey*, 7.

19. Ibid., 41.

20. John H. Wigmore, *Evidence in Trials of Common Law*, vol. 3 (Boston: Little, Brown, 1923), 1367.

21. Jethro K. Lieberman, *The Litigious Society* (New York: Basic Books, 1981), 169.

22. See John H. Langbein, *The Origins of the Adversary Criminal Trial* (Oxford, UK: Oxford University Press, 2003), 310.

23. It is interesting to note how deeply this perception of judging permeates the traditional conception of what a judge is. Even John Roberts at his confirmation hearing to be chief justice of the U.S. Supreme Court noted that the judge, in this case an appellate judge, is merely an umpire, calling balls and strikes. "Confirmation Hearing on the Nomination of John G. Roberts Jr. to Be Chief Justice of the United States: Hearing before the S. Comm. on the Judiciary," 109th Cong. 55 (2005).

24. Robert P. Burns, *The Death of the American Trial* (Chicago: University of Chicago Press, 2009), 115.

25. Jeffrey Abramson, *We, the Jury: The Jury System and the Ideal of Democracy* (New York: Basic Books, 1994), 2.

26. Marcus W. Reinkensmeyer and Chuck Oraftik, "Today's Version of Yesterday's Vision of Tomorrow's Courthouse," *Court Manager* 26 (Spring 2011): 24.

27. Theodore L. Becker, *Comparative Judicial Politics* (Chicago: Rand McNally, 1970), 26.

28. National Center for State Courts, *Trial Court Performance Standards with Commentary* (Washington, DC: Bureau of Justice Assistance, 1997), 13.

29. Becker, *Comparative Judicial Politics*, 13.

30. Stephen Landsman, "So What? Possible Implications of the Vanishing Trial Phenomenon," *Journal of Empirical Legal Studies* 1 (November 2004): 982.

31. Burns, *Death of the American Trial*, 122 (emphasis original).

32. Landsman, "Vanishing Trial Phenomenon."

33. William J. Stuntz, *The Collapse of American Criminal Justice* (Cambridge, MA: Harvard University Press, 2011), 302.

34. Ibid., 283.

35. Institute for the Advancement of the American Legal System, American Board of Trial Advocates, and National Center for State Courts, *A Return to Trials: Implementing Effective, Short, Summary, and Expedited Civil Action Programs 3* (Denver: Institute for the Advancement of the American Legal System, 2012), 1.

36. Ibid.

37. Justice at Stake and the National Center for State Courts, *Funding Justice: Strategies and Messages for Restoring Court Funding* (Williamsburg, VA: National Center for State Courts, 2012); James L. Gibson, *Electing Judges: The*

Surprising Effects of Campaigning on Judicial legitimacy (Chicago: University of Chicago Press, 2012).

38. Institute for the Advancement of the American Legal System, American Board of Trial Advocates, and National Center for State Courts, *Return to Trials,* 117.

39. Ibid., 4.

Chapter 5

1. Thomas A. Henderson, Cornelius Kerwin, and Hildy Saizow, *Structuring Justice: The Implications of Court Unification Reform* (Washington, DC: U.S. Department of Justice, 1984), 11, summarizes "decisional adjudication."

2. Lawrence M. Friedman, "The Day before Trials Vanished," *Journal of Empirical Legal Studies* 1 (2004): 693.

3. Malcolm Feeley, *The Process Is the Punishment: Handling Cases in a Lower Criminal Court* (New York: Russell Sage Foundation, 1979).

4. W. Redlich, *Albany Lawyer* blog (2007), available at http://albany-lawyer.blogspot.com/2007/04/assembly-line-justice.html, accessed November 22, 2011.

5. Colloquium, "What Is a Traditional Judge Anyway? Problem Solving in the State Courts," *Judicature* 84 (2000): 78.

6. James Eisenstein, *Politics and the Legal Process* (New York: Harper and Row, 1973), 103. See also Abraham Blumberg, *Criminal Justice* (Chicago: Quadrangle, 1967), 58, for a similar list of prosecutor duties.

7. William J. Stuntz, "Self-Defeating Crimes," *Virginia Law Review* 86 (2002): 1892.

8. David A. Jones, *Crime without Punishment* (Lexington, MA: D. C. Heath, 1979), 55.

9. *Bordenkircher v. Hayes,* 434 U.S. 357 (1978).

10. *Blackledge v. Allison,* 431 U.S. 63, 71 (1977).

11. Raymond Moley, *Politics and Criminal Prosecution* (New York: Minton, Balch, 1929), ch. 7. See also Lawrence M. Friedman, *Crime and Punishment in American History* (New York: Basic Books, 1993), 253; George Fisher, *Plea Bargaining's Triumph: A History of Plea Bargaining in the United States* (Palo Alto, CA: Stanford University Press, 2003); and Albert W. Alschuler, "Plea Bargaining and Its History," *Columbia Law Review* 79 (1979): 1.

12. Milton Heumann calculated the percentage of trials for the Connecticut Superior Court between 1880 and 1954 and found the trial rate to average 8.7 percent. Heumann, "A Note on Plea Bargaining and Case Pressure," *Law and Society Review* 9 (Spring 1975): 520. See also his *Plea Bargaining: The Experiences of Prosecutors, Judges and Defense Attorneys* (Chicago: University of Chicago Press, 1978).

13. "Sourcebook of Criminal Justice Statistics Online," *Bureau of Justice Statistics,* University of Albany, 2011, available at www.albany.edu/sourcebook/csv/t200312100.csv Table 2.0031.2011, table 5.57.

14. See Lawrence Friedman and Robert V. Percival, *The Roots of Justice: Crime and Punishment in Alameda County California, 1870–1910* (Chapel Hill: University of North Carolina Press, 1981), 166, table 5.8.

15. William J. Stuntz, *The Collapse of American Criminal Justice* (Cambridge, MA: Harvard University Press, 2011), 139.

16. Michael L. Rubenstein, Stevens H. Clarke, and Teresa J. White, *Alaska Bans Plea Bargaining* (Washington, DC: U.S. Department of Justice, 1980).

17. Michael L. Rubenstein and Teresa J. White, "Alaska's Ban on Plea Bargaining," *Law and Society Review* 13 (1979): 380.

18. Teresa White Carns and John Druse, *Alaska's Plea Bargaining Ban Re-Evaluated* (Anchorage, Alaska, Judicial Council, 1991).

19. Reported by David G. Savage, Washington Bureau of the *Tribune*. The Supreme Court cases discussed are *Missouri v. Frye* and *Lafler v. Cooper*.

20. Paula Hannaford-Agor and Nicole Waters, "Estimating the Cost of Civil Litigation," *Caseload Highlights* 20 (January 2013).

21. John Greacen, "How Fair, Fast, and Cheap Should Courts Be?" *Judicature* 82 (May–June 1999), 287–291.

22. William Glaberson, "In Misdemeanor Cases, Long Waits for Elusive Trials," *New York Times*, April 30, 2013, available at www.nytimes.com/2013/05/01/nyregion/justice-denied-for-misdemeanor-cases-trials-are-elusive.html?page wanted=all.

23. Forrest Mosten, "Unbundling Legal Services in 2014: Recommendations for the Courts," *Judges Journal* 53 (Winter 2014): 10–15.

24. Henry R. Glick, *Supreme Courts in State Politics: An Introduction to the Judicial Role* (New York: Basic Books, 1971), 30–34. See also Thomas Ungs and Larry R. Baas, "Judicial Role Perceptions: A Q-Technique Study of Ohio Judges," *Law and Society Review* 6 (1972): 343–348.

25. Keith Boyum, "A Perspective on Civil Delay in Trial Courts," *Justice System Journal* 5 (1979): 170.

26. David Golden and Martha Casey, "New York City Administrative Tribunals: A Case Study in Opportunity for Court Reform," *Judges' Journal* 49 (Winter 2010): 20–27. See also Richard Zorza, "Courts in the 21st Century: The Access to Justice Transformation," *Judges' Journal* 49, no. 1 (Winter 2010): 14–19, 34–36.

27. Personal communication, unpublished program evaluations from New Hampshire, Utah, Minnesota, and Oregon.

28. Victor E. Flango, "Is Procedural Fairness Applicable to All Courts?" *Court Review* 47 (2012): 92–95.

29. Tom R. Tyler, "Procedural Justice and the Courts," *Court Review* 44 (2009): 26–31.

30. Thomas A. Henderson and Cornelius M. Kerwin, "The Changing Character of Court Organization," *Justice System Journal* 7 (1982): 449.

31. The *Economist* describes an interesting situation where the types of controlled experiments ("randomized control trials") usually done in a lab or classroom were being applied to real-world problems. The balance point between

application of due-process safeguards on one hand and timely disposition on the other would make an excellent case study to determine the fastest disposition rate that does not sacrifice due process. "Random Harvest," *Economist*, December 14, 2013, 83.

32. *Mathews v. Eldridge*, 424 U.S. 319, 96 S.Ct. 893 (1976), and discussed in Craig R. Ducat, *Constitutional Interpretation*, 9th ed. (Belmont, CA: Wadsworth Publishing, 2009), 464. In *Goldberg v. Kelly*, 397 U.S. 254 (1970), the U.S. Supreme Court said the opportunity to present a case required (1) "timely and adequate notice"; (2) an opportunity to defend by confronting any adverse witnesses and by presenting his or her own arguments and evidence orally; (3) retained counsel, if desired; (4) a neutral decision maker; (5) a decision resting "solely on the legal rules and evidence adduced at the hearing"; and (6) a statement of reasons for the decision and the evidence supporting it. We are indebted to Professor Ducat for these references.

33. Hon. Ben F. Tennille and Corinne B. Jones, "Developments at the North Carolina Business Courts," in *Future Trends in State Courts 2010*, ed. Carol R. Flango et al. (Williamsburg, VA: National Center for State Courts, 2010), 90–93.

34. "Delaware's Corporate Courts," *Economist*, November 23, 2013, 67. The appeal was *Delaware Coalition for Open Government v. Strine*, U.S. Court of Appeals for the Third Circuit (Philadelphia).

35. See www.virtualcourthouse.com.

36. See www.rezoud.com.

37. A quick search found the following examples: eQuibbly (mediation and arbitration, primarily traffic tickets), ZipCourt (arbitration by trained lawyers), and Online Arbitration Network, or OAN (flat-rate lawyer arbitration). The latter also offers a Software as a Solution (SaaS) cloud platform that Court ADR offices may use.

Chapter 6

1. Lawrence Friedman and Robert Percival, "A Tale of Two Courts: Litigation in Alameda and San Benito Counties," *Law and Society Review* 10 (1976): 267, 286. But see Richard Lempert, "More Tales of Two Courts: Exploring Changes in 'Dispute Settlement Function' of Trial Courts," *Law and Society Review* 13 (1978): 91.

2. Simon H. Rifkind, "Are We Asking Too Much of Our Courts?" *F.R.D.* 70 (1976): 97.

3. American Bar Association, *Report of the Pound Conference Follow-Up Task Force* (1976), 3.

4. Ibid., 21.

5. William L. F. Felstiner, Richard L. Abel, and Austin Sarat, "The Emergence and Transformation of Disputes: Naming, Blaming, Claiming . . . ," *Law and Society Review* 15 (1980–1981): 634–636.

6. Richard E. Miller and Austin Sarat, "Grievances, Claims, and Disputes:

Assessing the Adversary Culture," *Law and Society Review* 15 (1980–1981): 538–541.

7. This is one of the eight purposes of courts identified by Ernest Friesen, but nevertheless, making a legal record does not require an adjudicatory process.

8. Richard Zorza, "Courts in the 21st Century, the Access to Justice Transformation," *Judges' Journal* 49 (Winter 2010): 17.

9. Keith Roberts, "What Judges Actually Do," *Judges' Journal* 49 (Winter 2010): 29.

10. Ibid., 30.

11. Victor E. Flango, "Is Procedural Fairness Applicable to All Courts?" *Court Review* 47 (2012): 92–95.

12. Fla. Stat. § 318.30 and 318.36.

13. See www.vermontjudiciary.org/GTC/judicial/default.aspx.

14. Charlotte Stockwell, "Managing the Transition from the Adversarial to the Non-adversarial Court: A Court Administrator's Perspective" (Evaluation Report of the Court Integrated Support Program, Magistrate's Court of Victoria, 2010).

15. David B. Goldin and Martha I. Casey, "New York City Administrative Tribunals: A Case Study in Opportunity for Court Reform," *Judges' Journal* 49 (Winter 2010): 21.

16. Robert A. Kagan, *Adversarial Legalism* (Cambridge, MA: Harvard University Press, 2001), 10.

17. Ibid., 238.

18. Takao Tanase, "The Management of Disputes: Automobile Accident Compensation in Japan," *Law and Society Review* 24 (1990): 651.

19. Kagan, *Adversarial Legalism,* 135.

20. J. Mark Ramseyer and Minoru Nakazato, "Why Is the Japanese Conviction Rate So High?" (discussion paper, John M. Olin Center for Law, Economics, and Business, Harvard Law School, 1989) quoted in Kagan, *Adversarial Legalism,* 136.

21. Daniel Foote, "Resolution of Traffic Accident Disputes and Judicial Activism in Japan," *Law in Japan* 25 (1995): 10.

22. Tanase, "The Management of Disputes," 660.

23. Richard H. Thaler and Cass R. Sunstein, *Nudge* (New York: Penguin Books, 2008), 209.

24. Ibid., 211. See also David A. Hyman and Charles Silver, "Medical Malpractice Litigation, and Tort Reform: It's the Incentives, Stupid," *Vanderbilt Law Review* 59 (2006): 1085–1136; and Tom Baker, *The Medical Malpractice Myth* (Chicago: University of Chicago Press, 2005).

25. Daniel Kessler and Mark McClellan, "Do Doctors Practice Defensive Medicine?" *Quarterly Journal of Economics* 111 (1996): 353–390.

26. Thaler and Sunstein, *Nudge,* 213. See also Russell A. Localio et al. "Relation between Malpractice Claims and Adverse Events Due to Negligence: Results of the Harvard Medical Practice Study III," *New England Journal of Medicine* 325 (1991): 245–251; and Michelle Mello and Troyen Brennan, "Deter-

rence of Medical Errors: Theory and Evidence for Malpractice Reform," *Texas Law Review* 80 (2002): 1597–1637.

27. Thaler and Sunstein, *Nudge,* 215

28. Kagan, *Adversarial Legalism,* 126.

29. The U.S. Congress legalized the term "black lung" as a synonym for that disease in Title IV of the Coal Mine Act. It was the first time that the Congress had mandated that an occupational disease occurring in a major industry must be eradicated. The Congress also established the black lung benefits program, the first and only federal compensation statute to compensate victims of occupational diseases. In 1977, amendments established a Black Lung Disability Trust Fund to provide compensation to miners whose employers no longer existed, financed by taxes paid by all coal operators. They also made coal companies directly responsible for compensation and medical costs for black lung victims who had worked for them. The UMWA has advocated legislative and administrative reforms to make it easier for black lung victims to establish eligibility for benefits.

Appendix to Chapter 6

1. This appendix was originally published as Victor E. Flango and F. Dale Kasparek, Jr., "Which Commercial Driving Cases Should Go to Court?" in *Trends in State Courts, 2013,* ed. Carol R. Flango et al. (Williamsburg, VA: National Center for State Courts, 2013), 66–70, and is used here with permission from the National Center for State Courts.

2. Federal Motor Carrier Safety Administration, "Commercial Motor Vehicle Facts" (March 2013), available at www.fmcsa.dot.gov/facts-research/art.htm.

3. Martin Shapiro, *The Supreme Court and Administrative Agencies* (New York: Free Press, 1968), 52, distinguishes "generalist" courts from "specialized" agencies—a distinction that becomes less relevant to the extent that "specialized" courts exist.

4. Available at http://legal-dictionary.thefreedictionary.com/Administrativ e+Law+and+Procedure (accessed November, 21, 2012).

5. *Gale Encyclopedia of US History: Administrative Justice,* available at www .answers.com/topic/administrative-justice (accessed November 21, 2012).

6. Shapiro, *Supreme Court and Administrative Agencies,* 44.

Chapter 7

1. Chief Justice Warren Burger, quoted in Gary Toohey, "The Civil Jury Trial: Going, Going, Gone," *Precedent,* Summer 2010, 7.

2. Robert W. Tobin, *Creating the Judicial Branch: The Unfinished Reform* (New York: Authors Choice Press, 1999), 210.

3. Donald J. Farole Jr., Nora K. Puffett, and Michael Rempel, *Collaborative Justice in Conventional Courts* (report prepared for the Judicial Council of Cali-

fornia, Administrative Office of the Courts by the Center for Court Innovation, 2005), available at www.courtinnovation.org.

4. See the Center for Court Innovation website: www.courtinnovation.org/index.cfm?fuseaction=page.viewPage&pageID=628&nodeID=1.

5. Quoted in Donald J. Farole, "Applying Problem-Solving Principles in Mainstream Courts: Lessons for State Courts," *Justice System Journal* 26 (2005): 65.

6. David Rottman and Pamela Casey, "Therapeutic Jurisprudence and the Emergence of Problem-Solving Courts," *National Institute of Justice Journal,* July 1999, 15. See also Peggy F. Hora, William G. Schma, and J. T. A. Rosenthal, "Therapeutic Jurisprudence and the Drug Treatment Court Movement: Revolutionizing the Criminal Justice System's Response to Drug Abuse and Crime in America," *Notre Dame Law Review* 74 (1999): 453.

7. National Association of Drug Court Professionals, Drug Court Standards Committee, *Defining Drug Courts: The Key Components* (Washington, DC: Drug Courts Program Office, 1997).

8. Greg Berman and John Feinblatt, "Problem-Solving Courts: A Brief Primer," *Law and Policy* 23 (2001).

9. Candace McCoy, "The Politics of Problem Solving: An Overview of the Origins and Development of Therapeutic Courts," *American Criminal Law Review* 40 (2003): 1526.

10. Michael Isikoff and William Booth, "Miami 'Drug Court' Demonstrates Reno's Unorthodox Approach," *Washington Post,* February 20, 1993.

11. C. West Huddleston III and Douglas B. Marlowe, *Painting the Current Picture: A National Report Card on Drug Courts and Other Problem-Solving Court Programs in the United States* (Washington, DC: Bureau of Justice Assistance, 2011), 1.

12. Morris B. Hoffman, "The Drug Court Scandal," *North Carolina Law Review* 78 (2000): 1479–1480.

13. For these and other related findings, see Shelli B. Rossman and Janine M. Zweig, "The Multisite Adult Drug Court Evaluation," (report prepared for National Association of Drug Court Professionals, Alexandria, Virginia, May 2012).

14. Steven Belenko, *Research on Drug Courts: A Critical Review* (New York: National Center on Addiction and Substance Abuse at Columbia University, 1998), 6–7.

15. Lawrence Baum, *Specializing the Courts* (Chicago: University of Chicago Press, 2011), 119.

16. See David B. Rottman, *Community Courts: Prospects and Limits* (Williamsburg, VA: National Center for State Courts, 2002).

17. See the discussion in Baum, *Specializing the Courts,* 126–128.

18. Jeffrey Fagan and Victoria Malkin, "Theorizing Community Justice through Community Courts," *Fordham Urban Law Journal* 30 (2003): 902.

19. Marty Price, "Personalizing Crime," *Dispute Resolution Magazine* 7 (2000): 8–11, available at http://dx.doi.org/10.1007%FBF02249525.

20. See the discussion in John Braithwaite, "Restorative Justice and De-Professionalization," *Good Society* 13 (2004): 28–31. See also M. Liebmann, *Restorative Justice: How It Works* (London: Jessica Kingsley Publishers, 2007).

21. Gordon Bazemore and Mark S. Umbreit, *Balanced and Restorative Justice for Juveniles: A Framework for Juvenile Justice in the 21st Century* (Washington, DC: Office of Juvenile Justice and Delinquency Prevention, U.S. Department of Justice, 1997).

22. David J. Wallace, "Do DWI Courts Work?" in *Future Trends in State Courts, 2008,* ed. Carol R. Flango et al. (Williamsburg, VA: National Center for State Courts, 2008), 92–95.

23. Jeffrey Tauber and C. W. Huddleston, *DUI/Drug Courts: Defining a National Strategy* (Washington, DC: National Drug Court Institute, 1999), 5.

24. Baum, *Specializing the Courts,* 122. See also John S. Goldkamp and Cheryl Irons-Guynn, *Emerging Judicial Strategies for the Mentally Ill in the Criminal Caseload* (Washington, DC, Bureau of Justice Assistance, 2000); Amy Watson et al., "Mental Health Courts and the Complex Issue of Mentally Ill Offenders," *Psychiatric Services* 52 (2001): 477–481; Henry J. Steadman, Susan Davidson, and Collie Brown, "Mental Health Courts: Their Promise and Unanswered Questions," *Psychiatric Services* 52 (2001): 457–458; and Robert Bernstein and Tammy Selzer, "Criminalization of People with Mental Illnesses: The Role of Mental Health Courts in System Reform," *University of the District of Columbia Law Review* 7 (2003): 143–162.

25. Henry J. Steadman et al., "Six Steps to Improve Your Drug Court Outcomes for Adults with Co- Occurring Disorders," National Drug Court Institute and SAMHSA's GAINS, *Drug Court Practitioner Fact Sheet,* April 2013, 2.

26. America's Law Enforcement and Mental Health Project, as cited in Baum, *Specializing the Courts,* 123.

27. Nicole L. Waters, Shauna M. Strickland, and Sarah A. Gibson, *Mental Health Court Culture: Leaving Your Hat at the Door* (Williamsburg, VA: National Center for State Courts, 2009), 34.

28. Council of State Governments Justice Center, *Mental Health Courts: A Primer for Policymakers and Practitioners* (New York: Council of State Governments Justice Center, 2008), 7.

29. Timothy S. Eckley, "Veterans Court in Session in Buffalo," *Judicature* 92 (2008): 43–44.

30. Robert T. Russell, "Veterans Treatment Courts Developing throughout the Nation," in *Future Trends in State Courts 2009,* ed. Carol R. Flango et al. (Williamsburg, VA: National Center for State Courts, 2009), 130–133.

31. Robert V. Wolf, Center for Court Innovation, *Reentry Courts: Looking Ahead* (Washington, DC: Bureau of Justice Assistance, 2011).

32. See http://csgjusticecenter.org/nrrc.

33. See Office of Juvenile Justice and Delinquency Prevention, "OJJDP Model Programs Guide," available at www.ojjdp.gov/mpg/progTypesReentry Court.aspx.

34. Bernard Flexner, Reuben Oppenheimer, and Katherine F. Lenroot, *The Child, the Family, and the Court: A Study of the Administration of Justice in the Field of Domestic Relations* (Washington, DC: U.S. Government Printing Office, 1929), 49.

35. Institute of Judicial Administration, American Bar Association, *Juvenile Justice Standards Relating to Court Organization*, Standard 1.1 Part 1, 5 (1980). The National Council of Juvenile and Family Court Judges recommended a similar jurisdiction for unified family courts; see Sanford N. Katz and Jeffrey A. Kuhn, *Recommendations for a Model Family Court: A Report from the National Family Court Symposium* (Reno, NV: National Council of Juvenile and Family Court Judges, 1991), recommendations 13–17.

36. H. Ted Rubin and Geoff Gallas, "Child and Family Legal Proceedings: Court Structure, Statutes and Rules," in, *Families in Court,* ed. Meredith Hofford (Reno, NV: National Council of Juvenile and Family Court Judges, 1989), 25–62.

37. See, for example, Virginia Family Court Pilot Project Advisory Committee, *Report on the Family Court Pilot Project* (unpublished report, Richmond, VA, 1992), 21, 28, which identifies problems of inconvenience, inefficiency, lack of coordination, backlog, and unpredictable outcomes for litigants; Governor's Constituency for Children, *A Family Court for Florida* (1988), 10–11, which identifies high volume, delay, lack of coordination, and inconsistency as problems; and State Bar of Georgia Commission on Family Courts, *Report and Recommendations* (1995), 13–14, which lists problems of confusion, inefficiency, delay, conflicting rulings, extended appeals, lack of services, and untrained or unqualified court personnel.

38. Catherine J. Ross, "The Failure of Fragmentation: The Promise of a System of Unified Family Courts," *Family Law Quarterly* 32 (1998): 8.

39. Paul A. Williams, "A Unified Family Court for Missouri," *University of Missouri Kansas City Law Review* 63 (1995): 383.

40. Robert Page, "Family Courts: A Model for an Effective Judicial Approach to the Resolution of Family Disputes," in *ABA Summit on Unified Family Courts: Exploring Solutions for Families, Women and Children in Crisis* (Chicago: American Bar Association, 1998), A3 (hereafter, *ABA Summit*). See also Linda Szymanski, Theresa Hornisak, and Hunter Hurst III, *Policy Alternatives and Current Court Practice in the Special Problem Areas of Jurisdiction of the Family* (Pittsburgh: National Center for Juvenile Justice, 1993), 6.

41. Judge Page regards jurisdiction over juvenile delinquency and divorce within one court as the primary indicator of a family court. Robert Page, "Family Courts," A-5. In New York, matrimonial matters, including divorce, annulment and separation, are heard in the Supreme Court. N.Y. FAM. CT. ACT § 115 (McKinney 1988 and Supp. 1997). For a discussion of subject-matter jurisdiction of family courts, see Robert E. Shephard Jr., "The Unified Family Court: An Idea Whose Time Has Finally Come," *Criminal Justice* 8 (1993): 37–38. See also William C. Gordon, "Establishing a Family Court System," *Juvenile Justice* 28 (1977): 9.

42. Steadman et al., "Six Steps to Improve Your Drug Court Outcomes for Adults with Co-Occurring Disorders," 7.

43. Nancy Ver Steegh, "Yes, No, and Maybe: Informed Decision Making about Divorce Mediation in the Presence of Domestic Violence," *William and Mary Journal of Women and the Law* 9 (Spring 2003): 145. See also Sarah Krieger, "Note: The Dangers of Mediation in Domestic Violence Cases," *Cardozo Women's Law Journal* 8 (2002): 235.

44. Erica F. Wood and Lori A. Stiegel, "Not Just for Kids: Including Elders in the Family Court Concept," in *ABA Summit*.

45. Interview with the Honorable Elizabeth Welch, quoted in Carol R. Flango, Victor E. Flango, and H. Ted Rubin, *How Are Courts Coordinating Family Cases?* (Williamsburg, VA: National Center for State Courts, 1999), 16.

46. Judge Patricia Banks, Judge Julie Conger, and Judge Joyce M. Cram, "Elder Protection Courts, "*Experience* 24 (2014): 12–16.

47. H. Ted Rubin and Victor Eugene Flango, *Court Coordination of Family Cases* (Williamsburg, VA: National Center for State Courts, 1992).

48. Carol S. Stevenson et al., "The Juvenile Court: Analysis and Recommendations," *Future of Children* 6 (Winter 1996): 6. Judge Edwards predicts that court jurisdiction over status offenses will be reduced in the future. See Hon. Leonard P. Edwards, "The Future of the Juvenile Court: Promising New Directions," *Future of Children* 6 (Winter 1996): 137.

49. Vaughn Stapleton, David P. Aday Jr., and Jeanne A. Ito, "An Empirical Typology of American Metropolitan Juvenile Courts," *American Journal of Sociology* 88 (November 1982): 549–564.

50. Ibid., 560.

51. Note that American Samoa (Ann. Code Sec 45.0103[8]; 45.0115) separates uncontested adoptions, which are heard in district court, from contested adoptions, which are heard in the trial division of the high court.

52. National Center for State Courts weighted caseload studies found that the typical dependency/neglect case required 149 minutes to resolve on average in Minnesota, 119 minutes in Washington, 172 minutes in North Dakota, 271 minutes in Michigan, 220 minutes in South Dakota, and 585 minutes in West Virginia. One reason for the differences in time to resolution, in addition to any defects in the methodology (including different time periods when the studies were conducted), is the fact that judges who specialize in dependency cases can resolve them much more quickly than judges who rarely encounter them. In addition to differences in use of specialized courts, states also differ in their use of quasi-judicial officers to hear portions of the cases.

53. Mark Hardin, "Determining Appropriate Caseloads for Judicial Officers and Attorneys" (unpublished paper, Washington, DC: American Bar Association Center on Children and the Law, 1998). Tables are reproduced and updated to 2008 in Mark Hardin et al., *Court Performance Measures in Child Abuse and Neglect Cases: Assessment Guide* (Washington, DC: Office of Juvenile Justice and Delinquency Prevention, 2008), 3–4.

54. Monica Singh, King County Unified Family Court Project, as reported in the "Pro Se Resource Center Task Force Report," December 31, 1995, in *ABA Summit on Unified Family Courts: Exploring Solutions for Families, Women and Children in Crisis* (Chicago: American Bar Association, 1998).

55. Victor E. Flango and Brian J. Ostrom, *Assessing the Need for Judges and Court Support Staff* (Williamsburg, VA: National Center for State Courts, 1997). See also Alicia Summers et al., "A New Method of Assessing Judicial Workload in Juvenile Dependency Cases," *Juvenile and Family Court Journal* 64 (Spring 2013): 35–47.

56. Fred Cheesman and Tara L. Kunkel, *Virginia Adult Drug Treatment Courts: Cost Benefit Analysis* (unpublished paper, National Center for State Courts, October 2012), available at http://ncsc.contentdm.oclc.org/cdm/ref/collection/spcts/id/245

57. Jelena Popovic, "Judicial Officers: Complementing Conventional Law and Changing the Culture of the Judiciary," *Law in Context* 20 (2002): 129 (special edition on "Therapeutic Jurisprudence," ed. Marilyn McMahon and David B. Wexler).

58. For a review of the research evidence on judicial stress and impaired career advancement in specialized courts, see Deborah J. Chase and Peggy Fulton Hora, "The Implications of Therapeutic Jurisprudence for Judicial Satisfaction," *Court Review* 37, no. 1 (Spring 2002): 12.

59. Popovic, "Judicial Officers," 128.

60. Greg Berman and John Feinblatt, *The Case for Problem-Solving Justice* (New York: New Press, 2005), 4–5.

61. Chase and Hora, "The Implications of Therapeutic Jurisprudence," 12.

62. James L. Nolan Jr., *Reinventing Justice: The American Drug Court Movement* (Princeton, NJ: Princeton University Press, 2001), 110.

63. Hon. Jeffrey S. Tauber, *Drug Courts: A Judicial Manual* (Sacramento: California Center for Judicial Education and Research, 1994), 14.

64. Morris B. Hoffman, "The Drug Court Scandal," *North Carolina Law Review* 78 (June 2007): 1437 at 1479.

65. Quoted in Greg Berman and John Feinblatt, *Judges and Problem-Solving Courts* (New York: Center for Court Innovation, 2002), 11.

66. Ibid.

67. Joseph Goldstein, Anna Freud, Albert J. Solnit, and Sonia Goldstein, *In the Best Interests of the Child: Professional Boundaries* (New York: Free Press, 1986), 52.

68. Roger Hanson, "The Changing Role of a Judge and Its Implications," *Court Review* 38, no. 4 (Winter 2002): 10.

69. David B. Wexler, "Therapeutic Jurisprudence and the Criminal Courts," *William and Mary Law Review* 35 (1993): 299.

70. Hanson, "Changing Role of a Judge," 10.

71. Also, "[n]ow, in drug treatment courts, judges are cheerleaders and social workers as much as jurists." Leslie Eaton and Leslie Kaufman, "In Prob-

lem-Solving Court, Judges Turn Therapist," *New York Times*, April 26, 2005, available at www.nytimes.com/2005/04/26/nyregion/26courts.html?pagewanted =2&ei=5070&en=17fc6df08c9c39e6&ex=1186632000.

72. Barbara A. Babb, "Fashioning an Interdisciplinary Framework for Court Reform in Family Law: A Blueprint to Construct a Unified Family Court," *Southern California Law Review* 71 (1998): 523.

73. Victor E. Flango, "Creating Family Friendly Courts: Lessons from Two Oregon Counties," *Family Law Quarterly* 34 (2000): 115–132.

74. Donald J. Farole Jr., Nora K. Puffett, and Michael Rempel, *Collaborative Justice in Conventional Courts: Phase II Stakeholder Perspectives in California* (report prepared for the Judicial Council of California, Administrative Office of the Courts by the Center for Court Innovation, 2005), 22, available at www .courtinnovation.org.

75. Ibid.

76. Donald C. Dahlin, *Models of Court Management* (Mullwood, NY: Associated Faculty Press, 1986), 4.

77. Larry C. Berkson and Susan J. Carbon, *Court Unification: History, Politics and Implementation* (Washington, DC: National Institute of Law Enforcement and Criminal Justice, 1978), 17.

78. Ibid., 4.

79. Allen Ashman and Jeffrey A. Parness, "The Concept of a Unified Court System," *DePaul Law Review* 24 (1974): 1–44.

80. David B. Rottman and William Hewitt, *Trial Court Structure and Performance: A Contemporary Reappraisal* (Williamsburg, VA: National Center for State Courts, 1996), 12.

81. To reinforce the point of a tendency to create a court to match every problem, see President Barack Obama's receptiveness of establishing a "drone court" to determine whom U.S. forces could legally kill via drone strikes. Anna Mulrine, "Would a US 'Drone Court' to Authorize Drone Strikes Be a Good Idea?" *Christian Science Monitor,* May 24, 2013. Note too the resistance of the judges on the Foreign Intelligence Surveillance Court to the recommendations of a presidential task force to add an independent advocate for privacy and civil liberties to the courts classified hearings because it would create "an adversarial legal process in the court, which now hears only from government lawyers." Ken Dilanian, "Secret Spy Court Opposes Changes," *Daily Press,* January 15, 2014, 13.

82. Isaac Unah, *The Courts of International Trade: Judicial Specialization, Expertise, and Bureaucratic Policy-Making* (Ann Arbor: University of Michigan Press, 1998), 7.

83. David B. Rottman, "Does Effective Therapeutic Jurisprudence Require Specialized Courts (and Do Specialized Courts Imply Specialist Judges)?" *Court Review* 37 (Spring 2000): 23.

84. National Center on Addiction and Substance Abuse at Columbia University, *No Safe Haven: Children of Substance Abusing Parents* (New York: National Center on Addiction and Substance Abuse, 1999).

85. N. Young, S. Boles, and C. Otero, "Parental Substance Use Disorders and Child Maltreatment: Overlap, Gaps, and Opportunities," *Child Maltreatment* 12 (2007): 137–149.

86. Honorable Judith S. Kaye, "Changing Courts in Changing Times: The Need for a Fresh Look at How Courts Are Run," *Hastings Law Journal* 44 (1997): 851.

87. See Meghan M. Wheeler and Carson L. Fox Jr., "Family Dependency Treatment Court: Applying the Drug Court Model in Child Maltreatment Cases," *Drug Court Practitioner Fact Sheet* (Alexandria, VA: National Drug Court Institute, 2006), 5.

88. Huddleston and Marlowe, *Painting the Current Picture,* available at www.ndci.org/sites/default/files/nadcp/PCP%20Report%FINAL.PDF.

89. See Stephen H. Legomsky, *Specialized Justice: Court, Administrative Tribunals, and a Cross-national Theory of Specialization* (New York: Oxford University Press, 1990), 38–39. See also Roger Peters and Fred Osher, *Co-occurring Disorders and Specialty Courts* (Delmar, NY: The National GAINS Center, 2004).

90. John Feinblatt, Greg Berman, and Derek Denckla, "Judicial Innovation at the Crossroads: The Future of Problem-Solving Courts," *Court Manager* 15, no. 3 (2000): 28–34. Note that in her article "Drug Courts" in that same publication, Caroline Cooper also notes the "shift to a post adjudication focus for many drug courts."

91. Steve Leben, "Thoughts on Some Potential Appellate and Trial Court Applications of Therapeutic Jurisprudence," *Seattle University Law Review,* 24 (2000): 467. See *Gonzalez v. Reno,* 215 F.3d 1243 (11th Cir. 2000); *Gonzalez v. Reno,* 212 F.3d 1338 (11th Cir. 2000).

Chapter 8

1. The philosophical basis of the problem solving movement is "therapeutic jurisprudence," unquestionably a medical approach. See Bruce J. Winick and David R. Wexler, eds., *Judging in a Therapeutic Key: Therapeutic Jurisprudence and the Courts* (Durham, NC: Carolina Academic Press, 2003); and Candace McCoy, "The Politics of Problem-Solving: An Overview of the Origins and Development of Therapeutic Courts," *American Criminal Law Review* 40 (2003): 1513–1539.

2. Donal E. J. MacNamara, "The Medical Model in Corrections," *Criminology* 14 (February 1977): 439–440.

3. MacNamara lists some of the new penologists as Norval Morris, Ernst van den Hagg, Andrew von Hirsch, and James Q. Wilson.

4. James L. Nolan, *Legal Accents, Legal Borrowing: The International Problem-Solving Court Movement* (Princeton, NJ: Princeton University Press, 2009), 10–11.

5. This concept, central to the notion of justice and the rule of law, has been traced back to Book 5 of Aristotle's *Nicomachean Ethics.*

6. Thomas A. Henderson and Cornelius M. Kerwin, "The Changing Character of Court Organization," *Justice System Journal* 7 (1982): 457.

7. Governor's Task Force on Family Law, Family Court and Court Services Committee, Recommendations and Procedures for E180 Governor's Task Force on Family Law, Family Court and Court Services Committee, *Recommendations and Procedures for Establishing a Family Court in Maryland, Final Report* (October 1992).

8. David Eagleman, "The Brain on Trial," *Atlantic* (July–August 2011): 121.

9. Quoted in William Doherty, "Bridging Psychotherapy and Moral Responsibility," *Responsive Community* 5 (Winter 1994–1995): 42; and in Amitai Etzioni, *The New Golden Rule* (New York: Basic Books, 1996), 135.

10. Dr. Karl Menninger, *The Crime of Punishment* (New York: Penguin Books, 1968).

11. Eagleman, "The Brain on Trial," 114.

12. Ibid., 118.

13. Ibid.

14. "Dr. Doug Marlowe on a Vision for the Future of U.S. Drug Policy," *All Rise: A Publication of the National Association of Drug Court Professionals,* Fall 2012, 4.

15. Roger K. Warren, "Reengineering the Court Process" (presentation to Great Lakes Court Summit, Madison, Wisconsin, September 24–25, 1998), reprinted in David Rottman and Pamela Casey, "Therapeutic Jurisprudence and the Emergence of Problem-Solving Courts, *NIJ Journal* (July 1999): 12–19.

16. Candace McCoy, "Review of *Good Courts: The Case for Problem-Solving Justice* by Greg Berman and John Feinblatt," *Law and Politics Book Review* 16 (2006): 964.

17. B. J. Winick and D. B. Wexler, *Judging in a Therapeutic Key: Therapeutic Jurisprudence and the Courts* (Durham, NC: Carolina Academic Press, 2003), 87.

18. Alexander B. Aikman, *The Art and Practice of Court Administration* (Boca Raton, FL: CRC Press, 2006).

19. Donald J. Farole Jr., Nora K. Puffett, and Michael Rempel, *Collaborative Justice in Conventional Courts* (report prepared for the Judicial Council of California, Administrative Office of the Courts by the Center for Court Innovation, 2005), 16, available at www.courtinnovation.org.

20. Ibid.

21. See http://ccj.ncsc.dni.us/CourtAdminResolutions/ProblemSolving CourtPrinciplesAndMethods.pdf.

22. Farole, Puffet, and Rempel, *Collaborative Justice,* 17.

23. John J. DiIulio, "The Coming of Super Predators," *Weekly Standard,* November 27, 1995, 23. DiIulio later regretted his theory, which did not pass the evidence test. See Elizabeth Becker, "An Ex-Theorist on Young 'Superpredators,' Bush Aide Has Regrets," *New York Times,* February 9, 2001.

24. Carol S. Stevenson et al., "The Juvenile Court: Analysis and Recommendations," *Future of Children* 6 (Winter 1996): 7.

25. Patricia Torbet et al., *State Responses to Serious and Violent Juvenile Crime* (Washington, DC: Office of Juvenile Justice and Delinquency Prevention, 1996).

26. Lawrence Baum, *Specializing the Courts* (Chicago: University of Chicago Press, 2011), 29.

27. Andrew J. Polsky, "The Odyssey of the Juvenile Court: Policy Failure and Institutional Persistence in the Therapeutic State," *Studies in American Political Development* 3 (1989): 176.

28. Robert M. Mennel, *Thorns and Thistles: Juvenile Delinquents in the United States 1825–1940* (Hanover, NH: University Press of New England, 1973), 144.

29. *In re: Gault*, 387 U.S. 1 (1967).

30. *Kent v. United States*, 383 U.S. 541 (1966): 556.

31. McCoy, "The Politics of Problem-Solving," 1528.

32. American Probation and Parole Association, *Effective Responses to Offender Behavior: Lessons Learned for Probation and Parole Supervision* (Lexington, KY: American Probation and Parole Association, 2013).

33. Ibid., 10.

34. Robert V. Wolf, Center for Court Innovation, *Reentry Courts: Looking Ahead* (Washington, DC: Bureau of Justice Assistance, 2011), 5.

Chapter 9

1. Anne L. Stahl et al., *Juvenile Court Statistics 2003–2004* (Pittsburgh: National Center for Juvenile Justice 2007), 70, available at www.ncjrs.gov/pdffiles1/ojjdp/218587.pdf. Percentages are from the National Center for State Courts' Court Statistics Project. The percentage for the states with unified courts is even higher.

2. Sara Mogulescu and Gaspar Caro, "Making Court the Last Resort: A New Focus for Supporting Families in Crisis" (report, Vera Institute of Justice, 2008), 2, available at http://verastage.forumone.com/download?file=1/96/status_offender_finalPDF.pdf.

3. Jane M. Spinak, "Reforming Family Court: Getting It Right between Rhetoric and Reality," *Washington University Journal of Law and Policy* 31 (2009): 36.

4. Ibid.

5. Center for Family Representation, "New Model of Legal Services—Community Advocacy Teams," available at www.cfrny.org/new_legal.asp, accessed November 5, 2009.

6. The study was commissioned by the Arizona Supreme Court in February 2004, with the final report completed August 18, 2004. Recommendations were implemented on a pilot basis, with the final plan submitted to Arizona Supreme Court on February 28, 2006, and implemented in the ensuing years. See www.superiorcourt.maricopa.gov/SuperiorCourt/FamilyCourt/docs/4th_Quarter_2005_Progress_Report.pdf.

7. Elkins Family Law Task Force, "Report to the Judicial Council" (California Judicial Council, San Francisco, 2010), 2, available at www.courtinfo.ca.gov/jc/documents/reports/20100423itemj.pdf

8. David B. Goldin and Martha I. Casey, "New York City Administrative Tribunals: A Case Study in Opportunity for Court Reform," *Judges' Journal* 49 (Winter 2010): 20–27. Admittedly, the housing court is not a traditional court but an administrative law court dealing with a high volume of relatively low-stakes cases, mostly involving self-represented litigants.

9. "Speedy Justice for Civil Cases in Multnomah County," available at www.mbabar.org/docs/SpeedyJusticeMediaRelease.pdf.

10. Minnesota Judicial Branch, "ECM/ENE Initiative (Early Case Management/Early Neutral Evaluation Pilot) Final Report to the State Justice Institute" (Minnesota Judicial Branch, St. Paul, 2010), available at www.mncourts.gov/?page=4145; T. K. Manrique and J. Goetz, "The Minnesota Model of Early Case Management/Early Neutral Evaluation" (Minneapolis, 2009), available at www.mncourts.gov/?page=4017.

11. Richard Zorza, "Access to Justice: The Emerging Consensus and Some Questions and Implications," *Judicature* 94 (2011): 157–158. An overview and examples of these suggestions can be found in *Best Practices in Court-Based Self-Represented Litigation Innovation,* 2nd ed. (Williamsburg, VA: National Center for State Courts, 2008), prepared by the Self-Represented Litigation Network and available at https://www.selfhelpsupport.org/library/item.223550-2008_edition_of_Best_Practices_in_CourtBased_Programs_for_the_Self Represent. This website is operated by the National Center for State Courts in cooperation with the Self-Represented Litigation Network and requires registration, which is free.

12. John Feinblatt, Greg Berman, and Derek Denckla, "Judicial Innovation at the Crossroads: The Future of Problem-Solving Courts," *Court Manager* 15, no. 3 (2000): 31.

13. Gordon M. Griller, "The Quiet Battle for Problem-Solving Courts," in *Future Trends in State Courts 2011,* ed. Carol R. Flango et al. (Williamsburg, VA: National Center for State Courts, 2011), 58–63.

14. See Roger K. Warren, *Evidence-Based Practices and Sentencing Policy: Ten Policy Initiatives to Reduce Recidivism* (Williamsburg, VA: National Center for State Courts, 2006).

15. Ryan S. King and Jill Pasquarella, *Drug Courts: A Review of the Evidence* (Washington, DC: Sentencing Project, 2009).

16. Personal communication, Tim Shea of the Utah Administrative Office of the Courts, June 25, 2010, with an attachment, "Proposed Rules Governing Civil Discovery," by the Utah Supreme Court Advisory Committee on the Rules of Civil Procedure.

17. Donald J. Farole Jr., Nora K. Puffett, and Michael Rempel, "Collaborative Justice in Conventional Courts" (report prepared for the judicial Council of California, Administrative Office of the Courts, by the Center for Court Innovation, New York, 2005), 12, available at www.courtinnovation.org.

18. See, for example, Deborah J. Chase and Peggy Fulton Hora, "The Implications of Therapeutic Jurisprudence for Judicial Satisfaction," *Court Review* 37, no. 1 (2000): 12.

19. Susan Daicoff, "Lawyer: Know Thyself: A Review of Empirical Research on Attorney Attributes Bearing on Professionalism," *American University Law Review* 46 (1997): 1337, at fn. 221.

20. Stephen H. Legomsky, *Specialized Justice: Court, Administrative Tribunals, and a Cross-national Theory of Specialization* (New York: Oxford University Press, 1990), 23.

21. Donald J. Farole Jr., Nora Puffett, Michael Rempel, and Francine Byrne, *Can Innovation Be Institutionalized?* (New York: Center for Court Innovation, 2004), 13.

22. Ibid., 12.

23. Greg Berman, *The Hardest Sell* (New York: Center for Court Innovation, 2004), 5.

24. Phillip Knox, Janet Cornell, and Peter Kiefer, "Did You See *That* Coming?" *Court Manager* 28, no. 4 (2013–2014): 13.

25. See *Wikipedia* entry under the title "collaborative law," which has found its way into several law school curricula.

Chapter 10

1. Paula Hannaford-Agor and Nicole L. Waters, "Estimating the Cost of Civil Litigation," *Caseload Highlights* 20, no. 1 (2013).

2. Brian Ostrom and Roger Hanson, *Achieving High Performance: A Framework for Courts* (Williamsburg, VA: National Center for State Courts, 2010), available at www.ncsc.org/hpc.

3. Tom R. Tyler, "Procedural Justice and the Courts," *Court Review* 44 (2007–2008): 26–31.

Bibliography

Abraham, Henry J. *The Judicial Process.* 3rd ed. New York: Oxford University Press, 1975.

Abramson, Jeffrey. *We, the Jury: The Jury System and the Ideal of Democracy.* New York: Basic Books, 1994.

"Administrative Law and Procedure." The Free Dictionary. Available at http://legal-dictionary.thefreedictionary.com/Administrative+Law+and+Procedure. Accessed November 21, 2012.

Aikman, Alexander B. *The Art and Practice of Court Administration.* Boca Raton, FL: CRC Press, 2006.

Alschuler, Albert W. "Plea Bargaining and Its History." *Columbia Law Review* 79, no.1 (1979): 1–43.

Alter, Jonathan. "The War on Addiction." *Newsweek,* February 12, 2001, 37–43.

American Bar Association. *Perceptions of the U.S. Justice System.* Chicago: American Bar Association, 1999.

———. *Report of the Pound Conference Follow-Up Task Force.* Chicago: American Bar Association, 1976.

Aristotle. *Nicomachean Ethics, Book 5.* Cambridge: Cambridge University Press, 2000.

Babb, Barbara A. "Fashioning an Interdisciplinary Framework for Court Reform in Family Law: A Blueprint to Construct Unified Family Court." *Southern California Law Review* 71 (1998): 469–546.

Baker, Elizabeth. "An Ex-theorist on Young 'Superpredators,' Bush Aide Has Regrets." *New York Times,* February 9, 2001.

Baker, Tom. *The Medical Malpractice Myth.* Chicago: University of Chicago Press, 2005.

Banks, Judge Patricia, Judge Julie Conger, and Judge Joyce M. Cram, "Elder Protection Courts," *Experience* 24 (2014): 12–16.

Barky, Allan E. "Parenting Coordination: The Risks of a Hybrid Conflict Resolution Process." *Negotiation Journal* 27, no. 1 (2011): 7–27.

Baum, Lawrence. *American Courts: Process and Policy.* Boston: Houghton Mifflin, 1998.

———. *Specializing the Courts.* Chicago: University of Chicago Press, 2011.

Bazemore, Gordon, and Mark S. Umbreit. *Balanced and Restorative Justice for Juveniles: A Framework for Juvenile Justice in the 21st Century.* Washington, DC: Office of Juvenile Justice and Delinquency Prevention, U.S. Department of Justice, 1997.

Becker, T. L. *Comparative Judicial Politics.* Chicago: Rand McNally, 1970.

Belenko, Steven. *Research on Drug Courts: A Critical Review.* New York: National Center on Addiction and Substance Abuse at Columbia University, 1998.

Berman, Greg. *The Hardest Sell.* New York: Center for Court Innovation, 2004.

Berman, Greg, and John Feinblatt. *The Case for Problem-Solving Justice.* New York: New Press, 2005.

———. *Judges and Problem-Solving Courts.* New York: Center for Court Innovation, 2002.

———. "Problem-Solving Courts: A Brief Primer." *Law and Policy* 23, no. 2 (2001): 125–140.

Bernstein, Robert, and Tammy Selzer. "Criminalization of People with Mental Illnesses: The Role of Mental Health Courts in System Reform." *University of the District of Columbia Law Review* 7 (2003) 143–162.

Best Practices in Court-Based Self-Represented Litigation Innovation. 2nd ed. Williamsburg, VA: National Center for State Courts, 2008.

Blumberg, Abraham. *Criminal Justice.* Chicago: Quadrangle, 1976.

Boyum, Keith. "A Perspective on Civil Delay in Trial Courts." *Justice System Journal* 5, no. 2 (1979): 170–186.

Braithwaite, John. "Restorative Justice and De-Professionalization." *Good Society* 13 (2004): 28–31.

Buenger, Michael L. "Of Money and Judicial Independence: Can Inherent Powers Protect State Courts in Tough Fiscal Times." *Kentucky Law Journal* 92 (1979): 979–1050.

Burger, Warren. "Isn't There a Better Way?" *American Bar Association Journal* 68 (1982): 274–277.

Burns, Robert P. *The Death of the American Trial.* Chicago: University of Chicago Press, 2009.

Byrne, Francine, Nancy Taylor, and Amy Nunez. *California Drug Court Cost Analysis Study.* San Francisco: Administrative Office of the Courts Center for Families, Children, and the Courts, 2006.

Carmichael, Mary. "The Doctor Won't See You Now." *Newsweek*, March 8, 2010, 47.

Carns, Teresa White, and John Druse. *Alaska's Plea Bargaining Ban Re-evaluated*. Anchorage: Alaska Judicial Council, 1991.

Casey, Pamela M., and David B. Rottman. *Problem-Solving Courts: Models and Trends*. Williamsburg, VA: National Center for State Courts, 2003.

Caulkins, Jonathan P., Peter H. Reuter, Martin Y. Iguchi, and James Chiesa. *How Goes the "War on Drugs"? An Assessment of U.S. Drug Problems and Policy*. Santa Monica, CA: RAND Corporation Drug Policy Research Center, 2005.

Chase, Deborah J., and Peggy Fulton Hora. "The Implications of Therapeutic Jurisprudence for Judicial Satisfaction." *Court Review* 37 (2000): 12–20.

Cheesman, Fred, and Tara L. Kunkel. "Virginia Adult Drug Treatment Courts: Cost Benefit Analysis." Unpublished paper. National Center for State Courts, 2012.

Cleveland, David R., and Steven Wisotsky. "The Decline of Oral Argument in the Federal Courts of Appeals: A Modest Proposal for Reform." *Journal of Appellate Practice and Process* 13 (2012): 119–125.

Cooper, Caroline. "Drug Courts." *Court Manager* 15, no. 3 (2000): 50–53.

Council of State Governments Justice Center, Criminal Justice/Mental Health Consensus Project. *Mental Health Courts: A Primer for Policymakers and Practitioners*. New York: Council of State Governments Justice Center, 2008.

"Court Statistics Project." National Center for State Courts. Available at www .courtstatistics.org/Other-Pages/StateCourtCaseloadStatistics.aspx.

Daicoff, Susan. "Lawyer: Know Thyself: A Review of Empirical Research on Attorney Attributes Bearing on Professionalism." *American University Law Review* 46 (1997): 1337–1427.

De Muniz, Chief Justice Paul J. "The Invisible Branch: Funding Resilient Courts through Public Relations, Institutional Identity, and a Place on the 'Public Radar.'" *Kentucky Law Journal* 100 (2012): 807–832.

Dewees, Donald, Michael Trebilcock, and Peter Coyte. "The Medical Malpractice Crisis: A Comparative Empirical Perspective." *Law and Contemporary Problems* 54 (1991): 217–251.

DiIulio, John J. "The Coming of Super Predators." *Weekly Standard*, November 27, 1995, 23–38.

"Disruptors, Health Care." *Forbes*, April 15, 2013, 96.

Doherty, William. "Bridging Psychotherapy and Moral Responsibility." *Responsive Community* 5 (1994): 41–52.

"Dr. Doug Marlowe on a Vision for the Future of U.S. Drug Policy." *All Rise: A Publication of the National Association of Drug Court Professionals* 4 (Fall 2012).

Ducat, Craig R. *Constitutional Interpretation*. 9th ed. British Columbia, Canada: Wadsworth Publishing, 2009.

Durham, Christine, and Dan Becker. *A Case for Court Governance Principles*. Executive Session for State Court Leaders in the 21st Century. Williamsburg, VA: National Center for State Courts, 2013.

Dwyer, Judge William L. *In the Hands of the People: The Trial Jury's Origins, Triumphs, Troubles, and Future in American Democracy.* New York: Thomas Dunne Books, 2002.

Eagleman, David. "The Brain on Trial." *Atlantic,* July–August 2011, 112–123.

Eaton, L., and L. Kaufman. "In Problem-Solving Courts, Judges Turn Therapist." *New York Times,* April 26, 2005. Available at www.nytimes.com/2005 /04/26/nyregion/26courts.html?pagewanted=2&ei=5070&en=17fc6df08c9e 6&ex=1186632000.

Eckley, Timothy S. "Veterans Court in Session in Buffalo." *Judicature* 92 (2008): 43–44.

Edwards, Hon. Leonard P. "The Future of the Juvenile Court: Promising New Directions." *Future of Children* 6, no. 3 (1996): 131–139.

Ehrenberg, Suzanne. "Embracing the Writing-Centered Legal Process." *Iowa Law Review* 89 (2004): 1159–1199.

Ehrlich, Thomas. "Legal Pollution." *New York Times Magazine,* February 8, 1976, 17.

Eisenstein, James. *Politics and the Legal Process.* New York: Harper and Row, 1973.

Elkins Family Law Task Force. *Report to the Judicial Council.* San Francisco: California Judicial Center, 2010.

Emery, Robert E. *Renegotiating Family Relationships: Divorce Child Custody, and Mediation.* New York: Guilford Press, 1994.

Etzioni, Amitai. *The New Golden Rule.* New York: Basic Books, 1996.

"Everybody Is Suing Everybody." *Chicago Times,* April 1983, 76.

Fagan, Jeffrey, and Victoria Malkin. "Theorizing Community Justice through Community Courts." *Fordham Urban Law Journal* 30 (2003): 897–953.

Farole, Donald J. "Applying Problem-Solving Principles in Mainstream Courts: Lessons for the State Courts." *Justice System Journal* 26, no. 1 (2005): 57–75.

Farole, Donald J., Nora Puffett, Michael Rempel, and Francine Byme. *Can Innovation Be Institutionalized?* New York: Center for Court Innovation, 2004.

———. "Collaborative Justice in Conventional Courts." *Center for Court Innovation.* 2005. Available at www.courtinnovation.org.

Federal Motor Carrier Safety Administration. "Commercial Motor Vehicle Facts." March 2013. Available at www.fmcsa.dot.gov/facts-research/art.htm.

Feeley, Malcom. *The Process Is the Punishment: Handling Cases in a Lower Criminal Court.* New York: Russell Sage Foundation, 1979.

Feinblatt, John, Greg Berman, and Derek Denckla. "Judicial Innovation at the Crossroads: The Future of Problem-Solving Courts." *Court Manager* 15, no. 3 (2000): 28–34.

Felstiner, William L. F., Richard L. Abel, and Austin Sarat. "The Emergence and Transformation of Disputes: Naming, Blaming, Claiming. . . ." *Law and Society Review* 15 (1981): 631–654.

Firestone, Gregory, and Janet Weinstein. "In the Best Interests of Children: A Proposal to Transform the Adversarial System." *Family Court Review* 42, no. 2 (2004): 203–215.

Fisher, George. *Plea Bargaining's Triumph: A History of Plea Bargaining in the United States.* Palo Alto, CA: Stanford University Press, 2003.

Flango, Carol R., Victor E. Flango, and H. Ted Rubin. *How Are Courts Coordinating Family Cases?* Williamsburg, VA: National Center for State Courts, 1999.

Flango, Victor. "Creating Family Friendly Courts: Lessons from Two Oregon Counties." *Family Law Quarterly* 34 (2000): 115–132.

———. "Is Procedural Fairness Applicable to All Courts?" *Court Review* 47, no. 4 (2012): 92–95.

Flango, Victor E., and Thomas Clarke. "Which Disputes Belong in Court?" *Judges' Journal* 50 (2011): 22–30.

Flango, Victor E., and F. Dale Kasparek Jr. "Which Commercial Driving Disputes Belong in Court?" In *Future Trends in State Courts 2013*, edited by Carol R. Flango, Deborah W. Smith, Nora E. Sydow, Charles F. Campbell, and Neal B. Kauder, 66–70. Williamsburg, VA: National Center for State Courts, 2013.

Flango, Victor E., and Brian J. Ostrom. *Assessing the Need for Judges and Court Support Staff.* Williamsburg, VA: National Center for State Courts, 1997.

Flango, Victor E., Robert T. Roper, and Mary E. Elsner. *The Business of State Trial Courts.* Williamsburg, VA: National Center for State Courts, 1983.

Flexner, Bernard, Reuben Oppenheimer, and Katherine F. Lenroot. *The Child, the Family, and the Court: A Study of the Administration of Justice in the Field of Domestic Relations.* Washington, DC: U.S. Government Printing Office, 1929.

Foote, Daniel. "Resolution of Traffic Accident Disputes and Judicial Activism in Japan." *Law in Japan* 25, no. 10 (1995): 23–31.

Fox, Sanford J. "The Early History of the Court." *Future of Children* 6, no. 3 (1996): 37.

Friedman, Lawrence M. *Crime and Punishment in American History.* New York: Basic Books, 1993.

———. "The Day before Trials Vanished." *Journal of Empirical Legal Studies* 1 (2004): 689–703.

Friedman, Lawrence, and Robert V. Percival. *The Roots of Justice: Crime and Punishment in Alameda County California, 1870–1910.* Chapel Hill: University of North Carolina Press, 1981.

———. "A Tale of Two Courts: Litigation in Alameda and San Benito Counties." *Law and Society Review* 10 (1976): 267–301.

Fuller, Lon L. "Adjudication and the Rule of Law." *Proceeding of the American Society of International Law* 2, nos. 1–8 (1960).

Fuller, Lon L., and Kenneth I. Winston. "The Forms and Limits of Adjudication." *Harvard Law Review* 92, no. 2 (1978): 353–409.

"Funding Justice: Strategies and Messages for Restoring Court Funding." *National Center for State Courts,* 2012, 3.

Galanter, Marc. "A World without Trials." *Journal of Dispute Resolution* 32 (2006): 7–33.

Galanter, Marc, and John Lande. "Private Courts and Public Authority." *Studies in Law, Politics, and Society* 12 (1992): 393–415.

Gale Encyclopedia of US History: Administrative Justice. Available at www .answers.com/topic/administrative-justice. Accessed November 21, 2012.

Garry, Patrick M. *A Nation of Adversaries: How the Litigation Explosion Is Reshaping America.* New York: Insight Books, 1997.

Glaberson, William. "In Misdemeanor Cases, Long Waits for Elusive Trials," April 30, 2013. Available at www.nytimes.com/2013/05/01/nyregion/justice-denied-for-misdemeanor-cases-trials-are-elusive.html?pagewanted=all.

Glick, Henry R. *Supreme Courts in State Politics: An Introduction to the Judicial Role.* New York: Basic Books, 1971.

Goerdt, John, Chris Lomvardias, and Geoff Gallas. *Reexamining the Pace of Litigation in 39 Urban Trial Courts.* Williamsburg, VA: National Center for State Courts, 1991.

Gold, Steven D., editor. "State Fiscal Problems and Policies." In *Fiscal Crisis of the States,* 34. Washington DC: Georgetown University Press, 1995.

Goldin, David, and Martha Casey. "New York City Administrative Tribunals: A Case Study in Opportunity for Court Reform." *Judges' Journal* 40, no. 1 (2010): 20–27.

Goldkamp, John S., and Martha Casey. *Emerging Judicial Strategies for the Mentally Ill in the Criminal Caseload.* Washington, DC: Bureau of Justice Assistance, 2000.

Goldstein, Joseph, Anna Freud, Albert J. Solnit, and Sonia Goldstein. *In the Best Interests of the Child: Professional Boundaries.* New York: Free Press, 1986.

Gordon, William C. "Establishing a Family Court System." *Juvenile Justice* 28 (1977): 9.

Governor's Constituency for Children. *A Family Court for Florida.* 1988.

Greacen, John. "How Fair, Fast, and Cheap Should Courts Be?" *Judicature* 82 (1999): 287–291.

Greve, Michael S. "Environmentalism and Bounty Hunting." *Public Interest* 97 (1989): 15.

Griller, Gordon M. "The Quiet Battle for Problem-Solving Courts." In *Future Trends in State Courts 2011,* edited by Carol R. Flango, Amy M. McDowell, Charles F. Campbell, and Neal B. Kauder, 58–63. Williamsburg, VA: National Center for State Courts, 2011.

Grossman, Joel B., Herbert M. Kritzer, Kristin Bumiller, Austin Sarat, and Stephen McDougal. "Dimensions of Institutional Participation: Who Uses Courts and How?" *Journal of Politics* 44, no. 1 (1982): 86–114.

Hannaford-Agor, Paula, and Nicole Waters. "Estimating the Cost of Civil Litigation." *Caseload Highlights* 20, no. 1 (2013): 1–9.

Hanson, Roger. "The Changing Role of a Judge and Its Implications." *Court Review* 38, no. 4 (2002): 10–16.

Hardin, Mark. "Determining Appropriate Caseloads for Judicial Officers and

Attorneys." Unpublished paper. Washington DC: American Bar Association Center on Children and the Law, 1998.

Hardin, Mark, Ying Ying Yuan, Judith Larson, Sophia I. Gatowski, and Dawn Marie Rubio. *Court Performance Measures in Child Abuse and Neglect Cases: Assessment Guide*. Washington, DC: Offices of Juvenile Justice and Delinquency Prevention, 2008.

Henderson, Thomas A., and Cornelius M. Kerwin. "The Changing Character of Court Organization." *Justice System Journal* 7 (1982): 449–469.

Henderson, Thomas A., Cornelius Kerwin, Randall Guynes, Carl Baar, Neal Miller, Hildy Saizow, and Robert Grieser. *The Significance of Judicial Structure: The Effect of Unification on Trial Court Operations*. Washington, DC: U.S. Department of Justice, 1984.

Henderson, Thomas A., Cornelius Kerwin, and Hildy Saizow. *Structuring Justice: The Implications of Court Unification Reform*. Washington, DC: U.S. Department of Justice, 1984.

Heumann, Milton. "A Note on Plea Bargaining and Case Pressure." *Law and Society* 9, no. 3 (1975): 515–528.

———. *Plea Bargaining: The Experiences of Prosecutors, Judges and Defense Attorneys*. Chicago: University of Chicago Press, 1978.

Hiefetz, Ronald, Alexander Grashow, and Marty Linsky. *The Practice of Adaptive Leadership*. Cambridge, MA: Harvard Business Press, 2009.

Hoffman, Morris B. "The Drug Court Scandal." *North Carolina Law Review* 78 (2000): 1437–1534.

Hora, Peggy F., William G. Schma, and J. T. A. Rosenthal. "Therapeutic Jurisprudence and the Drug Treatment Court Movement: Revolutionizing the Criminal Justice System's Response to Drug Abuse and Crime in America." *Notre Dame Law Review* 74, no. 2 (1999): 439–538.

"How Goes the 'War on Drugs': An Assessment of U.S. Drug Problems and Policy." *RAND Corporation Drug Policy Research Center*, 2005.

Huddleston, C. West, III, and Douglas B. Marlowe *Painting the Current Picture: A National Report Card on Drug Courts and Other Problem Solving Court Programs in the United States*. Washington, DC: Bureau of Justice Assistance, 2011.

Hyman, David A., and Charles Silver. "Medical Malpractice Litigation and Tort Reform: It's the Incentives Stupid." *Vanderbilt Law Review* 59 (2006): 1085–1136.

Institute for the Advancement of the American Legal System, American Board of Trial Advocates, and National Center for State Courts. *A Return to Trials: Implementing Effective, Short, Summary, and Expedited Civil Action Programs*. Denver: Institute for the Advancement of the Legal System, 2012.

Isikoff, Michael, and William Booth. "Miami 'Drug Court' Demonstrates Reno's Unorthodox Approach." *Washington Post*, February 20, 1993.

Jacob, Herbert. *Urban Justice*. Englewood Cliffs, NJ: Prentice Hall, 1973.

Jones, David A. *Crime without Punishment*. Lexington, MA: D. C. Health, 1979.

"Justice Center." The Council of State Governments. Available at http://csg justicecenter.org/nrrc.

Kagan, Robert A. *Adversarial Legalism: The American Way of Law*. Cambridge, MA: Harvard University Press, 2001.

Kaheny, Erin B. "Appellate Judges as Gatekeepers? An Investigation of Threshold Decisions in Federal Courts of Appeals." *Journal of Appellate Practice and Process* 12, no. 2 (2011): 255–257.

Katz, Sanford N., and Jeffrey A. Kuhn. *Recommendations for a Model Family Court: A Report from the National Family Court Symposium*. National Council of Juvenile and Family Court Judges, 1991.

Kaye, Judith S. "Changing Courts in Changing Times: The Need for a Fresh Look at How Courts Are Run." *Hastings Law Journal* 48, no. 5 (1998): 851–866.

———. "Constructive State Court Intervention: Turning Crisis into Opportunity." In *The Book of the States 2010*, edited by the Council of State Governments, 295–297. Lexington, KY: Council of State Governments, 2010.

Kelly, Joan B. "The Origins and Development of Parenting Coordination" In *Parenting Coordination Handbook*, edited by Stephen J. Lally and Shirley A. Higuchi, chap. 2. Washington, DC: American Psychological Association, 2000.

Kessler, Daniel, and Mark McClellan. "Do Doctors Practice Defensive Medicine?" *Quarterly Journal of Economics* 111 (1996): 353–390.

King, Ryan S., and Jill Pasquarella. *Drug Courts: A Review of the Evidence*. Washington, DC: Sentencing Project, 2009.

Knox, Phillip, Janet Cornell, and Peter Kiefer. "Did You See *That* Coming?" *Court Manager* 28 (Winter 2013–2014): 6–18.

Koelling, Peter M. "Caseflow Management and Its Effect on Timeliness in the Colorado District Court." Master's thesis, Delkab: Northern Illinois University, 2013.

Krieger, Sarah. "Note: The Dangers of Mediation in Domestic Violence Cases." *Cardozo Women's Law Journal* 8 (2002): 235–259.

LaFountain, R., R. Schauffler, S. Strickland, S. Gibson, and A. Mason. *Examining the Work of State Courts: An Analysis of 2009 State Court Caseloads*. Williamsburg, VA: National Center for State Courts, 2011.

Landsman, Stephen. "So What? Possible Implications of the Vanishing Trial Phenomenon." *Journal of Empirical Legal Studies* 1 (2004): 973–984.

Langbein, John H. *The Origins of the Adversary Criminal Trial*. Oxford, UK: Oxford University Press, 2003.

———. "Understanding the Short History of Plea Bargaining." *Law and Society Review* 13 (1979): 261–272.

Lee, S. Aos, E. Drake, A. Pennucci, M. Miller, and L. Anderson. *Return on Investment: Evidence-Based Options to Improve Statewide Outcomes*. Olympia: Washington State Institute for Public Policy, 2012.

Legomsky, Stephen H. *Specialized Justice: Court, Administrative Tribunals, and a Cross-national Theory of Specialization*. New York: Oxford University Press, 1990.

Lempert, Richard. "More Tales of Two Courts: Exploring Changes in 'Dispute Settlement Function' of Trial Courts." *Law and Society Review* 13, no. 1 (1978): 19–38.

Lieberman, Jethro K. *The Litigious Society*. New York: Basic Books, 1981.

———. *The Role of Courts in American Society: The Final Report of the Council on the Role of Courts*. St. Paul: West Publishing, 1984.

Liebmann, M. *Restorative Justice: How It Works*. London: Jessica Kingsley Publishers, 2007.

Lithwick, Dahlia. "Whose God Wins?" *Newsweek*, March 8, 2010, 22.

Localio, A. Russell, Ann G. Lawthers, Troyen A. Brennan, Nan M. Laird, Liesi E. Herbert, Lynn M. Peterson, Joseph P. Newhouse, Paul C. Weiler, and Howard A. Hiatt. "Relation between Malpractice Claims and Adverse Events Due to Negligence: Results of the Harvard Medical Practice Study III." *New England Journal of Medicine* 325 (1991): 245–251.

Manning, Christopher. "Hyperlexis: Our National Disease." *Northwestern Law Review* 71, no. 6 (1977): 767–782.

Manrique, Tanja, and James Goetz. *The Minnesota Model of Early Case Management/Early Neutral Evaluation*. Minneapolis: 2009.

McCoy, Candace. "The Politics of Problem Solving: An Overview of the Origins and Development of Therapeutic Courts." *American Criminal Law Review* 40 (2003): 1513–1539.

———. "Review of *Good Courts: The Case for Problem Solving Justice* by Greg Berman and John Feinblatt." *Law and Politics Book Review* 16 (2006): 864–969.

McKnight, David L., and Paul J. Hilton. "International Comparisons of Litigation Costs: Europe, the United States, and Canada." *NERA Economic Consulting* (May 2013).

McLauchlan, William P. *American Legal Processes*. New York: Wiley, 1977.

McNamara, Richard B. Memo. "Innovation Commission." June 8, 2010.

McQueen, Mary. *Governance: The Final Frontier*. Executive Session for State Courts Leaders in the 21st Century. Williamsburg, VA: National Center for State Courts, 2013.

McVey, Austin J. *The 1989 NCCD Prison Population Forecast: The Impact of the War on Drugs*. San Francisco: National Council on Crime and Delinquency, 1989.

Mello, Michelle, and Troyen Brennan. "Deterrence of Medical Errors: Theory and Evidence for Malpractice Reform." *Texas Law Review* 80 (2002): 1597–1637.

Mennel, Robert M. *Thorns and Thistles: Juvenile Delinquents in the United States 1825–1940*. Hanover, NH: University Press of New England, 1973.

Miller, Richard E., and Austin Sarat. "Grievances, Claims, and Disputes: Assessing the Adversary Culture." *Law and Society Review* 15 (1981): 525–565.

Minnesota Judicial Branch. *ECM/ENE Initiative (Early Case Management/Early Neutral Evaluation Pilot) Final Report to the State Justice Institute*. St. Paul: Minnesota Judicial Branch, 2010.

Mize, Hon. Gregory E., Paula Hannaford-Agor, and Nicole L. Waters. *The State-of-the-States Survey of Jury Improvement Efforts: A Compendium Report*. Williamsburg, VA: National Center for State Courts, 2007.

Mogulescu, Sara, and Gaspar Caro. "Making Court the Last Resort: A New Focus for Supporting Families in Crisis." Vera Institute of Justice. 2008. Available at http://verastage.forumone.com/download?file=1796/status_offender _finalPDF.pdf.

Moley, Raymond. *Politics and Criminal Prosecution*. New York: Minton, Balch, 1929.

Mulvey, Edward P. "Family Courts: The Issue of Reasonable Goals." *Law and Human Behavior* 6, no. 1 (1982): 49–64.

Murphy, Jane C. "Revitalizing the Adversary System in Family Law." *University of Cincinnati Law Review* 78 (2010): 891–927.

National Association of Drug Court Professionals, Drug Court Standards Committee. *Defining Drug Courts: The Key Components*. Washington, DC: Drug Courts Program Office, 1997.

National Center for State Courts. *Court Case Management System Functional Standards: A Development Road Map*. Williamsburg, VA: National Center for State Courts, 2005.

———. *Minnesota Judicial Workload Assessment, 2002*. Williamsburg, VA: National Center for State Courts, 2003.

———. *Trial Court Performance Standards with Commentary*. Washington, DC: Bureau of Justice Assistance, 1997.

National Center for State Courts: Court Statistics Project. *The State Court Guide to Statistical Reporting*. Williamsburg, VA: National Center for State Courts, 2009.

National Center on Addiction and Substance Abuse at Columbia University. *No Safe Haven: Children of Substance Abusing Parents*. New York: National Center on Addiction and Substance Abuse, 1999.

National Council of Juvenile and Family Court Judges. *Families in Court: Recommendations from a National Symposium*. Reno, NV: National Council of Juvenile and Family Court Judges, 1989.

Neely, Richard. *Why Courts Don't Work*. New York: McGraw-Hill, 1982.

Nolan, James L. *Legal Accents, Legal Borrowing: The International Problem-Solving Court Movement*. Princeton, NJ: Princeton University Press, 2009.

———. *Reinventing Justice: The American Drug Court Movement*. Princeton, NJ: Princeton University Press, 2001.

"OJJDP Model Programs Guide." Office of Juvenile Justice and Delinquency Prevention. Available at www.ojjdp.gov/mpg/progTypesReentryCourt.aspx.

Ostrom, Brian J., Victor E. Flango, and Heidi Green. *Determining the Need for Judgeships in Wisconsin.* Williamsburg, VA: National Center for State Courts, 1996.

Ostrom, Brian J., and Roger Hanson. *Achieving High Performance: A Framework for Courts.* Williamsburg, VA: National Center for State Courts, 2010.

Ostrom, Brian J., Shaunna M. Strickland, and Paula I. Hannaford-Agor. "Examining Trial Trends in State Courts: 1976–2002." *Journal of Empirical Legal Studies* 1 (2004): 755–782.

Page, Robert. "Family Courts: A Model for an Effective Judicial Approach to the Resolution of Family Disputes." American Bar Association Summit on Unified Family Courts: Exploring Solutions for Families, Women and Children in Crisis. 1998.

Peters, Roger H. and Fred C. Osher. *Co-occurring Disorders and Specialty Courts.* Delmar, NY: National GAINS Center, 2004.

Polsky, Andrew J. "The Odyssey of the Juvenile Court: Policy Failure and Institutional Persistence in the Therapeutic State." *Studies in American Political Development* 3 (1989): 157–198.

Popovic, Jelena. "Judicial Officers: Complementing Conventional Law and Changing the Culture of the Judiciary." *Law in Context* 20, no. 2 (2002): 121–137.

Powell, Edward. "Jury Trial at Gaol Delivery in the Late Middle Ages: The Midland Circuit, 1400–1429." In *Twelve Good Men and True: The Criminal Trial Jury in England, 1200–1800,* edited by J. S. Cockburn and Thomas A. Green, 78–116. Princeton, NJ: Princeton University Press, 1988.

Price, Marty. "Personalizing Crime." *Dispute Resolution Magazine* 7 (2008): 8–11.

Quam, Lois, Robert Dingwall and Paul Fenn. "Medical Malpractice in Perspective." *British Medical Journal* 294 (1987): 1529–1597.

Ramseyer, J. Mark, and Minoru Nakazato. "Why Is the Japanese Conviction Rate So High?" *John M. Olin Center for Law, Economics, and Business, Harvard Law School.* 1989.

Rausch, Hon. Jim, and Hon. Tom Rawlings. "Integrating Problem-Solving Court Practices into the Child Support Docket." *Juvenile and Family Justice Today* (Winter 2008): 16–19.

"Recommendations and Procedures for Establishing a Family Court in Maryland, Final Report." *Governor's Task Force on Family Law, Family Court and Court Services Committee* (October 1992).

Redlich, W. Personal webpage. 2007. Available at http://albany-lawyer.blogspot .com/2007/04/assembly-line-justice.html.

Reinkensmeyer, Marcus W., and Chuck Oraftik. "Today's Version of Yesterday's Vision of Tomorrow's Courthouse." *Court Manager* 26 (2011): 22–29.

Rifkind, Simon H. "Are We Asking Too Much of Our Courts?" *Federal Rules Decisions* 70 (1976): 96.

———. "Are We Asking Too Much of Our Courts?" *Judges' Journal* 15 (Spring–Summer 1976).

Roberts, Keith. "What Judges Actually Do." *Judges' Journal* 49 (2010): 28–31.

Rosenberg, Maurice. "Court Congestion: Status, Causes and Proposed Remedies." In *The Courts, the Public and the Law Explosion,* edited by H. W. Jones. Englewood Cliffs, NJ: Prentice-Hall, 1965.

Ross, Catherine J. "The Failure of Fragmentation: The Promise of a System of Unified Family Courts." *Family Law Quarterly* 32, no. 1 (1998): 3–30.

Rossman, Shelli B., and Janine M. Zweig. *The Multisite Adult Drug Court Evaluation.* Alexandria, VA: National Association of Drug Court Professionals, 2012.

Rottman, David B. *Community Courts: Prospects and Limits.* Williamsburg, VA: National Center for State Courts, 2002.

Rottman, David B., and Pamela Casey. "Therapeutic Jurisprudence and the Emergence of Problem Solving Courts." *National Institute of Justice Journal* (July 1999): 12–19.

Rottman, David B., and Randall M. Hansen. *How Recent Court Users View the State Courts.* Williamsburg, VA: National Center for State Courts, 2000.

Rottman, David B., and William Hewitt. *Trial Court Structure and Performance: A Contemporary Reappraisal.* Williamsburg, VA: National Center for State Courts, 1996.

Rottman, David B., and Alan Tompkins. "Public Trust and Confidence in the Courts: What Public Opinion Surveys Mean to Judges." *Court Review* 36 (1999): 24–31.

Rubenstein, Michael L., Stevens H. Clarke, and Teresa J. White. *Alaska Bans Plea Bargaining.* Washington, DC: U.S. Department of Justice, 1980.

Rubenstein, Michael L., and Teresa J. White. "Alaska's Ban on Plea Bargaining." *Law and Society Review* 13, no. 2 (1979): 367–383.

Rubin, H. Ted, and Victor Eugene Flango. *Court Coordination of Family Cases.* Williamsburg, VA: National Center for State Courts, 1992.

Rubin, H. Ted, and Geoff Gallas. "Child and Family Legal Proceedings: Court Structure, Statutes and Rules." In *Families in Court,* edited by Meredith Hofford, 25–62. Reno, NV: National Council of Juvenile and Family Court Judges, 1989.

Russell, Robert T. "Veterans Treatment Courts Developing throughout the Nation." In *Future Trends in State Courts 2009,* edited by Carol R. Flango, Amy M. McDowell, Charles F. Campbell, and Neal B. Kauder, 130–133. Williamsburg, VA: National Center for State Courts, 2009.

Schepard, Andrew, and Peter Salem. "Foreword of the Special Issue on the Family Law Education Project." *Family Court Review* 44 (2006): 513.

Shapiro, Martin. *The Supreme Court and Administrative Agencies.* New York: Free Press, 1968.

Shea, Tim. Personal communication with attachment. Utah Supreme Court Advisory Committee on the Rules of Civil Procedure. "Proposed Rules Governing Civil Discovery."

Shephard, Robert E., Jr. "The Unified Family Court: An Idea Whose Time Has Finally Come." *Criminal Justice* 8 (1993): 37–38.

Siegel, Jonathan R. "A Theory of Justiciability." *Texas Law Review* 86, no. 1 (2007): 73–78.

Silberman, Charles E. *Criminal Violence, Criminal Justice*. New York: Vintage Books, 1978.

Singh, Monica, King County Unified Family Court Project. "Pro Se Resource Center Task Force Report." In *ABA Summit on Unified Family Courts: Exploring Solutions for Families, Women, and Children in Crisis*. Chicago: American Bar Association, 1998.

Sipes, Dale Anne. *On Trial: The Length of Civil and Criminal Trials*. Williamsburg, VA: National Center for State Courts. 1988.

Solomon, Maureen. *Caseflow Management in the Trial Court*. Chicago: American Bar Association, 1973.

"Sourcebook of Criminal Justice Statistics Online." *Bureau of Justice Statistics, University of Albany*. 2011. Available at www.albany.edu/sourcebook/csv/t200312100.csv, Table 2.0031.2011.

"Speedy Justice for Civil Cases in Multnomah County." Available at www.mbabar.org/docs/SpeedyJusticeMediaRelease.pdf.

Spinak, Jane M. "Reforming Family Court: Getting It Right between Rhetoric and Reality." *Washington University Journal of Law and Policy* 31 (2009): 11–39.

Stahl, Ann L., Charles Puzzanchera, Sarah Livsey, Anthony Sladky, Terrence A. Finnegan, Nancy Tierney, and Howard N. Snyder. "Juvenile Court Statistics 2003–2004." *National Center for Juvenile Justice*. 2007. Available at www.cjrs.gov/pdffiles1/opjjdp/218587.pdf.

Stapleton, Vaughn, David P. Aday Jr., and Jeanne A. Ito. "An Empirical Typology of American Metropolitan Juvenile Courts." *American Journal of Sociology* 88 (1982): 549–564.

State Bar of Georgia Commission Family Courts *Report and Recommendations*. 1995.

"State Courts at the Tipping Point." *New York Times*, November 25, 2009.

Steadman, Henry J., Susan Davidson, and Collie Brown. "Mental Health Courts: Their Promise and Unanswered Questions." *Psychiatric Services* 52 (2001): 457–458.

Steadman, Henry J., Roger H. Peters, Christine Carpenter, Kim T. Mueser, Norma D. Jaeger, and Richard B. Gordon. "Six Steps to Improve Your Drug Court Outcomes for Adults with Co-occurring Disorders." *National Drug Court Institute and SAMHSA's GAINS, Drug Court Practitioner Fact Sheet*. 2013.

Steadman, Steven R. "Structured Factorial Sort Survey: Wisconsin Clerks of Courts' Perception on Compliance and the Need for Staff across Their Typology of Duties." In "Analysis of Court Support Staffing Levels in Wisconsin," by Steven R. Steadman and Kathleen M. Murphy. Unpublished paper, Institute for Court Management, National Center for State Courts, 1991.

Steelman, David C., John Goerdt, and James McMillan. *Caseflow Management: The Heart of Court Management in the New Millennium*. Williamsburg, VA: National Center for State Courts, 2004.

Stephens, Gene. "Participatory Justice." In *The 1990's and Beyond*, edited by Edward Cornish. Bethesda, MD: World Future Society, 1990.

Stevenson, Carol S., Carol S. Larson, Lucy Salcido Carter, Deanna S. Gomby, Donna L. Terman, and Richard E. Behrman. "The Juvenile Court: Analysis and Recommendations." *Future of Children* 6, no. 3 (1996): 4–28.

Stockwell, Charlotte. "Managing the Transition from the Adversarial to the Non-adversarial Court: A Court Administrator's Perspective." Evaluation report of the *Court Integrated Support Program, Magistrate's Court of Victoria* (2010).

Strick, Anne. *Injustice for All*. New York: G. P. Putnam's Sons, 1977.

Stuntz, William J. *The Collapse of American Criminal Justice*. Cambridge, MA: Harvard University Press, 2011.

Sullivan, Matthew J. "Parenting Coordination: Coming of Age?" *Family Court Review* 51, no. 1 (2013): 56–62.

Summers, Alicia, Stephanie O. Macgill, Sophia I. Gatowski, Jesse R. Russell, and Steve Wood. "A New Method of Assessing Judicial Workload in Juvenile Dependency Cases." *Juvenile and Family Court Journal* 64 (2013): 35–47.

Szymanski, Linda, Theresa Hornisak, and Hunter Hurst III. *Policy Alternatives and Current Court Practice in the Special Problem Areas of Jurisdiction of the Family*. Pittsburgh, PA: National Center for Juvenile Justice, 1993.

Talesh, Shauhin. "How Dispute Resolution System Design Matters: An Organizational Analysis of Dispute Resolution Structures and Consumer Lemon Laws." *Law and Society Review* 46 (2012): 463–492.

———. "The Privatization of Public Legal Rights: How Manufacturers Construct the Meaning of Consumer Law." *Law and Society Review* 43 (2009): 527–562.

Tanase, Takao. "The Management of Disputes: Automobile Accident Compensation in Japan." *Law and Society Review* 24, no. 3 (1990): 651–692.

Tauber, Hon. Jeffrey S. *Drug Courts: A Judicial Manual*. Sacramento: California Center for Judicial Education and Research, 1994.

Tauber, Jeffrey, and C. W. Huddleston. *DUI/Drug Courts: Defining a National Strategy*. Washington, DC: National Drug Court Institute, 1995.

Tennille, Hon. Ben F., and Corinne B. Jones. "Developments at the North Carolina Business Court." *National Center for State Courts, Future Trends in State Courts 2010*. 2010.

Thaler, Richard H., and Cass R. Sunstein. *Nudge*. New York: Penguin Books, 2008.

Tobin, Robert W. *Creating the Judicial Branch: The Unfinished Reform*. Williamsburg, VA: National Center for State Courts, 1999.

Toohey, Gary. "The Civil Jury Trial: Going, Going, Gone." *Precedent* (Summer 2010): 6–23.

Torbet, Patricia, Richard Gable, Hunter Hurst IV, Imogene Montgomery, Linda Szymanski, and Douglas Thomas. *State Responses to Serious and Violent Juvenile Crime.* Washington, DC: Office of Juvenile Justice and Delinquency Prevention, 1996.

Tyler, Tom R. "Procedural Justice and the Courts." *Court Review* 44 (2009): 26–31.

Ungs, T., and L. R. Baas. "Judicial Role Perceptions: A Q-Technique Study of Ohio Judges." *Law Society and Review* 6 (1972): 343–348.

U.S. Department of Justice, Office of Justice Programs. *Bureau of Justice Assistance Fact Sheet: Differentiated Case Management.* Washington, DC: U.S. Department of Justice, 1995.

Vallinder, Torbjorn. "When the Courts Go Marching In." In *The Global Expansion of Judicial Power,* edited by C. Neal Tate and Torbjorn Vallinder, 13–26. New York: New York University Press, 1995.

"Vermont Judicial Bureau." Vermont Judiciary. Available at www.vermont judiciary.org/GTC/judicial/default.aspx.

Ver Steegh, Nancy. "Yes, No, and Maybe: Informed Decision Making about Divorce Mediation in the Presence of Domestic Violence." *William and Mary Journal of Women and the Law* 9, no. 2 (2003): 145–205.

Virginia Family Court Pilot Project Advisory Committee. "Report on the Family Court Pilot Project." Unpublished report. 1992.

Wallace, David J. "Do DWI Courts Work?" In *Future Trends in State Courts, 2008,* edited by C. Flango, Amy M. McDowell, Charles F. Campbell, and Neal B. Kauder, 92–95. Williamsburg, VA: National Center for State Courts, 2008.

Waller, Mark, Shannon Carey, Erin Farley, and Michael Rempel. *Testing the Cost Savings of Judicial Diversion: Final Report.* New York: NPS Research and Center for Court Innovation, 2013.

Warren, Roger K. *Evidence-Based Practices and Sentencing Policy: Ten Policy Initiatives to Reduce Recidivism.* Williamsburg, VA: National Center for State Courts, 2006.

———. "Reengineering the Court Process." 1998. Reprinted in David Rottman and Pamela Casey, "Therapeutic Jurisprudence and the Emergence of Problem-Solving Courts," *NIJ Journal* (July 1999): 12–19.

Waters, Nicole L., Shauna M. Strickland, and Sarah A. Gibson. *Mental Health Court Culture: Leaving Your Hat at the Door.* Williamsburg, VA: National Center for State Courts, 2009.

Watson, Amy, Patricia Hanrahan, Daniel Luchins, and Arthur Lurigio. "Mental Health Courts and the Complex Issue of Mentally Ill Offenders." *Psychiatric Services* 52 (2001): 477–481.

"Welcome to the Family Court of the State of Delaware." Delaware State Courts. Available at http://courts.state.de.us/Courts/Family%20Court/?history .htm.

Wexler, David B. "Therapeutic Jurisprudence: It's Not Just for Problem-Solving Courts and Calendars Anymore." In *Future Trends in State Courts 2004,* edited by Carol R. Flango, Neal Kauder, Kenneth G. Pankey Jr., and Charles Campbell, 87–89. Williamsburg, VA: National Center for State Courts, 2004.

Wheeler, Meghan M., and Carson L. Fox Jr. "Family Dependency Treatment Court: Applying the Drug Court Model in Child Maltreatment Cases." *Drug Court Practitioner Fact Sheet* 5, no. 1 (2006): 1–7.

Wigmore, John H. *Evidence in Trials of Common Law.* Vol. 3. Boston: Little, Brown, 1923.

Williams, Paul A. "A Unified Family Court for Missouri." *University of Missouri Kansas City Law Review* 63 (1995): 383–384.

Wilson, James Q. *Varieties of Police Behavior: The Management of Law and Order in Eight Communities.* New York: Atheneum, 1970.

Winick, B. J., and D. B. Wexler. *Judging in a Therapeutic Key: Therapeutic Jurisprudence and the Courts.* Durham, NC: Carolina Academic Press, 2003.

Wolf, Robert V., Center for Court Innovation. *Reentry Courts: Looking Ahead.* Washington, DC: Bureau of Justice Assistance, 2011.

Wood, Erica F., and Lori A. Stiegel. "Not Just for Kids: Including Elders in the Family Court Concept." In *ABA Summit on Unified Family Courts: Exploring Solutions for Families, Women, and Children in Crisis.* Chicago: American Bar Association, 1998.

Young, N., S. Boles, and C. Otero. "Parental Substance Use Disorders and Child Maltreatment: Overlap, Gaps, and Opportunities." *Child Maltreatment* 12 (2007): 137–149.

Zorza, Richard. "Access to Justice: The Emerging Consensus and Some Questions and Implications." *Judicature* 94 (2011): 156–167.

———. "Courts in the 21st Century: The Access to Justice Transformation." *Judges' Journal* 49, no. 1 (2010): 14–19, 34–36.

Cases

Blackledge v. Allison, 431 U.S. 63 (1977).

Bordenkircher v. Hayes, 434 U.S. 357 (1978).

Crowell v. Benson, 285 U.S. 22 (1932).

Goldberg v. Kelly, 397 U.S. 254 (1970).

Gonzalez v. Reno, 212 F.3d 1338 (11th Cir. 2000).

Gonzalez v. Reno, 215 F.3d 1243 (11th Cir. 2000).

In re: Gault, 387 U.S. 1 (1967).

Kent v. United States, 383 U.S. 541 (1966).

Lafler v. Cooper, 132 S. Ct. 1376 (2012).

Mathews v. Eldridge, 424 U.S. 319 (1976).

Missouri v. Frye, 132 S. Ct. 1399 (2012).

Index

Page numbers followed by the letter *f* refer to figures; page numbers followed by the letter *t* refer to tables.

ABA. *See* American Bar Association

Adjudicatory processes, 25, 35, 38, 39t, 44; administrative, 50t, 85–95; adversary, 40–42; combinations used today, 35; dispositional, 42, 70–82; evolution of adjudicatory processes, 25–26; problem-solving, 42–45

Administrative agencies, 92–93

Administrative law courts, 155, 160

Administrative Office of Courts in California study on screening family cases, 119

Administrative process: alternatives, 88–91; caseload, 86; commercial driving violations, 93–95; courts as administrative agencies, 92–93; ideal case types, 50t; purpose, 85; role of the judge, 87–88; triage, 86–87

Administrative tribunals, 89–90

Adoption cases, 109

Adversary process, 5, 15, 40–42, 54–56; adversary system, 19, 61; comparison to transformed process, 133t; decline in trials, 64; differences from the problem-solving approach, 134; facilities, 62–63; role of court staff, 62; role of the judge, 61; shift away from, 6–12, 56–60; traditional, 35, 40

Aikman, Alex, 135

Alameda County, 73

Alameda County Superior Court, 107

Alaska, "cooling off periods" mandated for every case in, 160

Alternative dispute resolution: Early Neutral Evaluation program in Minnesota, 146; fast-track procedures, 83; as new functions of courts, 7

American Bar Association (ABA), 56; recommendations for family courts, 103; report on nonadversarial methods, 151; Task Force, 85

American Probation and Parole Association, 138

Arbitration, 9, 11, 41, 76, 83, 155; Delaware fast-track, 83; private, for civil cases, 74–75, 154

Assembly line dockets, 71–74, 78

Babb, Barbara A., 117

Baum, Lawrence, 35–36

Becker, Theodore L., 63, 64

Bell, Griffin B., 85

Berman, Greg, 113, 125, 147

Best practices, 52, 81–82, 104; procedural justice, 164

Blatz, Kathleen A., 71

Victor E. Flango has recently retired as Executive Director of Program Resource Development at the National Center for State Courts.

Thomas M. Clarke is Vice President for Research and Technology at the National Center for State Courts.